THE

International
Money Game

THE
International
Money Game

Robert Z. Aliber

FOURTH EDITION, REVISED AND EXPANDED

Basic Books, Inc., Publishers

NEW YORK

Library of Congress Cataloging in Publication Data

Aliber, Robert Z.
   The international money game.

   Includes index.
   1.   International finance.   I.   Title.
HG3881.A44   1983   332.4'5   82–72393
ISBN 0–465–03377–6
ISBN 0–465–03379–2 (pbk.)

CONTENTS

v

PART II
Living with the System

PREFACE

International finance is frequently viewed as esoteric, understood only by a few skilled speculators in the British pound and the Japanese yen, and central bankers. In part, the mystery results from the specialized use of everyday language—"gliding parities" and "sliding bands," "support limits" and "counterspeculation," "SDRs" and "Eurodollars," "cross-rates" and "intervention limits," "tax havens" and "transfer pricing." The words seem common enough, but the meanings and significance are elusive. The reader is deterred because of the effort required to learn an esoteric language.

As the jargon barrier is surmounted, a second problem appears—recognized experts in the field frequently disagree about the explanations for the same events. Is the dollar "strong" because U.S. imports are down due to the recession, or because U.S. interest rates are high, or because the U.S. inflation rate is down? Is the gold price down because the Russians are selling gold or because interest rates are rising? When the United States reports a trade deficit, the experts disagree about whether the problem is caused by an increase in U.S. imports of oil, the loss of a "competitive edge" by U.S. producers, rapid economic growth in the United States, or the desire of other industrial countries to maintain undervalued currencies to promote their exports.

And then, even if the experts agree, their recommendations for policy actions differ. They can't decide whether U.S. interests are better served by remaining with floating exchange rates or by returning to a pegged exchange rate system. Some experts propose an increase in the monetary gold price—the price at which central bankers buy and sell gold with each other—and several favor a return to a nineteenth-century gold standard. A few want to abandon national currencies in favor of a worldwide money, while others want to eliminate the use of the dollar and gold as international monies. The nonspecialist is left puzzled or bewildered—and skeptical of the value of expertise.

The International Money Game seeks to break the jargon barrier. Technical issues are presented in a straightforward manner with minimal use of specialized terms. Concepts are clarified by use of common metaphor. Explanations are given for the disagreements among the experts.

This book is now in its fourth edition. Previous editions were prepared in quite different economic contexts. The first edition was completed in the early 1970s as the Bretton Woods system of pegged exchange rates, established in the mid-1940s to avoid a repetition of the "beggar-thy-neighbor" policies of the 1920s and 1930s, was breaking down. The international economy was beginning to experience a severe peacetime inflation that had no good historical parallel in the last several hundred years.

The second edition was completed as the international economy was moving from boom to recession, one of the most severe of the postwar period. Movements in exchange rates appeared large, but it seemed that traders and investors required some time to adjust to the floating exchange rates system, which had replaced the pegged-rate system in 1973. Several smaller international banks failed, and a few larger banks incurred losses in the $50 to $100 million range, usually because of foreign exchange trading. International credit flows seemed precarious: the OPEC (Organization of Petroleum Exporting Countries) countries had large payments surpluses; the developing countries had modestly smaller payments deficits; and the major international banks, bridging borrowers and lenders, seemed threatened both by the inability of the borrowers to repay and the threats of the OPEC countries to shift or withdraw their deposits.

Preface

At the time of the third edition, written in the late 1970s, concern had shifted to whether the United States could significantly reduce its inflation rate. The supply of dollars was increasing more rapidly than the demand. Because of skepticism about U.S. price-level performance, the dollar had taken a tremendous beating in the foreign exchange market; in a relatively few years it had lost more than half of its value in terms of the German mark, the Swiss franc, and the Japanese yen. The dollar holdings of central banks in Western Europe and Japan increased sharply because private parties around the world were increasingly reluctant to hold dollar assets. Suddenly external factors became an important constraint on U.S. domestic policy choices. American policymakers were put on notice that their actions sometimes lacked credibility, and their need to regain votes of confidence prompted measures that brought the United States somewhat closer to the next recession. The investors and traders who set foreign exchange values had their own Proposition Thirteen referendum, and during the summer and fall of 1978 they voted no confidence in the credibility of U.S. economic policies.

In the early 1980s, contractive U.S. monetary policies have led to a sharp reduction in the inflation rate. High interest rates have depressed the housing and auto industries and have led to a sharp increase in the foreign exchange value of the U.S. dollar, stimulating U.S. imports and depressing U.S. exports. U.S. unemployment has reached postwar highs. Business bankruptcies are at their highest level since the Great Depression of the 1930s. There is a smell of financial disaster in the air.

Within the last decade the threat of financial crises has appeared with increasing frequency. Such crises have blurred the usual distinction between economics and politics. The Shah appeared tough on the oil price—and then, as he was forced from power, the future darkened. The oil price shot up again. Somehow the predicted disasters have never appeared, for the system has remarkable resiliency. But the expectation of future disasters has not abated. This series of financial crises and near-crises underlines the several themes of the fourth edition.

The question remains whether the U.S. economy can manage to achieve both high employment and reasonable price stability—and still retain minimal restrictions on international trade. Changes in exchange rates are inevitable because national economic policies diverge and national economic interests conflict. These exchange rate movements are much sharper and much larger than changes in relative national price levels might suggest. At times the U.S. dollar is substantially undervalued, at other times, greatly overvalued. The ups and downs of the dollar are part of the transition of the international monetary system from its U.S.-centered, dollar-oriented phase, probably to a more decentralized system. The efforts of other industrialized countries to devise rules to limit the external impact of American economic policies and to lessen the dominant U.S. international role will intensify, for monetary reform is a political process designed to accommodate changes in economic relationships. As long as national interests diverge, crises are certain, although their timing and form are unpredictable.

This revision of the *International Money Game* again provides an opportunity to reflect on recent events. The breakdown of the system of pegged exchange rates was inevitable once the world price level began to increase at rates approaching 10 percent a year. A pegged exchange rate system is incompatible with world monetary instability. The "date of no return" for the move to floating exchange rates occurred early in 1969, soon after Nixon became president. If the United States had successfully obtained a change in the alignment of exchange rates then and had adopted measures to ensure that the new structure of rates would be effective, the payment imbalances in 1970 and 1971 would have been modest, there would not have been an explosion in money supply growth outside the United States, the world inflation of the 1970s would have been much less severe, and much of the instability of the 1970s might have been avoided.

One reason these adjustments were necessary was that inflation rates in the major countries were high and variable. Another was that Germany and Japan had regained roles in the international economy appropriate to their economic size and power. In both cases the foreign exchange values of their currencies had been set twenty years earlier when Germany and Japan were still occupied by the allied powers and still far from regaining their productive potential. Finally, a change in monetary arrangements might have helped other countries cope with the retreat of American power. Yet the magnitude of the instability seems substantially larger in the obscure units in which such things are measured. Small policy errors appear to have major impacts. The explanation lies in the close links among national financial markets and the ease with which billions of dollars are moved internationally. In one hour in February 1973, the Bundesbank was obliged to buy $6 billion; a busy day's trading in the foreign exchange markets can reach $100 billion.

The mid-1970s proved to be a period of much greater instability than had been foreseen. Floating rates, while not yet the disaster that some of the critics had suggested, had proven to be far less of a panacea than the proponents had thought. The smooth, gradual adjustments predicted by the proponents of floating rates did not materialize. The movements in exchange rates were sharper, and within a substantially larger range, than had been anticipated. Moreover, the dominant position of the U.S. dollar has declined. Already there appears to be a reorganization of financial relationships in the international economy—the system centered around the dollar is breaking down, and from time to time a new currency bloc centered around the German mark and the Swiss franc appears to be developing. Whether there is a closely linked relationship between inflation and the rearrangement of financial relationships among the major countries remains conjectural and is not likely to be resolved until the next edition—or the sixth.

The decline in the U.S. inflation rate may presage a gradual move toward greater monetary stability. Yet the move toward greater price stability has shifted world concern toward the ability and the willingness of the developing countries to make their external debt service payments on schedule, and the ability and willingness of the industrial countries to arrest the movements toward higher trade barriers. So stability at the center may have accelerated the tendency of the system—or the arrangements—to fragment.

Several individuals have been important in the writing of this book. Martin Kessler provided the necessary condition, for he suggested that serious economic concepts could be discussed in a relatively light manner. And Fran Miller provided the sufficient condition; she cheerfully typed the N drafts of the first edition. Without her encouraging feedback, the project would have stalled with the $N - (N - 1)$ draft. Francine Spearman and Barbara Haskell were both diligent and patient with this edition.

PART I

The International Money System: Politics and Economics

 1

The Name of the Game Is Money

International finance is a game with two sets of players: the politicians and bureaucrats of national governments, and the presidents and treasurers of giant, large, medium-large, medium, medium-small, and small firms. The government officials want to win elections and secure a niche in the histories of their countries. The corporate presidents and treasurers want to profit—or at least avoid losses—from changes in exchange rates, changes that are inevitable in a world with more than 100 national currencies.

Under the pegged-rate system, the authorities in different countries disagreed over which country should take the initiative in changing the national currency price, so that the necessary change was frequently long delayed. From 1970 on, for example, it was obvious that, at a price of 360 yen to the dollar, the yen was too cheap in terms of the dollar; either the Japanese would have to reduce the yen price of the dollar, or the Americans would have to raise the dollar price of the yen. In either case, Japanese autos would cost more in the United States—and fewer U.S. workers in autos, steel, and textiles would lose their jobs because of imports from Japan. Eventually, the U.S. government took the initiative and forced a revaluation of the yen in 1971 and 1973. Three times in ten years (in 1961, 1969, and 1971) Germany raised the price of the mark in terms of the dollar to reduce its balance-of-payment surpluses. The Germans acted out of self-interest—and to reduce the likelihood that substantial numbers of American troops would be withdrawn from Europe to reduce the U.S. payments deficit. In the 1960s, French President Charles de Gaulle bought $2 billion worth of gold from the U.S. Treasury to force the United States to double the gold price, a move that would have benefited his domestic supporters, restored the prestige of France's monetary stability, and demonstrated that the dollar was a weak currency. The change in the dollar price of gold that he anticipated was delayed, but a first step in that direction occurred in 1971, when the gold price was raised to $39 an ounce, and a second step in 1973, when the price was increased to $42 an ounce. Private parties increasingly ignored the official price, and bid the price to nearly $200 in 1974 and then to $970 in January 1980.

Beginning in March 1973, the major industrial countries abandoned the system of pegged exchange rates that they had relied on for most of the twentieth century; since then, the foreign exchange value of their currencies has been set by market forces under the floating exchange rate system. The price of the dollar in terms of the European currencies began to vary extensively. Paradoxically, official intervention in the exchange market—purchases and sales of foreign exchange by national monetary authorities like the Bank of England and the Bank of Japan—was much more extensive with the floating exchange rate system.

Business fortunes are made on the ability to forecast changes in the values of national currencies, while political futures became frayed as a result of these changes. Under a pegged-rate system, the national monetary authority "fixes" the foreign exchange value of its currency—for a while. The direction of the change in exchange rates (and, frequently, the approximate amount) was predictable. What was less readily predictable were the dates when the change would occur. At one time, periodic cycles could be discerned. The pound sterling was devalued in 1914, 1931, 1949, and 1968; it began to seem that there was an eighteen-year cycle—wait until 1985. The French franc has generally been devalued every ten years—in 1919, 1939, 1949, 1959, 1969—and 1982 and 1983.

Devaluations and revaluations came much more frequently in the late 1960s and early 1970s than in previous decades. Exchange rate crises in each country occurred in November 1967 (British sterling), May 1968 (French franc), September 1969 (German mark), June 1970 (Canadian dollar), May 1971 (German mark, Dutch guilder, and Swiss franc), August 1971 (Japanese yen and all major European currencies), and June 1972 (British sterling and Italian lira). The increased frequency of such changes in exchange rates was closely associated with inflationary financial policies and the inability of countries to agree on an acceptable rate of inflation.

Movements in the exchange rates since the demise of pegged rates are clearly illustrated by sterling (see figure 1.1), which depreciated from $2.00 to $1.55 in 1976, and then, in 1977, appreciated to $1.97. By the end of 1979, with the run on the dollar, sterling climbed to $2.40. By the end of 1982, sterling had depreciated to $1.50. Swings in the Japanese yen have been nearly as extensive—in 1973 the yen climbed to 265 yen to the dollar; in 1975 it depreciated to over 300. By 1978, however, the yen had reached 175; it was worth twice as much as three years earlier. Yet, by the autumn of 1982, the yen had fallen again to 275 yen to the dollar.

The relations among countries and the positions of political leaders within those countries are affected by movements in exchange rates and the various measures employed to reduce payments imbalances. During the 1960s Germany had large payments surpluses and the United States had the large counterpart payments deficits. U.S. pressure on the German government to take measures to offset the foreign exchange costs of keeping

5

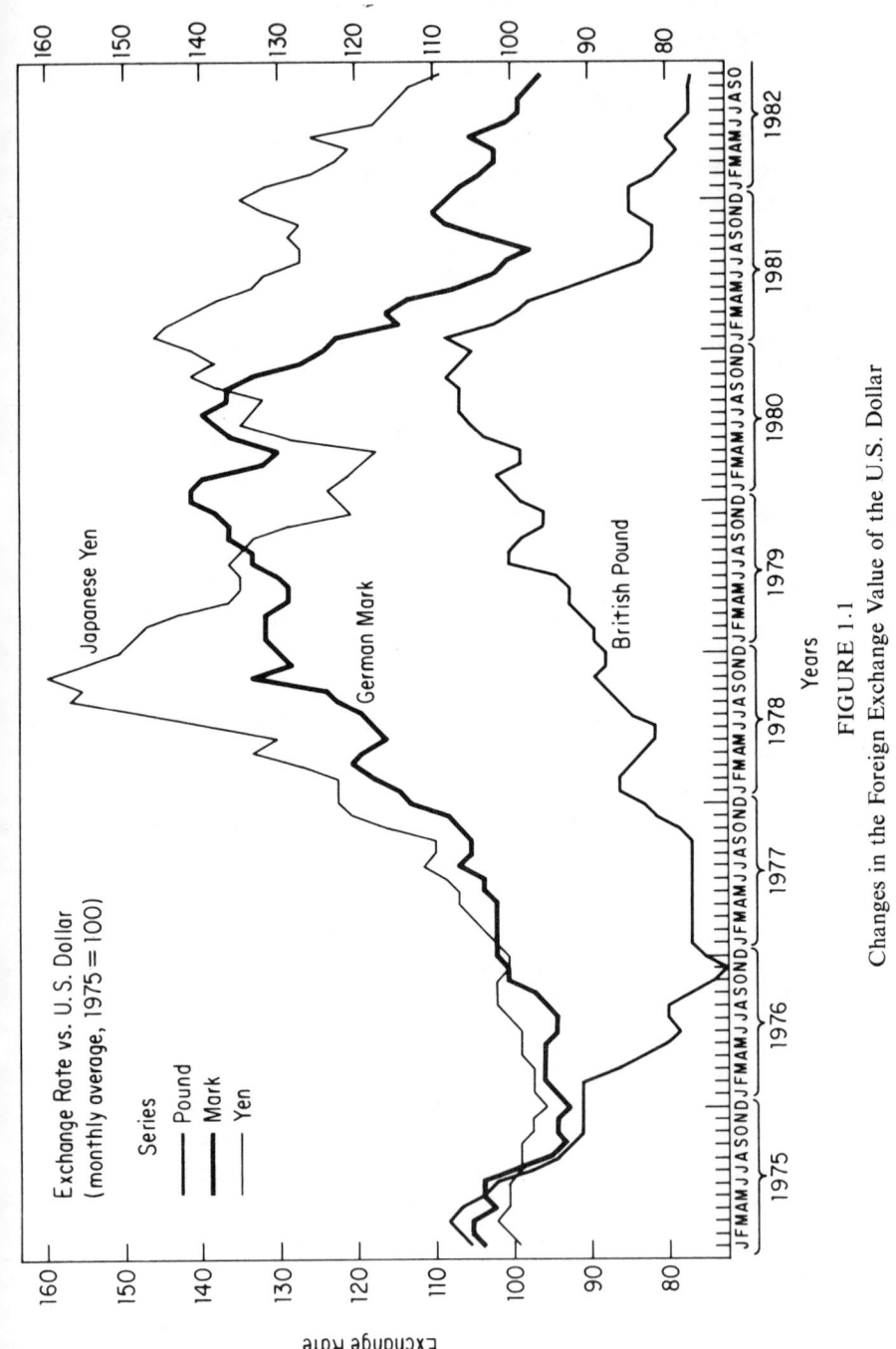

FIGURE 1.1

Changes in the Foreign Exchange Value of the U.S. Dollar

American troops in Germany forced the downfall of Ludwig Erhard as German prime minister. And the 10 percent import surcharge adopted by the U.S. government in August 1971, followed by the 17 percent revaluation of the yen, advanced the date of Prime Minister Sato's resignation in Japan.

British governments—especially Labour governments—resisted devaluing sterling in the 1960s because of the perceived costs in domestic support. The inevitable devaluation of sterling that should have occurred in 1964 was delayed until 1967. In 1974, even though sterling was floating, the British continued to support sterling rather than allow market forces to determine its value; eventually, as their ability to maintain the value of sterling diminished, they permitted it to depreciate.

Throughout the 1960s the U.S. government was extremely reluctant to recognize that an increase in the dollar price of gold was necessary. This change, when finally undertaken, was forced by foreign monetary authorities, especially those in France. Changing the price of gold was much more than a U.S. problem. All countries with large gold holdings were involved, for the change redistributed wealth among countries.

Finance ministers everywhere are continually concerned with changes in the price of their currencies relative to the dollar; they are also concerned with the price relationship between their currencies and gold. In the late 1970s, European governments complained that the U.S. dollar was too weak, and that U.S. exporters had a tremendous competitive advantage in international markets. In the early 1980s, they complained that the U.S. interest rates were too high, which greatly handicapped their ability to follow policies that might offset their own high levels of unemployment. Part of the job of being a finance minister in Europe involves complaining about U.S. policies.

Similarly, whether the yen price of the dollar should be raised is a question that involves not only the United States and Japan but also the many other countries which are customers of or competitors with Japan. Volkswagen's profits vary inversely with

the foreign exchange value of the yen, even though few Volkswagens are sold in Japan. When the yen is strong, the export
competitiveness of Japanese auto firms is diminished.

Changes in exchange rates redistribute payments surpluses
and deficits and, therefore, jobs and profits among countries.
The immediate consequence of revaluing the yen was to lower
profits and wages (or at least wage increases) in Japanese export
industries and to raise profits and permit more rapid wage increases in the competing U.S. industries. In 1974, Volkswagen
reported a loss of $350 million, partly because the appreciation
of the mark meant a sharp rise in the dollar price of Volkswagens. VW's share of the U.S. market for imported cars
dropped from 70 to 25 percent. When the yen depreciated, the
profits of Japanese automobile companies increased sharply, for
the yen equivalent of the U.S. selling price increased.

Exporting national problems is a classic form of international
behavior. Foreign votes do not count in national elections. The
political costs of domestic measures that might solve an unemployment problem, an inflation problem, or a "depressed industry" problem are higher than the political costs of exporting the
problem. Yet one country can export its problems only if some
other countries import them. In the Great Depression of the
1930s, nations sought to export their unemployment with "beggar-thy-neighbor" policies—raising import tariffs and devaluing
their currencies. Few countries were—or are—eager or willing to
import unemployment.

The Politics and Technology of Money

The politics of international money is decentralized. Each of the
100 countries producing money has its own interests and objectives. Each central bank wants to control the rate at which its
money supply grows so as to achieve its own objectives. Because

the objectives and economic structures of countries differ, so do their preferred rates of monetary growth.

The international monetary system must somehow accommodate these divergent national policies. International institutions such as the International Monetary Fund (IMF) in Washington, the Bank for International Settlements (BIS) in Basel, Switzerland, and the Organization for Economic Cooperation and Development (OECD) in Paris, seek to provide a coordinating mechanism for national monetary policies. The forms of international financial coordination vary: central banks borrow from each other when their holdings of foreign currencies decline, ministers of finance meet annually at the International Monetary Fund, and some steps have been taken to develop substitutes for gold. Such coordination, while useful as a counter to the decentralized decisions of national governments, is not an effective substitute for centralized decision making.

The "rules of the game"—the set of commitments that countries have accepted—also may not be effective. These rules seek to ensure that the conflicts among the nations' authorities are resolved in accord with established policies and procedures. When the rules constrain national policies, countries sometimes ignore the rules unilaterally and search for the legal justification later, as did President Nixon when he suspended the U.S. Treasury's gold transactions in August 1971. During the 1970s, the rules and procedures governing exchange market practices of central banks eroded and monetary practices were increasingly based on ad hoc decisions. Exchange crises were less frequent, yet conflict about currency values became more severe. And, at the same time, trade barriers which favored domestic producers were adopted with greater frequency, despite the cost advantages of foreign suppliers.

Firms and individual investors play their own games against this background of changing national currency values. They borrow currencies which they expect to fall in price, and lend currencies which they expect to rise. Sharp foreign exchange traders and corporate treasurers earned millions of dollars—and German marks and Swiss francs—for their companies in the late 1960s and early 1970s by correctly anticipating changes in exchange rates. Between 1967 and 1972, profits from such exchange-rate speculation probably reached $5 billion. Some major international commercial banks reported profits of $50 million in a quarter.

Not all corporate treasurers, however, participated in these profits. In the 1960s, some of them believed the statements of the authorities that parities would not be changed, invested accordingly, and lost their jobs—and others deserved to. During the mid-1970s, some firms reported losses in the tens of millions because of changes in exchange rates. The corporate treasurers of international firms are supposed to know all about profiting from differences in interest rates in various countries, from changes in exchange rates, and from the misfortunes of ministers of finance.

Many foreign exchange traders developed great confidence in their ability to predict changes in exchange rates during the pegged-rate period. Their confidence led them to continue speculating on a large scale during the period of floating exchange rates. Some did well. Some did not—Banque du Bruxelles reported losses of $60 million; Franklin National, $42 million; Herstatt, $400 million. These were the last losses ever reported by Franklin and Herstatt, for they were then losses forced into bankruptcy.

In addition to predicting exchange rate movements, the international money game involves firms and individuals circumventing the regulations of their countries. Indian peasants hoard gold because they believe gold is a better store of value than the rupee. Shoppers in Warsaw carry U.S. dollars. American banks establish branches in London and Nassau to avoid the regulations of U.S. monetary authorities. Italian investors smuggle lira notes into Switzerland because they want to reduce the tax bite of their government. All these moves are designed to protect wealth and increase personal income.

One view about the game—a view reinforced by the daily newspaper columns—is that changes in currency values and international business competition are independent of each other. A competing view—the view of this book—is that these events are related; patterns of international trade and investment are affected by changes in the exchange rates.

Bernie Cornfeld took the U.S. mutual fund industry to Europe, sold shares in U.S. firms to Europeans, and, for a brief period, beat the European financial establishment at its own game. U.S. companies compete aggressively in Canada, Europe, and Latin America, buying out some of their host country competitors and forcing others into insolvency. Machines Bull, the last independent French-owned computer firm, could not survive in the competitive international league because the world price level for computers, set by IBM, was too low relative to French costs. Nor could Rolls-Royce continue to compete in jet aircraft engines, for the prices set by its U.S. competitors—General Electric and the Pratt and Whitney division of United Technologies—were too low relative to British costs. British Leyland, the largest auto firm in Great Britain, was forced into bankruptcy because British costs were rising much more rapidly than the world price of automobiles.

The drama of international finance reflects the contrast between the politics and the technology of money. All the financial assets in the world—currency notes, bank deposits, government bonds, mortgages—must be denominated in one national currency or another. The advantages of having a national money are rarely questioned. To some they may seem intuitively obvious. A national money, like a national airline, a steel mill, and a branch of the Playboy Club, brings prestige. Control of the production of a national money also brings profit. Kings and presidents finance wars in Algeria and Vietnam and build monuments to themselves with newly produced money. Debasement of this money, reducing its purchasing power, occurs worldwide as an indirect or backdoor form of taxation. Taxation through the printing press and inflation is easier and less messy than raising tax rates. Sovereigns manipulate monetary policy because they want to secure full employment, speed growth and development, or accomplish some other worthy objective that will win the approval of their constituents.

Central bankers and finance ministers may not be able to make their country's economic policies effective unless they can isolate their national market for money and credit from the international market. The U.S. military draft provides an analogy: if too many potential draftees move to Canada or fail to register, the draft would not be effective. Similarly, if too many holders of dollar assets or sterling assets or franc assets anticipate the actions of the authorities and move their money abroad, their transactions frustrate the governments' policies.

Over the last several decades the links among national monies have become even stronger as a result of changes in technology. As the cost of transportation and communication across national borders continues to diminish, the effectiveness of national monopolies in the production of money declines. As knowledge about foreign investment opportunities grows and the cost of taking advantage of these opportunities declines, differences in national monetary systems become increasingly important.

In an isolated world, kings had monopoly power over their subjects money; there was no other place to send their wealth and no other currency in which they might hold their assets to escape the sovereign's tax. So the politics of money was largely national. But the monopoly power of kings and presidents is declining, and the constituents of various governments are adjusting to this new world more rapidly than the governments themselves. Governments frequently need international agreements to revise established institutions, and negotiating these agreements takes years. International conferences are becoming larger and more frequent. Meanwhile, established agreements fall into disuse before new agreements can be made.

Today, because of low-cost transportation and instantaneous communication, the several national markets for monies, bonds, deposits, and shares denominated in the various currencies are—in fact—more nearly parts of one international market. At any given moment, the price of IBM shares in Amsterdam and the price of IBM shares in London—and in the other foreign centers where IBM shares are traded—differ only by pennies from the New York price. Stockbrokers buy these shares where they are cheap and sell them where they are dear to profit from the difference, thus keeping the prices in line. The technology of money is international.

The Plan of This Book

The first part of the book examines the structure of national monies, focusing on the tension between economic pressures toward integration of national monetary policies and political pressures toward decentralization. The concern throughout is with the basic components of the international financial system—gold, the dollar, the foreign exchange market, the Eurodollar market—and with the problems created by changes in the price of oil and the inflation rate.

The second part of the book discusses some of the direct and indirect consequences of segmenting the world into 100 currency areas. Each chapter focuses on a particular issue. Thus, the chapter on taxation considers the impact of differences in national taxes on the competitive position of firms based in various countries. The chapter on commercial banking asks whether, as the technology of the banking industry changes so that the distance between banks and their customers becomes unimportant, banks in the United States, Europe, or Japan will have a competitive advantage in the international marketplace. The rise and fall of Bernie Cornfeld is generally seen as a tale of a swashbuckling entrepreneur; chapter 15 shows that the setting for his success, and failure—Europe—reflected financial events in the United States.

During the last 100 years, changes in technology have widened the marketplace for goods, services, and securities. For generations the market was smaller than the nation-state. The expansion of the boundaries of the market beyond the fixed boundaries of the state has threatened the viability of national economic independence and the future of many national industries. Adjustments to the problems created by efforts at national monetary independence are inevitable, but the form the adjustment will take is in doubt. One adjustment involves harmonizing national policies to reduce the competitive advantage—or disadvantage—encountered by firms in various countries as a result of policy differences. Firms in various countries would then be equally able to compete—and to fail. The scope of independent national financial policies would be narrowed. The alternative adjustment involves protecting national firms against more successful foreign competitors. A variety of discriminatory barriers could block the movement of goods and capital, thus protecting the efficacy of national policies.

Both types of adjustment are likely. Yet twenty, fifty, perhaps even one hundred years from now, the problems created by the multitude of national monies will remain. For inevitably the national authorities will manage their economies and develop regulations for their national constituents. And firms and investors will seek to profit from differences in national regulations and national policies.

A System Is How the Pieces Fit

The goal of every science is a conceptual model which shows how the pieces of its universe are related. An economist who seeks to become the Copernicus of the international financial system finds the task complicated because this system has changed substantially in the last 100 years. And in the last decade the pace of change has quickened.

Before World War I the system was described as the "gold standard." Then a change in concept led to a change in name, and "gold exchange standard" became the applicable term for the arrangement between World Wars I and II. From 1947 to 1971, the international monetary arrangements were known as the Bretton Woods system. Since 1971, the system has become a mixed set of arrangements to which no name has yet been attached. Indeed, in the absence of a descriptive term, it is sometimes called the "post-Bretton Woods system."

These changes have been more than cosmetic, for the systemic relationships among the key components—the mechanisms for setting exchange rates and for supplying the money to use in payments between central banks in different countries—were also revamped.

Changes in the system have usually been precipitated by a crisis over the relative values of different national monies, when the established arrangements for financing payments imbalances were about to break down. Thus, the move to the gold exchange standard reflected a prospective shortage of gold in the 1920s. The gold exchange standard failed in the Great Depression of the 1930s because of too-frequent changes in exchange rates. And the Bretton Woods system collapsed in 1971 because it was unable to cope with the large payments imbalances generated by inflation in the United States. The pattern is one of crisis, breakdown, and innovation.

The Copernicus of the international financial system must resolve two issues. First he must develop a model of the relationships among the major components of the system: the foreign exchange market in which national monies are traded, the monetary and fiscal policies of various countries, and the supply of international monies like gold. Then he must explain why these relationships change over time, and whether these changes follow a pattern or are random. This chapter discusses the relationships among these components, while the next chapter reviews the changes in the system over the last 100 years.

Fitting the Pieces: The Foreign Exchange Market

International transactions have one common element that makes them uniquely different from domestic transactions—one of the participants must deal in a foreign currency. When an American buys a new Toyota, he pays in either dollars or yen. If he pays in dollars, the Toyota company must convert the dollars into yen. If the Toyota company receives payment in yen, the buyer must first exchange dollars for yen. At some stage in the chain of transactions between the American buyer and the Japanese producer, dollars must be converted into yen. This transaction is inevitable, since Toyota pays its labor force and its suppliers in yen, while the American buyer receives his salary in dollars. Either the American buyer or the Japanese seller takes the dollars to the foreign exchange market to buy yen.

The foreign exchange market is a market in national monies; the exchange rate is the price. There are two basic types of exchange rate systems—two basic ways of organizing this market. One involves *floating exchange rates;* the price of foreign monies in terms of domestic money rises and falls in response to changes in the supply and demand, much as the prices of shares on the stock market or the price of wheat on the commodity market rise and fall. As U.S. residents pay for their Toyotas, the increase in their demand for yen leads to an increase in the dollar price of the yen, or, what is the same thing, a decrease in the yen price of the dollar.

The concept of a floating exchange rate system is simple: the exchange rate or price moves freely in response to market forces. National governments may participate in the exchange market to raise or lower the price of their money; they might seek to dampen daily or weekly movements in the exchange rate.

Despite the simplicity and neatness of the concept, few countries have permitted their currencies to float for very extended periods. Among developed countries, Canada has the longevity record for using a floating rate (1950–1962 and 1970 to the present). Lebanon holds the record for developing countries (1950 to the present). On three occasions, a substantial number of countries have used the floating-rate system at the same time. The first time came after World War I, between 1919 and 1925, when most European countries were adjusting to the inflationary impacts of the war. The second time, August to December 1971, most Western European countries and Japan permitted their currencies to float as an interim measure: they anticipated that the prices of their currencies would rise in terms of the U.S. dollar. Finally, the currencies of the major industrialized countries have been floating since early 1973, but the extent of central bank participation in the foreign exchange market has been much greater than in the two previous periods. The Bank of Japan has intervened extensively in the foreign exchange market to ensure smooth rate movements.

The alternative to a floating exchange rate is a *pegged-rate system*. This system has two main features. First, the government authority, usually the central bank, limits variations in the prices of foreign monies in terms of its own national money within a more or less narrow range. The price at the center of this range is the parity or peg for the currency, a reference point for the price of the currency in terms of some other asset. At one time, most currencies were pegged to gold. For more than 100 years the historic peg for the U.S. dollar was $20.67 per fine ounce of gold; the $35 parity was adopted in 1934. Alternatively, some countries use the currency of another country as the peg; the Mexican peso was pegged to the U.S. dollar from 1953 to 1975. After 1945 most foreign countries pegged their currencies to the U.S. dollar.

The second feature of a pegged-rate system is that on occasion—perhaps once a generation, or once a decade, or once a year, or once a month—the government may change the peg for its currency, as the British did when they altered the dollar price of sterling from $2.80 to $2.40 in November 1967 and to $2.60 in December 1971.

Pegged-rate systems are more complex than floating-rate systems, for the authorities must limit variations in the price of their currencies in the foreign exchange market so that the market price does not differ significantly from the parity. Usually each central bank buys its own currency to prevent its price from falling substantially below the peg and sells its own currency to prevent its price from rising substantially above the peg. Such purchases and sales prevent any significant deviation of the market exchange rate from the parity. The boundaries within which the market price of the currency may vary before the central bank is obliged to intervene are known as the support limits or margins. For example, the Bank of England bought sterling in exchange for dollars when the demand for sterling was weak, thus limiting the decline in the price of sterling in terms of the dollar. And the Bank of England sold sterling when the demand was strong to limit the increase in the price of sterling. In the 1960s, when sterling was pegged at $2.80, the support limits were $2.78 and $2.82, or about 0.75 percent on either side of the parity. When sterling was pegged at $2.60 at the end of 1971, these limits were widened to 2.25 percent, or to about $2.54 and $2.66.

Under pegged-rate systems, countries incur payments imbalances—surpluses and deficits—which reflect the central bank's transactions in the foreign exchange market. A payments surplus occurs when the central bank sells its currency in the foreign exchange market and buys gold or other international monies (the concept of international money is discussed later in this chapter). Conversely, a payments deficit occurs when the central bank buys its currency and sells international money.

From time to time, the authorities must change the value of the parity to reduce a payments deficit or surplus. A country with a payments deficit devalues its currency by increasing the price at which it buys and sells foreign money in terms of its own money. Conversely, a country with a surplus revalues its currency by reducing the price at which it buys and sells foreign monies.

During the 1960s, as in earlier periods, most countries were reluctant to change their parities (the basis of their concern is discussed in chapter 4) despite large payments imbalances; thus the pegs tended to become somewhat frozen. Still, measures had to be taken to limit payments deficits. So governments raised taxes and imposed controls on foreign payments, and they also subsidized exports. Some importers found that they had to pay more for foreign exchange than they would have if the currency had been devalued. In effect, such controls devalued the currency on a selective "backdoor" basis. Conversely, countries with large payments surpluses reduced controls on foreign payments rather than revalue.

In the decades since World War II, exchange rate pegs have been changed more than 100 times, an average of slightly more than one change per country. But this average covers a wide range of behavior. Several countries have maintained the same peg throughout this period, while a few have changed their peg every six or eight weeks for three or four years.

Central bank transactions in the foreign exchange market under a pegged-rate system are the counterpart of changes in the exchange rate under a floating-rate system—they match the demand for foreign exchange with the supply. If a central bank does not intervene in the exchange market under a floating-rate system, payments surpluses and deficits do not occur; the exchange rate changes to balance supply and demand. The floating-rate system's equivalent of a payments deficit is an increase in the price of foreign monies in terms of domestic money.

Although the two exchange systems are by no means identical, the distinction between them can become fuzzy, for the more frequently the exchange rate pegs are changed, the more nearly the pegged-rate system resembles a floating-rate system. Conversely, the more frequently authorities in countries with floating exchange rates intervene in the exchange market to dampen the movements in the foreign exchange price of their currency, the more nearly the floating-rate system resembles the pegged system.

Changes in the exchange rate pegs and variations in the price of foreign exchange under the floating-rate system are not economic accidents. Such changes are primarily results of differences in the monetary and fiscal policies of various countries; they are also the results of major disturbances like crop failures or oil price increases.

Fitting the Pieces: National Financial Policies

One approach toward the formulation of national monetary and fiscal policies involves managing these policies so the existing exchange rate peg can be maintained. A competing approach is to aim these policies in the direction of full employment, price stability, rapid economic growth, or financing government expenditures. If the second approach is followed, then changes in the exchange rate are necessary; the authorities may either opt for a floating rate or alter their exchange rate peg and/or their controls of international payments as frequently as necessary.

The monetary policies of the central bank and the fiscal policies of the national treasury have a major impact on each country's international financial position, affecting, for example, whether a country with pegged rates will be in deficit or surplus or whether a country with floating rates will find the price of its currency rising or falling. Monetary policy changes the amount of money held by the public; central banks increase or reduce the money supply to induce changes in the public's spending for goods and services. Fiscal policy involves changes in government expenditures relative to its revenues. Monetary and fiscal policies are manipulated to help the government achieve its employment, income, and price level objectives.

Changes in monetary and fiscal policies affect a country's payments balance by altering the demand for foreign goods and foreign securities. These policies lead to changes in national income; the demand for foreign goods increases when national income increases, and exports may increase less rapidly. Moreover, the change in income may cause domestic prices to increase; and if prices of domestic goods rise relative to prices of foreign goods, the country's international competitive position becomes less favorable. Then imports grow more rapidly, and exports more slowly. Monetary and fiscal policies also cause changes in interest rates; as domestic interest rates rise relative to interest rates abroad, the demand for foreign securities falls while exports of domestic securities may increase.

Some countries change their exchange rate pegs relatively infrequently because their monetary and fiscal policies are geared to maintaining a particular peg. Haiti holds the longevity record—the Haitian gourde has been pegged at 5 to the U.S. dollar since 1907. The Haitian record is no accident; Haiti's monetary and fiscal policies have been geared to maintaining a fixed parity. Similarly, the Mexican peso was pegged to the U.S. dollar for more than twenty years, from the mid-1950s to the mid-1970s; the central objective of Mexican monetary policy was to keep the peso at 12.5 to the dollar. In the early 1970s, Mexican monetary policy became much more expansive, and eventually the more rapid increase in Mexican than U.S. prices led to a progressively larger payments deficit, so the established parity was no longer viable.

In contrast, Brazil, Israel, and Denmark change their parities frequently because they direct their monetary and fiscal policies to domestic objectives, whether they be economic growth, full employment, or fighting wars in the Sinai and the Golan Heights. For these countries the retention of a particular exchange rate peg is neither an important policy objective nor a significant constraint on the choice of domestic policies. Thus, Brazil adjusts its monetary and fiscal policies to maintain a rapid rate of economic growth, Israel to finance its defense expenditures, and Denmark to pay for its welfare programs. Instead of adjusting its domestic economy to the prevailing exchange rate peg, each of these countries adjusts its exchange rate peg so that international payments and receipts will be roughly equal. The monetary policies of these countries are independent of their balance-of-payments positions.

The objectives of national economic policies change over time. U.S. history provides a good example. During the Civil War, monetary policies in both North and South were highly expansive, and both Union and Confederate governments printed large supplies of bank notes to finance their war expenditures. Commodity prices rose rapidly. After the war, the U.S. government sought to offset the wartime inflation by pursuing deflationary policies. The objective was to peg the dollar at its prewar parity with gold—which finally happened in 1878.

During World War I, as in the Civil War, the money supply grew rapidly; again commodity prices increased sharply. Price stability did not become an important objective of U.S. policy until the 1920s. Substantial up-and-down price-level variations, tolerable in the largely agricultural society of the nineteenth century, were unacceptable in an industrial society because falling prices led to large increases in rates of business failure and unemployment. During World War II, full employment became an important objective of national policy. In the 1950s, largely in response to the threat of Soviet economic and technological achievements, economic growth became an important objective. The realization of the Great Society—raising the economic welfare of the millions of Americans who lived below the poverty line—became a prime objective in the mid-1960s. Shortly thereafter, the preservation of freedom and the stability of the dominoes in Southeast Asia meant that security expenditures went to the head of the list. As these U.S. objectives have changed, so have the targets for monetary and fiscal policies.

Several themes emerge. Wars lead to inflation, and inflation leads to large payments deficits. No payments imbalance can persist forever; ultimately an adjustment is needed. As populations have become industrial and urban, governments have become increasingly concerned with economic welfare. Full employment, rarely a problem in an agricultural economy, became a matter of crucial importance as U.S. society became increasingly urban. The fiscal role of governments has increased; taxes in some countries now amount to 50 percent or more of national income. As expectations of higher living standards have become more widespread, raising the economic growth rate has grown increasingly important as a national objective.

National economic policies have stressed domestic objectives in recent years, while maintenance of a particular exchange rate peg has been slighted. The international system has had to accommodate these increasingly inward-looking national policies. At first, the combination of domestically oriented financial policies and a pegged-rate system led to increasingly large international payments deficits—and surpluses. The size of these imbalances was limited by the ability of individual countries to finance larger deficits, and, eventually, changes in parities were forced. Now, to the extent that each country allows its currency to float in the foreign exchange market, the diversity is reflected in movements in the exchange rates; the currencies of countries with relatively high rates of inflation tend to depreciate. The movements in exchange rates are continuous rather than abrupt—although changes in exchange rates have been both sharp and abrupt in the floating system.

Fitting the Pieces: The Supply of International Money

A central bank can buy its own currency in the foreign exchange market only by selling some other asset, and it can sell its own currency only if it buys some other asset. By definition, any asset which central banks buy and sell when they support their currencies in the exchange market is an *intervention* asset. And the assets which central banks acquire with intervention assets comprise the set of international monies. An international money is a necessary component of a pegged exchange rate system; a floating-rate system, in contrast, has no need for an international money.

One key question is what determines which assets qualify as international money: Why is gold an international money, while silver is not? Why are U.S. dollar assets considered international money, while Canadian dollar assets are not? A related question involves how much of each asset is held as international money.

Given that central banks need an international money because they peg their currencies, each central bank must decide which

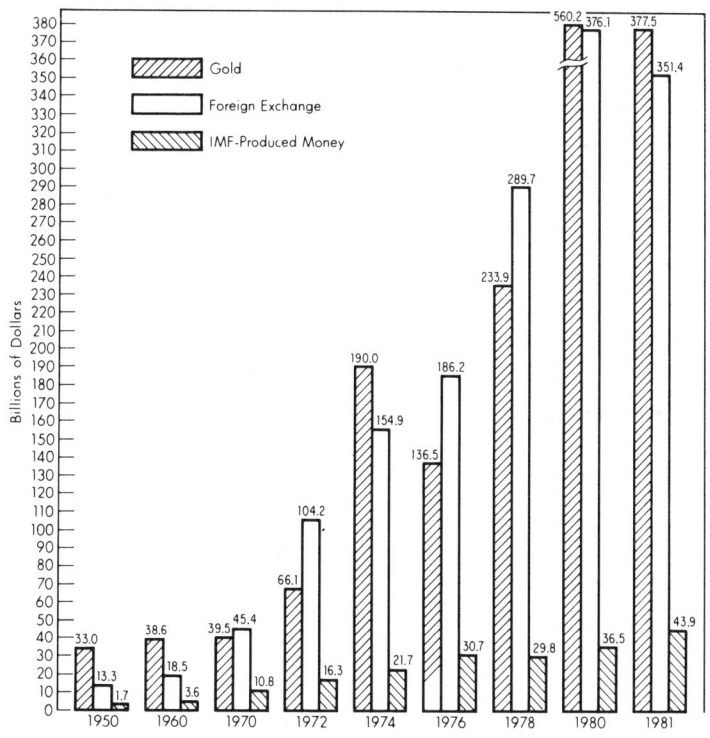

FIGURE 2.1

The Supply of International Money

(Billions of U.S. dollars, end of period)

SOURCE: International Monetary Fund, *International Financial Statistics* (Washington, D.C., March 1982).

NOTE: Gold excludes holdings in international institutions. Since 1972, gold is valued at the free-market dollar price.

asset has the most attractive combination of attributes in the form of interest income, future purchasing power, transaction costs, and storage costs.

Until the mid-1960s, holdings of gold were the largest component of international money (see figure 2.1). Then holdings of foreign exchange, largely dollars, surged. Now, because of the surge in the market price of gold, the gold component of reserves has increased sharply; the value of these holdings fluctuates with changes in the dollar price of gold. The third and the smallest component of international monies are those produced by international institutions, primarily the International Monetary Fund. Such institutions are groups of countries acting jointly. Negotiations among the members determine how much of each type of money will be produced each year and how the newly produced money will be distributed among the member countries.

The use of gold as an international money is explained by its history. (Chapter 5 examines gold's future as an international money.) For centuries, gold was the world's principal money. Gold bullion and then gold coins were used to make payments, both within countries and across national boundaries. Because gold was used in so many countries, payments between countries frequently did not involve any foreign exchange transactions, for foreign gold coins circulated together with domestic coins within many countries.

The volume of gold held as an international money represents the cumulative acquisitions of national central banks, or the difference between the amount of gold produced and the amount absorbed by jewelry, the arts, dentistry, industry, and private hoards. New gold discoveries led to sharp increases in price levels. Gold mining costs then increased, and gold production tended to decline.

For most of the last 300 years, central banks have bought and sold gold at their parities. If the amount of gold produced during a period exceeded the amount demanded by private parties at the central bank's price, the mining companies in effect sold their gold to the central banks, because the companies could obtain a higher price from the banks than in the commodity market. When private demand was weak, central banks acquired a large share of new production; when private demand was strong, they acquired a smaller share.

Several factors explain the central banks' preference for gold. A central bank holds gold because it feels it will be able to sell gold to some other central bank when the need arises. Even if this expectation should prove wrong, gold could still be sold in the commodity market, perhaps at a price not far below the price set by the mint.

Over the last several hundred years, as national currencies have become more important, gold's role as a money in domestic economies has declined. Initially, national monies in the form of bank notes and deposits could be easily used to buy gold from central banks. But as the amount of national monies increased relative to the amount of gold, sovereigns found it difficult to maintain the national money and gold in circulation at the same time, for gold was often hoarded. This problem was eventually resolved by eliminating the use of gold in domestic transactions. In the last fifty years, monetary gold transactions have been increasingly restricted to dealings among national central banks. For example, the Bank of England would sell gold to the U.S. Treasury to get dollars to support sterling in the exchange market; conversely, the Bank of England would acquire dollars in the exchange market, knowing that it could use these dollars to buy gold at the U.S. Treasury.

The severe gold shortage of the 1950s and 1960s led to renewed efforts to reduce the demand for gold. U.S. citizens, who had been prohibited from owning gold domestically in 1933, were prohibited from owning gold abroad in 1961. Foreign central banks were encouraged to acquire dollar assets rather than gold to meet their demand for international money. A major international negotiation to produce a "paper gold"—an asset which was supposed to have all of the attributes of gold except its weight, durability, and glitter—was set in motion. The objective of all such measures was to forestall the sure cure for any shortage—an increase in the price.

These measures proved ineffective. As long as private parties could buy gold in private markets at $35 an ounce, central banks were obliged to let private demand determine how much of new production would flow into private uses and how much would accrue to central banks and thus add to the stock of international monies. Indeed, maintaining one price for both private parties and central banks meant that central banks were required to sell gold from their own holdings to private parties if private demand in any period exceeded new production.

The inevitable occurred; by 1965 private demand exceeded new production, and sales from central banks as a group mounted to $2 billion by early 1967. The major central banks, following the U.S. lead, arranged a two-tier market: central banks would continue to buy from and sell gold to each other at $35, while private parties would buy and sell gold in a free market where the price might rise above the parity or fall below it. Gold producers would be tempted to sell new output to private parties if they would pay a higher price than the central banks.

Soon after this two-tier system was adopted, the price of gold in private markets began to rise modestly above the official price. Paradoxically, the gold shortage intensified; central banks were reluctant to sell gold to other central banks at $35 if its value in the private market was $40. If gold was to remain in the system, an increase in the monetary price was necessary.

The customary economic response to any shortage is a price rise. The gold price rose slowly in the late 1960s, and then very rapidly in the early 1970s. The price increase led to a very sharp increase in the value of gold held by monetary authorities. At a price of $200, central bank gold holdings exceeded $225 billion. And the gold shortage had disappeared.

The gold shortage of the 1960s was similar to that of the

1920s; then, too, central bankers were concerned that there wasn't enough gold. Not enough gold was being produced, and too much of the production was going into various private uses. There was a similar search for substitutes for gold. Some countries began to acquire assets denominated in dollars. The Bank of Canada and the Bank of Mexico, for example, held most of their international money in the form of dollar assets—U.S. Treasury bills and time deposits in U.S. banks. Similarly, the Bank of Malaysia held international money in the form of sterling assets deposited in London.

Dollar assets had several attractive attributes for foreign central banks: they provided interest income, and they could readily be exchanged for gold at the U.S. Treasury. For a long time, U.S. dollar assets appeared more likely to remain acceptable and retain value than assets denominated in other currencies. Dollars could be used to buy goods and securities in a country with a large, productive economy which seemed militarily secure and politically stable. And the dollar had—and still has—a better long-term record for retaining its purchasing power than most other currencies. Whether dollar assets will continue to have these qualities is examined in chapter 8.

As foreign holdings of dollar assets increased, however, countries became increasingly reluctant to acquire more dollar assets, in part, because the U.S. Treasury's ability to convert these assets into gold had come into question. Nevertheless, the dollar holdings of foreign central banks surged in 1970 and 1971, for business firms, banks, and private investors began to anticipate that the price of the West German mark, the Swiss franc, and the Japanese yen would rise in terms of the dollar, either because the dollar would be devalued in terms of gold or because these currencies would be revalued in terms of gold. So foreign central banks ended up with the dollars these other investors were selling; the foreign central banks were caught between their reluctance to acquire more dollar assets and their reluctance to revalue their currencies. The indecision proved costly, since these central banks first acquired the dollar assets and then revalued anyway. In the last several years, foreign holdings of dollars have surged; at the end of 1981, the dollar component of international money was eight times as large as at the end of 1970 (see figure 2.1).

The use of gold as money, because of its underlying value as a commodity, points to a unique problem of the international economy. In the domestic economy, paper money (in the form of bank notes and checks) has value because the government declares that it has value—sellers and tax collectors are obliged to accept the money. No government has similar power in the international economy; no sovereign can compel another sovereign to accept an asset as money, and neither can any international agency. Some countries may be reluctant to acquire assets as international money unless they are confident that the assets will retain value and remain acceptable.

The persistent gold shortage, together with the reluctance of central banks to acquire more dollar assets, led some observers to suggest that the demand for international money should be satisfied by increased reliance on the monies produced by international institutions. Perhaps. But the question remains whether countries would have confidence in this money, an issue discussed in chapter 11.

Who Fits the Pieces Together?

The gold and exchange crises of the last decade can be explained by the absence of institutions to ensure that the growth in the supply of international monies matches the growth in demand. The larger problem is that there is no mechanism to ensure that the three major components of the system—the exchange rate system, national monetary and fiscal policies, and the supply of international monies—are consistent with each other. Political forces within the individual countries explain the change in orientation of national financial policies. The adjustment of the foreign exchange market and the supply of international monies to the increased diversity in national financial policies has lagged because of difficulties in securing agreement among the sovereigns.

"The Greatest Monetary
Agreement in History"

The Smithsonian Institution in Washington, D.C., is the repository for the nation's artifacts. Lindbergh's *Spirit of St. Louis* hangs from the rafters. The Hope Diamond is there. So are George Washington's uniforms and the largest blue whale ever caught. And in December 1971 the finance ministers of the largest non-Communist industrialized countries met at the Smithsonian and agreed to set new foreign exchange values for their currencies. President Nixon called the Smithsonian Agreement "the greatest monetary agreement in history."

The remarkable accomplishment of the agreement was that more exchange rates were simultaneously realigned in a multinational framework than ever before. By mid-summer 1972 Great Britain ceased pegging sterling, and sterling depreciated immediately. Then early in 1973 Germany permitted the mark to float, and most other industrial countries followed Germany. So the major countries backed into a system of floating exchange rates. The "Greatest Monetary Agreement in History" lasted for a year. In effect, the breakdown of the agreement meant that the existing machinery for resolving exchange rate disputes could itself be sent to some monetary counterpart of the Smithsonian Institution to take its place alongside earlier monetary arrangements and agreements as yet another relic.

Rules and Myths of the Gold Standard

A hundred years ago, according to popular economic history, the world was on the gold standard. Participation in the gold standard was open to any country which agreed to buy and sell at a fixed price set by the national government, the mint parity. The gold standard was not based on a formal international agreement. The exchange rate between any two national currencies was set by the ratio of their mint parities, adjusted for any difference in the gold content of their coins. For example, the mint parity for the U.S. dollar was $20.67 in 1900, while the mint parity for the pound sterling was 3 pounds, 17 shillings, 10½ pence. The dollar-sterling exchange was $20.67 divided by 3/17/ 10½, or $4.86 per pound sterling after adjustment for the somewhat greater gold in U.S. coins than in British coins.

Moreover, each central bank was, on demand of private parties, ready to buy and sell gold at its mint parity. Whenever exporters within a country acquired gold from their foreign customers, they could sell the gold to their central bank in exchange for domestic currency. The central bank would then print more money to pay for the gold; the domestic money supply and the central bank's gold holdings would increase. Conversely, the domestic money supply would decline whenever importers, in order to make payments abroad, sold domestic money to the central bank to buy gold.

The attraction of the gold standard—the reason a return to this type of arrangement appears so attractive—is that the price levels were remarkably stable in the long run. The U.S. price level in 1900 was only two thirds as high as a century earlier—

although there had been sharp changes, both increases and decreases, in the price levels during much shorter intervals. The price level increased modestly in the 1850s, and then nearly doubled during the Civil War. Thereafter the price level decreased slowly. And during various financial crises—1847, 1873, 1884, 1890, 1893, 1907—the price level frequently fell sharply.

Market forces automatically and simultaneously answered two important questions: How rapidly should the domestic money supply grow in each country, and how rapidly should the international money supply grow? The theory held that a country's money supply increased when it achieved a payments surplus, and declined when there was a payments deficit. Exchange rate arrangements and monetary policies were compatible; there was never any risk that monetary policy would be so inflationary that the central bank might sell all its gold and not be able to retain its gold parity.

The flow of gold from new production meant that the gold holdings of all central banks could increase together; every country could have a payments surplus simultaneously. In the 1850s, after the discovery of gold in California, and again at the end of the nineteenth century following gold discoveries in the Yukon, Alaska, and South Africa, the rapid growth in gold holdings led to sharp increases in the supply of domestic monies and to worldwide increases in commodity prices. Increases or decreases in price levels were accepted as a natural part of economic life, much like the weather.

Market forces also determined how rapidly the supply of international money should grow. The amount of gold produced during any period depended on the relationship between the price that central banks would pay for gold and the costs of mining gold. These costs in turn depended on the general price level. When commodity prices increased, so would these costs. Gold production would then decline, since producers were caught between rising costs and a fixed selling price, the mint parity. Gold holdings would then increase less rapidly—and so would national money supplies. On the other hand, when the commodity price levels declined, so would gold-mining costs. Gold producers would then increase their output. Money supplies would grow more rapidly, thus checking the decline in commodity prices. So, the price level and the supply of gold were components of a consistent system. The pieces fit, at least in theory.

In practice, the gold standard was less systematic than the model suggests. Often, changes in the gold supply reflected the chanciness of new gold discoveries and innovations in gold ore-refining processes rather than changes in the price level or mining costs. Some central banks directed their monetary policies toward domestic objectives, especially during wars. Many countries were more frequently off the gold standard than on. Nevertheless, the automatic, anonymous, and consistent attributes of the system attracted numerous supporters who advocated adherence to the system as a basis for monetary policy.

Several developments associated with World War I reduced the relevance of the gold standard model. The war demonstrated that nationalism was a powerful force in Britain and France as well as in Germany and Austria. The monetary counterpart of nationalism was that central banks managed monetary policies to help finance their own war efforts. The cohesiveness of the international system was fragmented.

Wartime inflation, moreover, pushed commodity prices in the 1920s to levels at least twice as high as in 1913. Higher prices meant both an increased demand for money and gold and, because of higher gold production costs, a reduced level of output. A gold shortage ensued. Few countries were willing to accept the substantial reductions in commodity prices that would have been needed to raise gold output. If the demand for international money was to be satisfied, either the price of gold in terms of national currencies would have to be increased or new international monies would have to be developed.

Finally, the war brought about a sharp rise in U.S. economic power. The stimulus of the war tied the regional economies of the nation together, a linkage that would otherwise have developed more slowly. The United States, moreover, escaped both the material destruction and the postwar economic turmoil that pervaded much of Europe. After World War I, the U.S. economy was about as large as the combined economies of the ten next largest countries—a much more dominant position than Great Britain had ever enjoyed.

The monetary problems of the half century following World War I revolve around these three themes: nationalism, the shortage of international money, and shifts in economic power toward—and, later, from—the United States. The disintegration of the international system in the 1930s resulted from the failure to adjust institutional arrangements to these realities.

The breakdown of the gold standard became starkly evident in the economic behavior of nations during the 1920s and 1930s. At the beginning of World War I, most European countries left the gold standard, since their rates of inflation exceeded that of the United States; indeed, the dollar was the only major currency that remained convertible into gold. During the early 1920s the European currencies floated in the foreign exchange market, and many of them depreciated sharply in terms of gold and the dollar. Floating exchange rates were viewed as an interim measure, for most governments in Europe wanted to return to the gold standard at their prewar mint parities. But this objective could be achieved only if they permitted their domestic price levels to decline substantially—or if there was a substantial rise in the U.S. price level. Few countries were willing to adopt the deflationary policies needed to make a return to the 1913 parities feasible, and the United States was unwilling to inflate.

By the mid-1920s, some countries had changed their minds and most currencies were again pegged to gold. Sterling, the Swiss franc, and a few other currencies—those of countries that were neutral during the war—were again at their 1913 parities.

Many more currencies had been devalued extensively in terms of both gold and the dollar. For example, the French franc, which had been worth 18.3 cents in 1913, sold for 3.9 cents in 1926.

This system of pegged rates held together for several years. But there were too many inconsistencies for the pieces to fit together for long. Sterling was overvalued; the British had not deflated sufficiently so that the prewar parity was viable. In contrast, the French franc was undervalued; the decline in its foreign exchange value was much greater than was justified by the increase in the French price level relative to the price levels of its trading partners.

In the late 1920s, the central banks of the agricultural countries were again forced to permit their currencies to float because the prices and export earnings of farm products fell sharply. In July 1931, Germany went off the gold standard. Then, in September 1931, the Bank of England suspended gold transactions, and sterling again became a floating currency. In 1933, immediately after President Franklin D. Roosevelt took office, the U.S. government ceased pegging the dollar to gold at the $20.67 parity. The dollar floated until early 1934, when a new $35 parity was established. Two years later, other currencies—the French and Swiss francs and the Dutch guilder—were also devalued in terms of gold. Within a six-year period, nearly every currency had been devalued in terms of gold, many by as much as 50 to 70 percent.

In this sequence of currency devaluations in the 1930s, the industrial countries—Great Britain, the United States, France, the Netherlands, and Switzerland—were each pursuing what became known as a "beggar thy neighbor" policy. Each country devalued its currency because of high domestic unemployment. Each was concerned that more expansive policies would lead to large balance of payments deficits. Each country wanted to import jobs by reducing the price of its goods in foreign markets and raising the price of foreign goods in its domestic market. But no country wanted to export jobs at a time of substantial unemployment.

The Bretton Woods System

The interwar period demonstrated the need for an institutional framework that would enable countries to follow policies directed toward domestic objectives without exporting their problems. Somehow the system seemed unable to cope with the problem of obtaining consistency among the policies of the major countries. During World War II, the United States and Great Britain took the initiative in developing an international treaty to constrain the financial behavior of individual countries. This treaty—the Articles of Agreement of the International Monetary Fund (informally called the Bretton Woods Agreement after the New Hampshire resort where the final negotiations took place)—had two major components. One was a set of rules or constraints directed at the exchange rate behavior of member countries, especially their freedom to change their exchange rate parities. The thrust of the IMF Agreement was that unnecessary changes in exchange rates should be avoided, while desired and justifiable changes should take place in an orderly manner. The second was a pool of member countries' currencies. The IMF would be a "lender of last resort," lending currencies from this pool to its members to help them finance payments deficits. These two components were part of a package; it was believed that members would be more likely to accept the constraints on changing their exchange rates to reduce their payments deficits if they were assured that they could borrow foreign currencies from the Fund to finance these deficits.

The agreement proved to have two shortcomings. First, there was no mechanism to induce countries to change their parities when they became inappropriate. And this defect was especially relevant for countries with persistent payments surpluses. Second, the components of the system were not compatible: the agreement focused on the behavior of individual member countries, but not on consistency among national monetary policies, the exchange rate system, and the supply of international money.

The emphasis of national monetary policies on domestic objectives and the desire of most countries to retain pegged exchange rates subjected the Bretton Woods system to increasing stress. With most countries pursuing independent national monetary policies, changes in parities became inevitable. But national authorities were reluctant to recognize the implications of their monetary policies for their exchange rates: they retained the exchange market arrangements of the gold standard. The IMF rules sought to minimize unnecessary changes in the exchange parities, but, in fact, changes in parities proved too infrequent and too long-delayed; the adjustable parities of the IMF system were sticky or frozen.

During the 1950s and 1960s, the supply of international money increased less rapidly than the demand. The analogy with the 1920s is strong. In both periods, the problem was aggravated by the sharp rise in national price levels during and after a world war; the higher price levels led to an increase in the demand for international money. At the same time, higher production costs deterred increases in gold output. The increase in the central bank demand for gold was greater than the increase in monetary gold stocks resulting from new production. As a result, individual central banks could satisfy their demand for gold only by buying it from other countries. Between 1950 and 1970, U.S. gold holdings declined from $23 billion to $11 billion. One alternative to increased central bank holdings of gold was increased holdings of short-term assets denominated in dollars, sterling, and other major currencies. Foreign countries could add to their holdings of liquid dollar assets if they achieved payments surpluses. This meant that the United States would incur payments deficits. Foreign holdings of dollars increased from $8 billion in 1950 to $47 billion in 1970.

The United States could supply dollars to meet the international money demands of other countries without limit; there was a virtually inexhaustible supply of U.S. Treasury bills and deposits in U.S. banks. (Whether U.S. interests or the system's interests would be served by the continued exports of these bills and deposits is a different issue.) But U.S. ability to supply gold to foreign central banks was limited; each million dollars of gold sold to foreign central banks was a million dollars less in the holdings of the U.S. Treasury. The U.S. dilemma was that it was unable to distinguish, in the design of its balance-of-payments policies, between those foreign countries that wanted to add to their holdings of dollar assets and those countries that wanted to add to their gold holdings.

For most of the postwar period (probably until 1967 or even 1968), foreign holdings of dollars increased and the U.S. Treasury's gold holdings declined, not because U.S. goods were overpriced or foreign goods were underpriced, but because foreign central banks wanted to add to their holdings of international money. During this period, the United States was the principal source of international money because other sources were inadequate. But the United States could not sell dollars or gold to foreign central banks without incurring a payments deficit, at least as a payments deficit had been traditionally defined.

Numerous causes were given for the deficit: increased U.S. imports of Scotch whiskey, French brandy, and German beer; increases in U.S. military expenditures in Western Europe and Southeast Asia; and decreases in U.S. exports of automobiles and steel. But these factors derived from the foreign demand for dollars and gold. For if other countries want to add to their holdings of gold and dollars, they must cut the price of their goods relative to the price of U.S. goods to secure a payments surplus.

The implication of the worldwide gold shortage was that central banks were buying and selling gold at a price that was too low relative to the production costs of gold. One solution was an increase in the price of gold in terms of all currencies. Gold production would be stimulated; the amount of gold mined each year would increase, and the value of gold output would increase even more rapidly. And the private demand for gold would be lower because gold would be more expensive, so more of the newly produced gold would be sold to central banks. In this way, the central banks in Europe would be able to satisfy their demand for gold without forcing the U.S. Treasury to sell gold. Instead, they could purchase it from the gold-producing countries. At some price—$40 or $50 or $70—everyone's demand for gold could be satisfied.

If, on the other hand, the monetary price of gold were to remain unchanged, then the gold shortage would disappear only if the demand fell. One way to reduce the demand would be to stem the flow of dollars to foreign central banks, thus reducing their ability to buy gold from the U.S. Treasury. During the 1960s the U.S. authorities adopted a series of such measures. Foreign recipients of economic aid were obliged to spend the money on U.S. goods, even though foreign goods were cheaper. U.S. government agencies were directed to buy their goods from domestic sources unless foreign prices were lower, first by 6 percent, then by 12 percent and then by 50 percent. The U.S. Army began to ship Milwaukee beer to Munich. Purchases of foreign securities by U.S. residents were taxed, initially at a rate of 1 percent, then 2 percent. Purchases of foreign securities by U.S. firms and U.S. financial institutions were subjected to "voluntary" controls in 1965, and the controls became mandatory in 1968. Measures were also taken to increase U.S. receipts from foreigners—for example, U.S. domestic airlines offered special low fares to foreign tourists visiting the United States. Germany and several other countries were induced to buy more military equipment in the United States; if they did not, U.S. authorities indicated they might reduce the number of U.S. troops stationed overseas.

These measures effectively devalued the dollar by the "back door," because taxes and other barriers to U.S. purchases of foreign goods and securities raised their prices to U.S. residents. Individually, some of these measures were probably effective, but the annual U.S. payments deficit remained about as large as

41

it had been in the late 1950s and early 1960s. These measures appeared to affect the composition of U.S. payments and receipts, but not the payments balance.

One explanation for the apparent failure of these measures was that U.S. tourist expenditures abroad were increasing; another, that U.S. firms were investing more abroad. The list of special factors is long. An alternative explanation is that, as a group, other countries wanted to increase their holdings of international money at an annual rate of $2 to $3 billion a year.

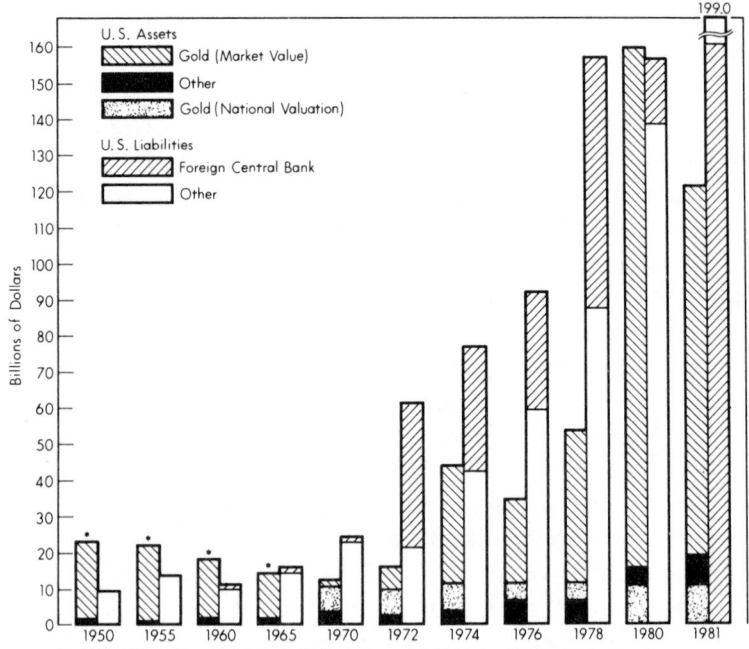

FIGURE 3.1
U.S. International Monetary Position[a]
(Billions of U.S. dollars)

SOURCE: International Monetary Fund, *International Financial Statistics* (Washington, D.C., 1982).
[a] Gold at market value.

Whenever their payments surpluses were too low, measures were taken to increase them. So the measures taken by the United States to reduce the U.S. payments deficit were more or less neutralized.

A different type of measure involved reducing the official foreign demand for gold. U.S. Treasury secretaries cajoled their foreign counterparts not to buy gold. The level of U.S. troops in Germany was tied to Germany's commitment not to buy more gold. The U.S. Treasury issued special securities denominated in the German mark, the Swiss franc, and other foreign currencies for foreign central banks in the hope that they would find these securities effective substitutes for gold. By 1965 the U.S. government began to recognize that its payments deficit could be better explained by the foreign demand for gold and liquid dollar assets than by the overvaluation of the dollar.

Devising new institutional arrangements that would satisfy the foreign demand for international money without forcing the United States to incur chronic payments deficits was a complex undertaking. The countries with surpluses were not convinced that the U.S. deficit was a problem of the system; rather, they believed that mismanagement of U.S. monetary and fiscal policies had led to the large deficits. Moreover, some countries— France, the Netherlands, Belgium, Switzerland, and to a lesser extent, Italy and Germany—had strong preferences for holding most of their international money in the form of gold. They favored a worldwide increase in the price of gold. The United States opposed such an increase, almost exclusively for political reasons. Domestically, a devaluation of the dollar in terms of gold might be regarded as evidence of poor financial management. And internationally, revaluation profits would go to gold speculators and to South Africa and the Soviet Union, countries not high on the list of those that the United States wanted to benefit from windfalls.

The U.S. government wanted the International Monetary Fund to produce an international money. This money, colloquially termed "paper gold," would have the monetary but not the physical attributes of gold—it would not glitter. Paper gold could be produced at a rate which would satisfy demand, and political negotiations would determine what this rate should be. European governments—especially the French—were reluctant to accept the U.S. initiative until the U.S. payments deficit was eliminated. But the U.S. deficit could not be eliminated until the foreign demand for international money declined.

The U.S. view eventually prevailed, and an international treaty was signed providing for the production of a new international money, known as Special Drawing Rights (SDRs), within the IMF framework. Some $10 billion of SDRs were produced between 1970 and 1972.

Perhaps the SDR arrangement would have been successful in resolving the system's needs. But with the Vietnam war and world inflation, the SDR arrangement became irrelevant even before it became operational.

The Monetary Impact of Vietnam

The irony of the late 1960s was that just as the Europeans came to accept the view that their demand for payments surpluses might be connected with the persistence of the U.S. payments deficit, the cause of the U.S. deficit changed. In 1969 the U.S. payments deficit of $6 billion was substantially larger than could be explained by the demands of other countries for international money. The overseas spending of U.S. military forces increased sharply and more importantly, U.S. prices rose rapidly, reducing the competitiveness of U.S. exports. As U.S. incomes and U.S. prices rose rapidly, so did the demand for imports.

The United States wanted other countries to take the initiative in restoring the payments balance. Whenever the international money holdings of one or two countries increase at a faster rate than they wish—a not unlikely event in a world of more than 100 currencies—these countries have an exchange rate problem, which they can resolve either by revaluing their currencies or by other measures to increase their international payments. From time to time in the 1960s, Germany and perhaps Switzerland were in this position; so, in 1969 and 1970, were Canada and Japan. When a few countries have excessively large payments surpluses, it does not follow that the United States should limit its payments to all countries, as it did from 1960 on. But when many countries have excessively large surpluses, there is a much stronger case for the U.S. government to take initiatives to reduce the payments imbalance.

The European governments were in a delicate position. They wanted to force the United States to reduce its payments deficit. They might threaten to buy gold from the U.S. Treasury with some of their dollar assets, dollars that had initially been acquired in the belief that the U.S. Treasury would convert them into gold on demand. But this premise obviously was no longer tenable. A few countries might buy small amounts of gold—$10 million or $25 million at a time—from the U.S. Treasury. But for Germany, Italy, Japan, and other countries with large dollar holdings, the dollar was effectively inconvertible into gold. The European threat to convert dollars into gold was no longer credible, for the U.S. Treasury might stop selling gold.

If the Europeans could no longer buy gold with their dollars, the wisdom of their acquiring substantial amounts of both gold and dollars would be questioned. Their acquisitions of dollar assets would be criticized because the dollars would no longer be convertible into gold. And their purchases of gold would be criticized because a decision by the U.S. Treasury not to buy or sell gold would cloud the future of gold as an international money.

From 1969 through the summer of 1971, the underlying issue was whether the United States or the European countries and Japan would take the initiative in altering the exchange parities, for it was increasingly obvious that the parities would have to be changed. Germany revalued the mark in October 1969. Canada returned to a floating rate in June 1970. Through late 1970 and the beginning of 1971, speculative pressure against the dollar mounted, as it became more and more evident that the European currencies and the Japanese yen would rise in price in terms of the dollar. What remained unclear was when the change would take place.

In May 1971 speculative pressure increased still further; Germany and the Netherlands followed the Canadian example and permitted their currencies to float, while Switzerland and Austria each revalued its currency by about 5 percent. But investors were not assuaged, and the pressure against the dollar increased further. Within three months, speculators converted billions and billions of dollars into yen, marks, Swiss francs, sterling, and other strong currencies.

The crisis came to a head in early August. The leading U.S. congressional authority on international finance, Representative Henry Reuss, suggested that the dollar price of gold be raised slightly—that the U.S. dollar be devalued. Speculative pressure against the dollar greatly intensified. Finally, on August 15, President Nixon announced that as part of his New Economic Policy, the Treasury would suspend gold sales and purchases. (Once it became obvious that the $35 parity would not remain viable until November 1972, it was in President Nixon's domestic political interest to advance the suspension of U.S. gold sales as far as possible before the 1972 election if closing the gold window could not be delayed until after the election.) However, the decision to suspend gold transactions did not automatically lead to changes in the exchange rates. Most foreign countries were reluctant to revalue their currencies because of the adverse impacts on jobs and profits in their export industries. Because of this concern, the U.S. government also adopted a surcharge of 10 percent on all imports subject to tariffs as a way to raise the dollar price of these goods. U.S. government officials made it clear that the surcharge would remain in effect until the exchange rate structure was realigned, discriminatory trade barriers against U.S. imports were reduced, and Europe and Japan agreed to begin negotiations toward a new international monetary system. The Europeans and Japanese stopped pegging their currencies in terms of the dollar, and their currencies began to rise in price in terms of the dollar. The U.S. authorities were content with a floating-rate system; the pressure for returning to the pegged-rate system—and eliminating the U.S. tariff surcharge—came from abroad.

Much of the monetary history of the 1970s is traceable to the delay in changing the parities in 1969, which was necessary because of the inflationary aspects of the Vietnam war. Because of this delay, the United States incurred a $40 billion payments deficit in the 1969–1971 period. The counterpart of the U.S. deficit was a surplus in most other countries. Their purchases of $40 billion led to a very rapid expansion in their money supplies, which in turn contributed greatly to worldwide inflation.

Much of history has a "what if" quality. Assume the U.S. government had been much less resistant to raising the monetary price of gold in 1961 and altering the exchange rate alignment in 1969. Both changes were made—too late. If they had been made on a more timely basis, the monetary history of the 1970s would be very different.

Monetary Artifacts and the Smithsonian Agreement

The suspension of U.S. gold sales was inevitable; the 10 percent surcharge was not. The surcharge was levied when most countries were in a recession—and, as in the 1930s, these countries found it attractive to import jobs by increasing their exports of goods. But they could only do this by maintaining an undervalued currency. In the first test in twenty years of its ability to prevent "beggar thy neighbor" policies, the Bretton Woods system had failed.

Two complex questions complicated the realignment of exchange rates. One was whether European and Japanese currencies should be revalued around the dollar while the dollar remained pegged to gold at $35, or whether the dollar price of gold should be increased so that the dollar would depreciate in terms of some of the European currencies. The second question concerned the amount of the revaluations of the various currencies in terms of the dollar. The first question involved political issues, the second, economic issues.

The political aspect was especially clear in the context of U.S.-French relations. President Nixon would lose points with his domestic constituency if the dollar were devalued in terms of gold, while President Pompidou would gain support with his Gaullist followers if it appeared that the dollar had been dethroned as the center of the international system. An increase of 10 or 15 percent in the dollar price of gold and other currencies would have no significant impact on gold output. But such an increase would win points for Pompidou.

The economic issues involved the effect of changes in the exchange rate structure on the competitive position of firms in different countries. Germany, for example, would not set a new parity for the mark until Japan had set a new parity for the yen. The Germans wanted to be sure that the yen would be revalued by a larger amount than the mark, so that German producers would be in a more favorable position relative to their Japanese competitors in world export markets. And the French would not set a new value for the franc until the rate for the mark had been set.

In mid-December 1971, agreement was reached on a currency realignment: the United States would increase the dollar price of gold by 8 percent, to $38; the other countries would realign their exchange rate pegs about the dollar. The yen was revalued by 17 percent from its May 1971 parity, the mark by 14 percent. But U.S. authorities would still not sell gold.

Thus, the Smithsonian Agreement—"The Greatest Monetary Agreement in History"—may have resolved the imbalances resulting from Vietnam war inflation, but it did not solve the gold problem or the inconsistencies between national monetary policies and the exchange rate system. While it was agreed that a new monetary system was needed, there was no agreement on what such a system should look like.

Any new system, regardless of its name, had to accommodate itself to several realities. Most countries continued to prefer pegged to floating exchange rates as a way to reduce the uncertainty associated with international trade and investment. More and more countries gave greater priority to independent monetary policies. Countries then adjusted to external disturbances by altering controls to increase or reduce net international payments. There was a widespread belief that the international role of the dollar would have to be diminished—a euphemism for attempting to reduce the economic power and influence of the United States. And somehow the new system would have to be built through multilateral agreement.

In June 1972 a speculative attack against sterling forced the British authorities to stop supporting the pound, which promptly floated to its pre-Smithsonian parity. Speculation against the dollar increased in early 1973; in less than a day, the Bundesbank was obliged to buy $6 billion. It was too much: the monetary authorities permitted their currencies to float, while U.S. authorities agreed to increase the dollar price of gold to $42. The greatest monetary agreement in history lasted little more than one year.

A new Smithsonian-style accord was virtually out of the question. While the national monetary authorities might again commit themselves to a new set of pegged rates, few investors would believe in their commitments to these rates. National treasuries were obliged to adopt floating rates because there was no feasible alternative. And so, beginning in late February 1973, the major currencies began to float against the dollar.

The changes in the price of the U.S. dollar in terms of European currencies and the Japanese yen were much sharper than had been anticipated. Foreign central banks intervened extensively in the foreign exchange market to limit the variations in the foreign exchange values of their currencies. One of the ironies was that central bank purchases and sales of foreign exchange were much more extensive under the floating-rate system than under the pegged-rate system. Despite this extensive intervention, the price of the dollar in terms of the German mark, the Swiss franc, and the Japanese yen varied by as much as 50 percent.

The Committee of Twenty Exercise

The signers of the Smithsonian Agreement concurred on the need for monetary reform. Monetary reform required a plan—a proposal for how institutional arrangements should be revamped. To develop such a plan, a small secretariat was established within the IMF; the staff members would serve the national representatives. The committee met frequently in 1972 and were about to propose a more relaxed form of pegged rates when currencies began to float in February 1973. The plan was obsolete before it could be adopted.

With the move to floating rates, member countries of the IMF were in violation of the rules requiring them to state parities and to limit variations in the foreign exchange value of their currencies. Since it was impossible for them to abide by their commitments, the rules were changed to permit each member to follow almost any set of exchange market practices that it wished. This rule change—the Jamaica Agreement of 1974—basically said: Whatever is, is OK. The official gold price was abandoned. Within a few years, all that remained of the IMF system was the IMF—a pool of currencies modest in size and largely irrelevant in function, given the rapid growth of international reserves, and 1,800 highly paid international civil servants, to police a set of rules that no longer existed.

 4

"The Gnomes of Zurich"—A London
Euphemism for Speculation
Against Sterling

Between 1967 and 1982 speculators in foreign exchange—private firms, banks, and individuals—netted $20 billion. In 1967 they sold British sterling; in 1969 they sold French francs and bought German marks. From 1970 on they sold massive amounts of U.S. dollars to buy most European currencies and Japanese yen. Few banks or firms admit that they speculate; it sounds antisocial. Rather, they maintain that they are solely engaged in hedging their risks. Everyone points instead to the "Gnomes of Zurich."

The brotherhood of Gnomes is worldwide. There are chapters in London, Paris, Tokyo, New York—indeed, in every financial center where banks and firms and investors deal in foreign exchange. Membership in the brotherhood is open to anyone willing to take the risks; all that is necessary is a willingness to play by the rules of the market economy. The Gnomes are on *Fortune*'s lists of the 500 largest U.S. corporations and the 300 largest foreign corporations.

Successful currency speculation is highly profitable. Speculators who bought dollars with sterling near the $2.80 parity, just before the November 1967 devaluation, and then repurchased sterling near the new $2.40 parity made a 16 percent profit. In the months prior to the revaluation of the mark in September and October 1969, speculators sold dollars to get marks at a parity of about 4 marks to the dollar. After the revaluation they bought dollars at about 3.67 marks, giving them a profit of 8 percent. Note that many speculators secured these profits in a month or two, so on an annual basis their profit may have been as high as 50 or 100 percent. If, for example, a speculator sold sterling for dollars in the middle of September 1967, about two months before the devaluation, his profit of 16 percent on the investment of two months equals an annual profit of 96 percent. In a world in which annual rates of return of 8 or 10 percent are the norm, such extremely high annual rates of profit attract risk takers.

Profits can be earned by playing the movements in the floating exchange rates—by buying currencies when they are cheap and selling them when they are dear. Some commercial banks have reported that they have earned as much as $50 million and $100 million each quarter from foreign exchange trading. Part of these profits may have been earned from acting as brokers in transactions with firms engaged in foreign trade and investment. Most of these profits, however, were made from being quicker than others in predicting the trend movements in the exchange rates.

Someone must pay for the revaluation profits earned by the Gnomes; for every winner there's a loser, or two. In part, one Gnome loses what another wins; speculators deal with each other. Still, the $20 billion earned between 1967 and 1982 is the net overall estimate of the Gnomes' profits. Part of this profit was earned at the expense of central banks. In the months prior to the 1967 devaluation, for example, the Bank of England sold $2 billion from its own holdings of dollars and $3 billion of borrowed dollars. Various firms and investors earned $800 million on the Bank's transactions—the product of the 16 percent devaluation and the $5 billion decline in their sterling position. After devaluation the Bank of England bought $3 billion from British exporters to get the dollars to repay its foreign creditors. In effect, it paid £1 for $2.40; before devaluation it had sold $2.80 for £1.

The revaluation losses of the Bank of England—and of the Bank of Japan, the Bank of France, the Bundesbank, and numerous other central banks—fall on their stockholders. And since these institutions are owned by their governments, the taxpayers pay the bill. Despite massive losses, the taxpayers rarely complained. Perhaps this explains why, despite the increased search for speculative profits by firms during the late 1960s and early 1970s, the authorities were slow to revise obsolete exchange market arrangements.

Foreign exchange speculation is not without risk. Nor is it costless—anticipated changes in exchange rates may not occur, or they may be long delayed. But under the exchange market arrangements that prevailed until the end of 1971, the risks and costs were low.

The Gnomes of Zurich were a handy scapegoat for the problems besetting sterling in the mid-1960s, problems that had their source in London, not Zurich. Sterling's weakness was a result of British monetary policy; $2.80 had ceased to be a viable parity by 1964, if not by 1962. Speculators sought revaluation profits at low risk because the British authorities retained archaic exchange market arrangements with an increasingly overvalued currency.

With the move to floating exchange rates in early 1973, central banks greatly reduced their subsidies to business firms willing to speculate in the exchange market, at least for a while. Many firms and banks had developed great confidence in their ability to predict changes in exchange rates during the pegged period. When currencies began to float, they continued to speculate. In the summer of 1974, numerous private banks began to report substantial foreign exchange losses. In some cases, including Herstatt Bankhaus, Westdeutsche Girozentral, and Franklin

National, top management participated in the decisions to profit from changes in exchange rates. In other cases, exchange speculation occurred at the distant branches or by surreptitious activities of the bank's traders. Altogether, some privately owned banks lost over $1 billion, not large by the standards of central banks, but enough to force Herstatt and Franklin National to go out of business. And the foreign exchange traders associated with the losing banks frequently changed careers.

Gnomes and Non-Gnomes

Gnomes (and non-Gnomes) who deal in foreign exchange buy and sell bank deposits denominated in different currencies. A turn of events—an election, the quarterly report on exports and imports, a dock strike, this month's report on changes in wholesale prices—can alter expectations about the future price of a currency. Gnomes sell and buy in order to profit from anticipated changes in exchange rates.

A market in national monies is inevitable as long as there are separate national currencies. Domestic monies—primarily bank deposits—are traded against similar deposits denominated in other currencies. In New York, U.S. dollars are traded against Canadian dollars, sterling, French francs, Swiss francs, marks, and more than 100 other currencies. In the United States, there are foreign exchange dealers in New York, Chicago, San Francisco, and Los Angeles; in Switzerland, in Zurich, Geneva, and Basel. But in reality, New York, London, Brussels, Zurich, and the other financial centers are the geographic extensions of one international market.

Because the costs of foreign exchange transactions are extremely low, the sterling-dollar exchange rates in New York and Zurich are virtually identical with the rates quoted in London, the principal center of trading in the dollar-sterling market. The deposits are not moved from one country to another; rather the ownership of deposits shifts from domestic residents to foreign residents. Foreign exchange traders find it financially rewarding to keep the rates in different centers in line whenever deviations appear. Assume an extreme example: the price of £1 is $2 in New York and $3 in London; that is, sterling is cheap in New York and dear in London. Foreign exchange traders buy sterling with dollars in New York: they receive a sterling deposit in a bank in London which they pay for with a dollar deposit in New York. Each pound sterling costs them $2. At the same time, they buy dollars with sterling in London and receive $3 for each pound; they receive a dollar deposit in New York and pay with a sterling deposit in London. Thus, their profit per "round trip" for each $2 investment is $1. Their activity is riskless, for the two transactions occur simultaneously. Riskless transactions designed to take advantage of price discrepancies in different geographic centers are known as *arbitrage*.

Investors continue this pattern of transactions until the dollar price of sterling rises in New York and falls in London, the two prices converge, and the remaining spread between them is insufficient for any additional arbitrage to be profitable. In practice, this means that the spread can be as low as several thousandths of 1 percent.

Arbitragers also ensure that the exchange rate between the guilder and the mark is consistent with the price of the dollar in terms of the guilder and the price of the dollar in terms of the mark. Once the price of the dollar in terms of each of these currencies is known, then the guilder price of the mark (the cross-rate) can be determined arithmetically. Arbitragers see to it that the arithmetic is correct. Assume, for example, that the dollar costs 4 marks, the mark costs 2 guilders, and the dollar costs 6 guilders. These rates are inconsistent; the cross-rate for the mark in terms of the guilder, given their rates against the dollar, is 1.5 guilders to the mark. So the arbitragers sell guilders to buy dollars, then sell the dollars to buy marks, and finally sell marks to buy guilders; 6 guilders buy $1, which buys 4 marks, which in turn buy 8 guilders. Arbitrage continues until the riskless profit opportunities are eliminated. The mark price and the dollar price of the guilder decline, while the dollar price of the mark rises.

Some foreign exchange dealings are *spot* transactions: buyers and sellers agree to transfer bank deposits immediately after they enter into the contract, which in practice means two days later. Most transactions in foreign exchange, however, involve trades in *forward* contracts, which differ from trades in spot transactions in only one important respect—the exchange of deposits occurs at a more distant future date, often thirty days or ninety days after the date of the contract.

Gnomes prefer forward transactions because they can buy a foreign currency without having to make an immediate large cash payment. But Gnomes can only buy forward contracts if some non-Gnomes sell forward contracts. If, for example, speculators believe that sterling will depreciate, they may want to sell sterling forward, which means they will want to buy dollars forward. Most participants in the exchange market would be reluctant to buy forward sterling if they thought sterling might depreciate. Some arbitragers, however, may buy forward sterling, but only after selling sterling in the spot market. By combining a sale of spot sterling with the purchase of forward sterling, they protect themselves against a loss from a depreciation of sterling. Thus, the arbitragers might sell spot sterling at $1.50 and at the same time buy forward sterling at $1.45. Regardless of changes in the dollar price of sterling, they would profit, since the forward contract protects them against any loss from a change in the exchange rate. While speculators seek to profit from anticipated changes in the exchange rates, arbitragers (who are reluctant to bear the risk associated with such changes) profit from the differences in the price of foreign exchange in the spot market and the forward market.

The foreign exchange market is distinguished from the commodity, stock, and bond markets by the pervasiveness of the government's role, especially the central bank's intervention to maintain the foreign exchange price of its currency. Under the Bretton Woods system, exchange rates were free to float within a narrow "band" around par values. Under the old IMF rules, support limits of the band could be no greater than 1 percent on either side of par; these limits were increased to 2.25 percent under the Smithsonian Agreement.

Speculation about changes in the exchange rate then centered largely on changes in the central bank's parity. Exchange speculators bought and sold foreign exchange with the large commercial banks, but these banks were not eager to hold large amounts of currencies which might be devalued. They were more likely to be sellers of the weak currency; indeed, many qualified for senior membership in the Brotherhood of Gnomes. Since for every seller there must be a buyer, the central banks were obliged to buy their own currencies to prevent the exchange rate from moving beyond the support limits.

Ten Things Your Mother Never Knew
About the Foreign Exchange Market

1. The foreign exchange market is the largest market in the world. On a busy day, the volume of transactions may reach $100 billion, fifty times the volume on the New York Stock Exchange.

2. Most foreign exchange transactions—90 to 95 percent—involve only banks: interbank transactions are undertaken to adjust their positions in currencies in order to offset the imbalances caused by purchases and sales with customers.

3. For the major currencies the larger banks act as *market makers:* they hold inventories of foreign currencies and stand ready to deal in large amounts at stated prices. In other currencies, in contrast, banks operate as brokers and avoid the price risk.

4. The exchange market is the most efficient market in the

---

world, at least as judged by transactions costs. Assume you started with $1 million U.S. and bought Canadian dollars. Then you realized you had made a mistake, so you sold the Canadian dollars for U.S. dollars. You would end up with less than $1 million U.S. by the amount of two commissions—equal to the bid-ask spread. Query: How much less?*

5. The foreign exchange market never (well, hardly ever) closes. When it is 3 P.M. Tuesday in Tokyo, it is 2 P.M. in Hong Kong; when it is 3 P.M. in Hong Kong, it is 1 P.M. in Singapore. When it is 3 P.M. in Singapore, it is noon in Bahrein; when it is 3 P.M. in Bahrein, it is 1 P.M. in Beirut. When it is 3 P.M. in Beirut, it is 1 P.M. in London; when it is 3 P.M. in London, it is 10 A.M. in New York. When it is 3 P.M. in New York, it is noon in San Francisco; when it is 3 P.M. Tuesday in San Francisco, it is 9 A.M. Wednesday in Sydney. So the center of trading moves with the sun around the world.

6. About 99.44 percent of all trades involve the U.S. dollar. If a Swiss importer wants to pay his German supplier, the bank calculates the Swiss franc–German mark rate as the combination of the Swiss franc–dollar rate and the German mark–dollar rate. Most trades in Frankfurt are marks against dollars.

7. The largest volume of foreign exchange trading occurs in London, with Zurich a distant second and Frankfurt third.

8. Most customer transactions in foreign exchange involve forward transactions—the corporate client makes a commitment to buy or sell forward exchange at a future date at a rate agreed to today.

9. Since 1973, about twenty firms have been established to sell forecasts on exchange rate movements. One inference is that they can make more money selling forecasts than using them.

10. A good foreign exchange trader can earn $100,000 a year—and lose $1 million in a day.

* The cost is 230 Canadian dollars. The comparable estimates for other currencies are: mark, $503; sterling, $514; yen, $1,041; and Swiss franc, $1,229.

While countries were reluctant to change the parity formally, they could not avoid or even postpone changes in the effective exchange rate. So ad hoc measures were adopted to prevent exceptionally large and persistent losses in central bank holdings of international money. Purchases of foreign exchange were restricted, taxed, delayed, and licensed. Supplemental tariffs were levied on commodity imports. A ceiling or tax might be placed on overseas spending by tourists. Government agencies were directed to supply their needs from domestic sources even though foreign sources were cheaper. Such taxes and restrictions increased the effective price of foreign exchange. In effect, the currency was devalued through the back door.

Once the ability to buy foreign exchange freely at the established price is restricted or taxed, a black market in foreign exchange almost inevitably develops. Rather than pay the taxes or wait in line at the central bank to buy the foreign exchange at the legal parity, some importers decide that it is cheaper to buy the currency they need in the black market. Some exporters increase their income by selling their foreign exchange earnings in the black market. Some governments profit by offering to sell foreign exchange to importers at the artificially low price, and then taxing their purchases. And various government officials in the agencies which ration foreign exchange and import licenses may place individual importers in a favored position, in return for side bets, private payments, commissions, or promises of future employment opportunities.

Surprisingly, most governments tolerate black markets in foreign exchange. Legal penalties are rarely imposed in spite of the pervasiveness of apparently illegal transactions. In many cases the black market permits the government to delay the political costs of formally devaluing the rate, while minimizing the economic costs of maintaining an overvalued currency.

The Source of Exchange Crises

Crises in the exchange market reflect two underlying factors. The first—and necessary—factor is the desire of many countries to pursue independent monetary policies. Price levels rise rapidly in some countries and slowly in others. The resulting changes in the relationships between the prices of domestic goods relative to the prices of comparable foreign goods affect patterns of imports and exports. The imports of countries whose prices are rising increase rapidly while their exports increase at a slower rate or may even fall. The international money holdings of their central banks decline, and ultimately a devaluation is necessary. Meanwhile, in the countries with more stable prices, exports grow more rapidly than imports and holdings of international money increase. A revaluation of the currency may be necessary in countries with payments surpluses.

The second factor in the exchange crises of the past is that the IMF rules for regulating exchange rates were archaic, if not when they were adopted in the 1940s, then by the early 1960s. These exchange rate provisions—a combination of narrow support limits around the parity and measures that sought to constrain countries from changing their parities by too large an amount—proved unworkable when changes in parities became necessary as national price levels began to increase.

The anomaly of the Bretton Woods system, which ultimately led to its breakdown, was that the exchange market arrangements of the gold standard were retained even though many central banks had switched from dependent monetary policies appropriate for the gold standard to independent monetary policies—that is, producing money at rates which satisfied their domestic economic objectives. Predictably, an exchange rate system designed in accordance with the gold standard worked less well in a period when central banks gave higher priority to domestic employment and price stability.

The Politics of Parity

The decision to change an exchange parity is ultimately political. Necessary changes in parities have often been delayed because of the political costs. One holdover from the gold standard era is the notion that there is something sacrosanct about a parity and that devaluation is an admission that domestic financial policies have failed. The monetary authorities always hope that events will somehow save them from the need to devalue—the next month's trade data will show a healthy rise in exports, or other countries will revalue their currencies making their own devaluation unnecessary.

No one needs any private knowledge to recognize when a currency is overvalued or undervalued. Because changes in parities are usually delayed, investors do not need remarkably accurate foresight to anticipate them. With a narrow band between the support limits, the cost of guessing wrong is minimal, since the transactions could be easily reversed and at modest cost. And because the authorities are often reluctant to change the parities by small amounts, speculators can be confident that the eventual changes will be substantial.

Take sterling. By 1964 sterling was clearly overvalued. British prices had been rising more rapidly than those of Britain's competitors, the British share of the world export market was declining, and its payments deficit was large. Many observers felt that the Labour government should have devalued immediately on coming to power in October 1964, for at that time the need for devaluation could have been blamed on the outgoing Conservatives. But the Labour party did not take advantage of its opportunity. Labour governments had been in power before when sterling was devalued—in 1931 and again in 1949—and party leaders were fearful of being tagged the "Devaluation Party." For at least three years, Britain's economic policies, as well as its international and domestic security policies, were constrained by the need to defend an overvalued currency.

By November 1967 nearly everyone except Prime Minister Harold Wilson was willing to admit that sterling would have to be devalued. While the size of the required devaluation could not be determined exactly, it was almost certain to be greater than 10 percent, since a smaller change would not have seemed worthwhile. And it was almost certain to be smaller than 20 percent, since a larger change would almost surely have resulted in retaliatory devaluations by other European countries whose trade positions would have been excessively threatened.

The Brussels Caper

In the mid-1960s, a foreign exchange trader in the Brussels branch of a major New York bank fell in love with sterling. The Gnomes were bearish on sterling; they anticipated a devaluation. Forward sterling was at a substantial discount—when spot sterling was at $2.79, forward sterling was cheaper. Moreover, the discounts on twelve-month forward contracts were substantially larger than on one-month forward contracts. So the trader bought the long sterling contracts, which were cheap, and sold one-month forward sterling contracts, which were more expensive. Thus, his position in sterling was more or less even, at least for one month; from the beginning of the second month until the end of the twelfth, he was long sterling. And he had a potential profit, which was the difference between the cheap sterling he had bought and the dear sterling he had sold.

A month later, he again bought one-month sterling forward to offset his position in the long forward contract, which had eleven months to run until maturity. At the same time, he bought more long sterling contracts and sold an equal amount of short sterling contracts; his long and short positions were offsetting, and he still had a nice potential profit.

A month later he repeated the process; he repeated it for several more months. The potential profit kept increasing.

When the bank learned of its extremely large position in long sterling contracts, the position was closed, at a loss of $8 million.

Eventually, in November 1967, sterling was devalued because the British authorities could no longer maintain the parity; their holdings of international money were exhausted and it was virtually impossible to borrow. Great Britain had already borrowed the maximum amount possible from IMF and large loans were being negotiated with other countries. But the conditions on British domestic policy attached to these loans, especially by France, were deemed too onerous.

The devaluation of the French franc in August 1969 was similarly influenced by political factors. To restore the domestic peace and harmony that had been threatened by the student riots of May 1968, General de Gaulle's government approved nationwide wage increases of 15 percent. Price increases were inevitable; otherwise firms could not afford to pay the higher wages. The prospect of a one-shot increase in the price level of 10 to 15 percent meant that the franc would have to be devalued. The anticipated price increases and the political uncertainty associated with the riots triggered a sharp speculative attack against the franc.

Yet the necessary change in the parity was delayed for political reasons. President de Gaulle would not devalue the franc; after all, he had given France ten years of price stability (1959–1968) following fifty years of inflation. To maintain that stability, payments abroad were restricted, and price and wage ceilings were adopted; the franc was being devalued by the back door. Only the date of the "front door" devaluation and the amount of the change remained uncertain. Less than four months after de Gaulle resigned, the franc was formally devalued.

The way election results can influence an exchange parity was dramatically shown by the revaluation of the German mark in October 1969. The Christian Democrats wanted to maintain the existing parity until the German parliamentary elections in September. The business community, an important supporter of the Christian Democratic Party, favored retaining the 4-mark parity with the dollar, since a revaluation of the mark would mean that the prices of German goods in the United States and other foreign markets would rise relative to the prices of U.S. goods, and that German export sales and German profits would decline. Revaluation of the mark would also lead Germans to buy more foreign goods, since they would then decline in price relative to German goods. Thus, the mark prices of Germans goods competing with imports would have to fall, and the profits of German firms producing these goods would decline.

The major constituency of the Social Democrats was—and is—the workers, who are interested in higher incomes and lower prices, not in business profits. Thus, a revaluation would benefit the Social Democrats, and a revaluation was widely expected—if the Social Democrats won the election. Had the Christian Democrats won, the outcome would have been more uncertain, for their constituency and the economic realities were pulling in opposite directions.

As soon as preliminary election results indicated that the voters preferred the Social Democrats, the speculative demand for the mark soared. On September 29 the Bundesbank ceased pegging the mark at the parity of 4 marks to the dollar, and the mark floated upward until October 24, when it was pegged at 3.67 marks by the newly installed Social Democratic government.

On two occasions in twenty years, once in 1950 and again in 1970, the Canadian government shifted from a pegged to a floating rate. In both instances, the cause was the same: Canada wanted to minimize the increase in the Canadian price level resulting from inflation in the United States. The dominant factor in Canada's exchange rate policy is the economic fit of the Canadian economy with the U.S. economy. The close economic and geographic relationship with the United States means that Canada has an automatic tendency to import U.S. problems. Moreover, because raw materials are such a large part of Canadian exports to the United States, U.S. economic developments have an exaggerated impact on Canada. When the U.S. economy has a little boom, U.S. imports of raw materials soar, and the Canadian economy has a big boom. Both in 1950 and again in the late 1960s, as a result of the U.S. booms, Canadian exports surged and large payments surpluses brought about large increases in Canada's money supply.

The Canadian government sought greater control over its price level by shifting to a floating exchange rate. Thus, in June 1950, the Canadian dollar (which had been pegged at the rate of $1.10 Canadian to $1.00 U.S.) was permitted to float, and shortly appreciated by 10 percent. Similarly, when in June 1970 the Canadian authorities again freed their dollar from a parity of $1.08 Canadian to $1.00 U.S., it appreciated by 8 percent.

Canada wants more independence from the United States. Since Canada cannot readily move to Europe or to the Far East, it has sought mechanisms that would disengage its economy from the U.S. economy. Both in 1950 and in 1970, the Canadians hoped that a floating rate would provide increased insulation from U.S. inflation. In contrast, in 1962 both the U.S. and Canadian economies were in recessions and the Canadian government returned to a pegged exchange rate to stimulate its economy; the Canadian dollar was pegged at a rate below the market level to increase Canadian exports.

Until 1971 most exchange crises involved only one currency; there was no systematic relation between the problems of sterling, the Canadian dollar, and the French franc. But the exchange rate changes of May 1971 and of February 1973—both those that did occur and those that should have occurred but did not—involved more than ten countries. The U.S. payments deficit associated with the Vietnam war led foreign central banks to acquire more dollars than they wished. As a result, their domestic money supplies were growing rapidly; they imported the U.S. inflation. One of the few options open to foreign central banks was to use the dollars to buy gold from the U.S. Treasury and hope that the gold losses would force U.S. authorities to take measures to reduce the payments imbalances. Another option was to revalue their currencies and incur costs in terms of their own constituencies.

Murphy's Law—anything that can go wrong will go wrong—went to work. The other industrial countries imported the U.S. inflation and then they revalued. Their price levels increased about as rapidly as the U.S. price level, because the revaluation was too long delayed.

The Search for Flexibility— Floating Rates and Sliding Parities

Since 1960, more than thirty countries have devalued their currencies. A few—including West Germany, Austria, the Netherlands, Switzerland, Japan, Canada, France, Italy, and Great Britain—have revalued. Small wonder that speculators appear increasingly sensitive to the possibility of changes in exchange parities. Whenever it has appeared likely that a parity might be changed, the volume of funds shifted in anticipation of such a change has increased greatly year after year. The odds in the game have increasingly favored the speculators.

Inevitably, the central bankers have been forced to deny they would change their parities; not to deny is to admit. But the sequence of a succession of denials followed by a succession of parity changes quickly reduced the value of their denials. Central bankers' public statements about the exchange rate have lost credibility, and speculation about changes in exchange parities has come to resemble a game of wits between government authorities and private parties. The participants in the exchange market must constantly decide how much importance to attach to those official denials.

The inconsistency between national monetary policies and the exchange rate system—and the resulting speculation—might be reduced by a return to a gold-standard monetary policy, that is, a return to dependent national monetary policies. For many countries, however, monetary independence is the essence of sovereignty. In the "Me Generation" each country wants to do its own thing.

Given each nation's desire for monetary independence, greater flexibility is obtained through floating exchange rates, or with more frequent changes in the parity so as to reduce the scope for speculative profits. Under a floating exchange rate system, the exchange rate varies in response to changes in supply and demand, just like any other price. Central banks are not required to support their currencies in the exchange market, although they may intervene to smooth movements in the exchange rate to accommodate the needs of traders and investors. Changes in the exchange rate are supposed to be less sudden than under the pegged system. New information about future events—and hence about future exchange rates—is supposed to be immediately reflected in the exchange rate. Thus, as the domestic price level increases or the foreign demand for domestic products declines, the price of foreign exchange increases. Investors can still speculate on changes in the exchange rate, but they no longer have the relatively riskless, one-way option available under the pegged exchange rate system. For one thing, the amount of the change is smaller, since the rate is adjusted continuously. And the costs of being wrong can be much greater, since the currency may appreciate by a larger amount if speculators are wrong. The need to apply controls and restrictions to limit purchases of foreign exchange should disappear, and so should currency black markets.

Academic economists—perhaps a majority of them—favor floating exchange rates. Some—those who advocate a fixed money supply growth rule of 5, 6 or 10 percent a year—favor independent monetary policies; they abhor the idea that the growth of the money supply within a country should be affected by whether the country has a payments surplus or deficit. And economists who do not accept a fixed monetary growth rule want

67

to eliminate both the external constraint on the choice of domestic policies and the need to balance international payments and receipts at one particular exchange rate. Most economists believe that the variations in exchange controls that would have been needed to maintain national parities indicated either that the pegged-rate system was badly managed or that it was obsolete—and that even the best central bankers could not make it work effectively.

Yet floating exchange rates were criticized extensively by men of affairs, especially during the pegged-rate period. Their reasons differed. Some believed that daily, weekly, and monthly movements in the exchange rate would retard the growth of international trade and investment because the increased uncertainty about future exchange rates would deter some individuals and firms from undertaking international transactions.

The rationale for pegged exchange rates is that central bankers are more astute in setting the price of foreign exchange—speculating in the exchange market—than are private investors. Central banks are government-owned public utilities, and they are supposed to provide public services—if necessary, at a loss. Their transactions in the exchange market are supposed to reduce uncertainty about future exchange rates. Exporters and importers benefit from the reduction of uncertainty. And since their costs decline, the benefits are passed on both to those who produce export goods (and would thus have a larger foreign market) and to those who consume imports.

The rationale for floating exchange rates, on the other hand, is that changes in the exchange rate should be depoliticized. Even if the foreign exchange traders in the central banks are more skillful than their private-sector counterparts, they cannot alter the exchange peg on their own; these changes reflect political decisions. Needed changes in parities almost always are long delayed. Thus, in most periods, any reduction in exchange market uncertainty stemming from central bank intervention may be offset by the sharp rise in uncertainty whenever expectations develop that the exchange parity will be altered—and while politicians are mustering the political will to make that alteration.

In general, proponents of floating exchange rates emphasize the ease with which the market rate changes over time. Exchange rate movements are supposed to be continuous and gradual rather than sudden and sharp. In contrast, the critics of floating exchange rates are worried that movements in exchange rates will be extensive.

In choosing between pegged and floating exchange rates, one of the major questions concerns the impact of uncertainty on trade and investment. Ideally, the effects and relative costs of uncertainty under the two systems might be measured and compared. Yet until 1973 the opportunities for comparison were infrequent. Floating exchange rate systems did not work well in the 1920s, but the relevance of this experience is questionable, as is the failure of the pegged-rate system during the 1930s. The twelve-year Canadian experience with floating exchange rates between 1950 and 1962 was generally acknowledged a success, except by the governor of the Bank of Canada, who in 1962 shifted back to a pegged system. Lebanon has used a floating exchange rate since 1950, and the system has worked well despite wars, revolutions, and other sources of political uncertainty in the Middle East. But Lebanon has not followed an independent monetary policy.

In addition, experience with pegged rates has been biased. Since most countries have been on pegged rates during the postwar period, the problems of this system have been most evident. Thus, however dramatic the exchange crises have been, their economic cost may not have been so great. In any case, the cost derived both from delays in changing the exchange rate and from changing the effective rate by administrative controls—in effect, from the way the system had been managed rather than from the system itself. Perhaps, however, it is inevitable that a pegged system would be poorly managed.

Another issue in choosing between these two exchange rate

systems concerns the likelihood that a floating exchange rate will be manipulated by governments. The fear is that some countries might manipulate their exchange rates to enhance their national advantage. Without established parities, governments cannot be prevented from manipulating the foreign exchange price of their currency. Perhaps international rules could be developed that would define acceptable and unacceptable forms of central bank intervention under a system of floating exchange rates. Perhaps—but the likelihood that such roles would be adopted seems low. And the likelihood that they would be followed, if adopted, is lower still.

The academic arguments between the proponents of pegged rates and the proponents of floating rates usually ignore the success of the Bretton Woods system in the 1950–1965 period, and concentrate instead on the exchange crises in the next few years, and the increasing problems thereafter. A pegged-rate system will work well whenever there is reasonable price stability in the major countries; crises will be infrequent because the need to change parities will also be infrequent. Floating rates would also work well in this monetary environment. As price stability begins to erode, the need to change parities will become increasingly frequent, and ultimately the authorities will permit their currencies to float.

Strong resistance to floating rates stimulated the search for greater flexibility within the pegged-rate system. The widening of the support limits around parities to 2.25 percent in 1971 was a response to this search. The advantage of a wider spread is that it tends to increase the risks associated with shifts of funds between assets denominated in various currencies, since the possible exchange losses are greater. Investors have less of a one-way option. Whether 2.25 percent is sufficient is not yet clear— a somewhat wider spread, perhaps 4 or 5 percent, might be preferable. But even if there were international agreement on a wider spread, some central banks might intervene to hold rate movements within a narrower range.

Even with wider spreads between exchange rate support limits, exchange crises might still arise because independent monetary policies tend to make established parities obsolete. Unless authorities manage to change their parities before they are forced to do so by speculative pressure, crises are inevitable. And the authorities have rarely changed their parities on a timely basis.

Another approach toward greater flexibility involves various mechanisms which make it easier to change parities. Such devices, called sliding parities, crawling pegs, or gliding rates, are all minor variations on a single theme: when a country begins to move into a position of persistent payments surplus or deficit, the parity should be changed quickly. Small, frequent changes in a parity then replace large, infrequent ones. These changes might be triggered automatically by changes in a country's holdings of international money, or by the decision of the authorities, since a formula-approach might circumvent the reluctance of the authorities to change the peg.

Brazil used a floating peg approach for more than a decade; every three or four weeks the authorities devalued the cruzeiro by 2 or 3 percent. The amount of the change was so small, and its exact timing so uncertain, that investors did not find it worthwhile to seek to profit from the predictably small change in the peg. But most governments are skeptical of using a formula to determine the amount and timing of rate changes in the foreign exchange values of their currencies; the domestic political consequences might be too severe. And many governments have shown an unusual reluctance to use any variant of the sliding parity approach.

That the Bretton Woods system would break down was inevitable; the system was fast becoming obsolete in a world of independent monetary policies and accelerating inflation. It became too easy for investors to profit from changes in parities. Central bankers continued to play by the Bretton Woods rules even while they sought to negotiate modifications. Changes in institutional arrangements occur slowly, especially when the number of na-

tional participants is large and their interests diverse. The negotiations proved unsuccessful; currencies were allowed to float because agreement could not be reached on any other exchange
rate regime.

The move to floating rates in 1973 did not occur because the
proponents of floating rates won the arguments; rather, pegged
rates were simply no longer credible in a period when inflation
rates began to exceed 10 percent. Eventually, it was realized that
authorities had only modest freedom to change the exchange
rate once they had selected a monetary policy. In a period of
monetary stability, the differences between the two exchange
rate systems were of the Tweedledee-Tweedledum variety. And,
given the monetary background of the 1970s, the concerns of the
critics of floating rates have been substantiated. Exchange rates
have moved very sharply, not gradually, much more than is war-
ranted by changes in relative prices. Governments have intervened extensively to advance their own interests without the constraint of rules. The criticism, however, should be directed at
monetary instability, and not at the exchange rate system.

Floating Rates—The Arguments and the Experience

The years since February 1973 provide the first extensive experience since the 1920s for testing the arguments for floating rates.
Even so, most currencies remain pegged; the floating currencies
are almost exclusively those of the industrial countries. And
there have been wide differences in the scope for changes in exchange rates, for most central banks have intervened extensively
in the exchange market to dampen movements in the foreign
exchange values of their currencies.

For a while, the Bank of Canada took a hands-off approach to
the exchange rate, until the Canadian dollar weakened. The
Bank of Japan has traditionally smoothed the daily movements

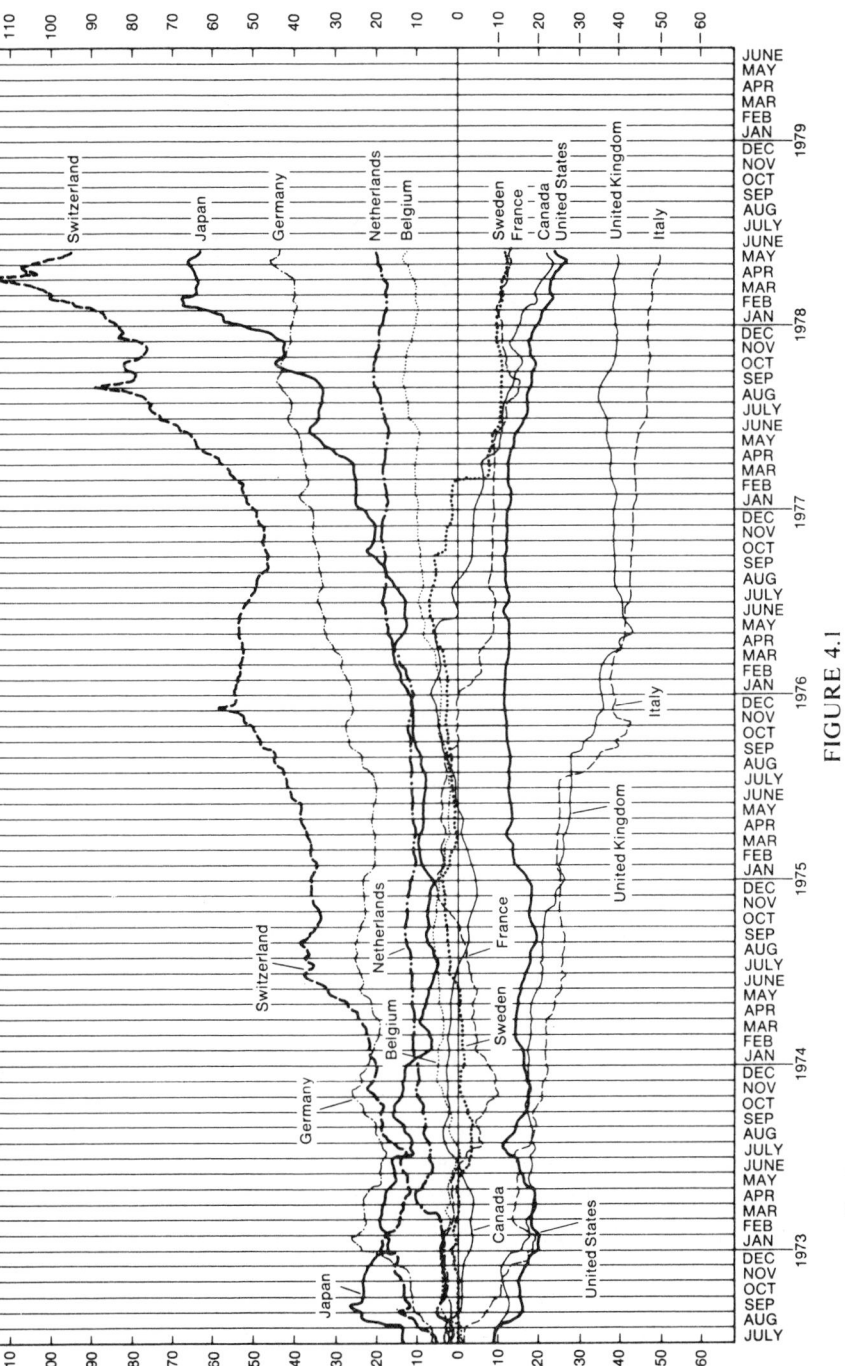

FIGURE 4.1

Effective Exchange Rates (*Percentage changes from 1st quarter, 1970, weekly averages of daily figures*)

SOURCE: Organization for Economic Cooperation and Development, *OECD Economic Outlook* (Paris, December 1978).

in the rate and has sought to moderate the tendency toward sharp cyclical swings. Sterling has been another managed floating currency. The U.K. authorities have decided on the range within which they want sterling to trade and have bought and sold dollars to achieve their objective. In both the Japanese and British cases, floating has largely meant the absence of a commitment to a particular parity.

The continental European countries have participated in a joint currency float as an initial step toward the eventual unification of their currencies. In effect, countries participating in the joint float peg their currencies to each other, and these currencies appreciate and depreciate together in terms of the dollar; the more or less parallel movement is called "the snake." The percentage changes from peak to trough and from trough to peak are sharp in terms of the dollar, as much as 15 to 20 percent in a relatively short interval. Moreover, these currencies also float relative to each other within a range of little more than 2 percent (see figure 4.1).

One advantage of floating rates is that the movements of the rates are no longer the occasion for great crises; the monetary authorities are no longer subject to the political embarrassment associated with changes in parities. But the quieter life for the authorities is not a free lunch for everyone; business firms and investors are concerned with the impact of exchange rate movements on their competitive position and on their profits. While international trade and investment have not declined, their rates of growth appear smaller than they would have been had currencies remained pegged.

Another major argument for floating rates has been that countries would be able to pursue independent monetary policies. Perhaps they tried. Yet one remarkable feature of the period since 1973 has been the similarity of movements of price levels and incomes among the major European countries. Intervention practices have, for example, led to the evolution of a German mark currency area.

Playing the Exchanges

The move to floating exchange rates signaled a boom for foreign exchange traders. The demand for their services skyrocketed—and so did their salaries. Success was measured by advancement, and advancement by profits earned for their employers. The foreign exchange departments of some banks made the major contribution to their profits.

These profits arose from two sources. First, banks could buy currencies at one price and sell them at a slightly higher price. Even when the bid-ask spread is small, the sums mount if the volume of business is large. The second source of profits comes from holding long positions in currencies that appreciate and short positions in currencies that depreciate.

In the spring of 1974, traders in a number of banks believed the dollar would appreciate, so they bought dollars forward. The dollar depreciated; they incurred losses. Rather than take these losses, they bought more dollars; in effect, it was the exchange market equivalent of double-or-nothing. The dollar depreciated further, so they doubled up again. The greater their losses, the more they increased their positions. Eventually, a few banks reported losses in the tens of millions of dollars.

Exactly how many foreign exchange traders—and how many banks—played the same game, incurred unrealized losses, yet managed to break even before their losses became so large that they had to be revealed is an unsettled question. The extent to which the managements of these banks were aware of the activities of their traders—and, if so, how they could have believed that such large profits came from the bid-ask spread is also unsolved.

One obvious feature of floating rates is that investors have caused market exchange rates to deviate sharply from the levels suggested by changes in national price levels. The stronger currencies have tended to appreciate sharply, the weaker currencies have tended to depreciate sharply. For example, in the decade since floating began, the U.S. dollar price of the German mark has varied from $.175 to $.260. The dollar has been on a seesaw, moving quickly from undervaluation to overvaluation. As the experience with floating rates has accumulated, the analogies with the 1920s seem stronger and stronger. In both cases, currencies became even more extensively overvalued or undervalued than under the pegged-rate system.

Frequently, the choice of exchange rate systems seems much like the choice among automobiles or brands of soap—any of the available brands might do. But the analogy is misleading, since floating rates were inevitable given the worldwide inflation of the 1970s. The historical record suggests that countries move to floating rates whenever rates of price change—or intended price change—deviate sharply. Sterling floated in terms of gold from 1803 to 1815 during the Napoleonic Wars. The U.S. dollar floated from 1862 to 1878 because Civil War finance was highly inflationary and the dollar remained overvalued for a substantial period after the war ended. That most European currencies were floating in the early 1920s was not an accident; floating rates were necessary as long as countries sought to deflate their price levels relative to the U.S. price level as a prelude to pegging their currencies to gold at the 1913 parities.

As long as the world economy continues to be subject to the disruptions of inflationary booms and sharp recessions, floating rates are likely to be retained. The major uncertainties then revolve around the extent of central bank intervention in the exchange market and the possibility that some countries might adopt exchange controls to limit abrupt changes in the foreign exchange values of their currencies.

Which Way After Floating?

The historical experience suggests that floating rates are inevitable in an era of double-digit inflation and world-wide recession. The record also suggests that countries will move back toward some form of pegged rates once the monetary environment is more stable. Individual countries will decide on their own when the time is appropriate to peg their currencies. Such a move might follow an international conference or agreement which recognizes that a move toward pegged rates is desirable; alternatively, individual countries might unilaterally peg their currencies to that of a major trading partner after they have achieved monetary stability.

Ultimately, a new agreement might be reached on pegged rates. Such an agreement would differ from the Bretton Woods system in several important ways. The support limits are likely to be wider, probably even wider than the 2.25 percent limits of the Smithsonian Agreement. The rules concerning parity changes would place greater emphasis on the need to change rates which are inappropriate. And the rules are likely to be more permissive, so that some countries might permit their currencies to float while others might peg their currencies.

Just as it is predictable that there will be a move back to pegged rates and a new exchange rate arrangement, so it is inevitable that this agreement too will eventually become outdated and will be shelved with the gold standard and the Bretton Woods system in the monetary counterpart of the Smithsonian Institution. Monetary agreements are matters of convenience which last for a decade or two; as the economic conditions which made the agreement feasible change, the agreement becomes obsolete.

Gold—How Much Is
a Barbarous Relic Worth?

President John F. Kennedy once observed that the U.S. balance-of-payments problem was one of the two most complex issues he had to deal with; the other was avoiding nuclear war. What worried him about the payments problem was that he might have to change the dollar price of gold. Yet when President Richard Nixon suspended gold sales by the U.S. Treasury in August 1971, and then agreed to increase the dollar price of gold to $38 (and subsequently to $42), the domestic political fallout was mild. Actually the Nixon decision was ironic. In his 1960 bid for the presidency, Nixon had suggested that the dollar would be devalued if Kennedy were elected president. Nixon was right—Kennedy was elected president and the dollar was devalued! Kennedy's estimates of the political costs of devaluation, domestic and foreign, were much too high. A number of U.S. decisions have proved more costly, including Nixon's temporary tariff surcharge of 10 percent, U.S. quotas on textile imports, and the invasion of Cambodia.

Gold's role in monetary affairs has periodically been subject to such ironic twists. John Maynard Keynes called gold a "barbarous relic." Charles de Gaulle said only gold could be the cornerstone of a new international monetary system. Both were probably right.

The U.S. government's suspension of gold transactions in 1971 raised the question of whether gold could continue as an international money. Demonetizing gold would have greatly reduced the supply of international money, since gold was the second largest component of international reserves. Indefinite suspension of the U.S. Treasury's gold transactions would have amounted to effective demonetization.

One solution for the gold problem that was suggested in the mid-1960s was to double the monetary price; the U.S. gold parity would have been $70. The rationale was that since the world commodity price level had more or less doubled since the monetary gold price was last increased in the mid-1930s, it was appropriate that the monetary gold price should also be doubled. Then, as world inflation proceeded apace, the goldbugs began to talk about a $100 parity.

In 1973 and 1974, when the price of gold in the private market began to rise, first to $100 and then to $150, the newspaper explanation was that investors around the world were losing confidence in paper monies. Perhaps. But an alternative explanation was that they were betting that the monetary price of gold would increase. An investor would pay $100 for gold only if the price was expected to rise; he would pay $150 or $200 only if the anticipated price was higher. Indeed the calculating investor was likely to acquire gold only if he expected that the price would rise by more than the rate of interest.

In January 1980, the gold price reached a peak of $970 an ounce. And for much of 1980, the gold price exceeded $600. In 1981, the average price was $450; in 1982, $350.

In 1982, the U.S. government set up a Gold Commission to analyze and evaluate gold's future role in both the domestic and the international monetary systems. The establishment of the commission was in response to several factors, including a statement in the Republican Party's 1980 campaign platform urging that the United States return to the gold standard. The Reagan administration loaded the membership of the commission with individuals not sympathetic to any new monetary role for gold. So most of the commission's report was predictable; the only positive recommendation was that the U.S. Treasury mint a new gold coin—one that would not have any fixed monetary value. Yet the commission also recommended that the U.S. Treasury hold on to its gold because such gold holdings might be valuable in international monetary negotiations in the future. The market prices of $900 or $350 for gold would be viable only if central banks continued to consider gold an international money. If gold were to be demonetized, the market price would tumble, for the central banks would find ways to sell gold and take their profits. For better or worse, investors have already indicated that the probability of the demonetization of gold is very low.

Before Gold Was a Barbarous Relic

The use of gold as money predates written history. How did gold develop its monetary role? In order to answer this question, two more are relevant. Why was a money necessary, and why did gold satisfy this need better than the other commodities?

Without money, goods had to be exchanged through barter, a time-consuming process. First, an individual who wished to sell his output had to find a buyer with a desirable product to exchange. Next, buyer and seller had to agree on a price, since there was no standard way to determine price. Finally, the values in the transaction had to match—if buyer and seller agreed that the fair price for one horse was three cows, the seller of the horse acquired three cows, perhaps one or two more than he wished or needed.

5 / Gold—How Much Is a Barbarous Relic Worth?

Someone realized that an intermediate good might lead to more efficient transactions. Producers could sell their output in exchange for the intermediate good, so that they need not spend the time finding a buyer for their product. Prices of goods might be expressed in terms of this intermediate good. If the intermediate good was divisible into smaller units, the amount of the payment in each transaction could be matched to the price. The intermediate good could thus perform the several functions of a money—it could serve as a medium of exchange, a unit of account, and a store of value.

Gold had several attributes that enhanced its attractiveness as the intermediate good. Gold was durable; it did not "wear out." Gold was homogeneous; one unit was virtually identical with another. Its value-to-weight ratio was high, so transport and storage costs were relatively low. Gold could be manufactured in large coins and small coins. Because of the high costs of gold mining, moreover, the supply of gold did not change rapidly—which meant that the price of a market basket of commodities was likely to be more stable in terms of a unit of gold than in terms of other commodities whose supplies changed more rapidly. So gold became a commodity money.

Other commodities with an attractive set of attributes have also been used as money. Silver, for example, had a somewhat lower value-to-weight ratio than gold, so it proved more useful for coins and transactions of lower value. The costs of transporting and storing silver were many times greater than those of transporting gold of equal value.

When different types of commodity monies were used at the same time, a major problem arose in that efficiency in transactions required that the price relationship between the different monies had to remain constant; otherwise, producers would have had to quote a price for each good in terms of gold coin and silver coin. A constant price relationship could not simply happen; government policies were necessary to peg the price of one commodity money in terms of any other. At one time, the U.S.

government set the price ratio of 15:1 (15 ounces of silver had the same value as 1 ounce of gold). But this ratio proved unsatisfactory in response to new silver discoveries, so pressures developed to alter the price ratio to 15.5:1. It proved impossible to find a price ratio that would work forever, so the idea of having two commodity monies was discarded. Gold eventually dominated silver as the paramount commodity money.

Over the last several hundred years, the authorities in virtually every country have supplemented gold's domestic role with paper monies—note issues and bank deposits. Such paper monies were easier to use in making payments than gold, for their storage and transportation costs were lower. Initially, individuals were dubious about the value of paper monies. One concern was that excessive production of paper monies might raise the commodity price level and lead to a reduction in the monies' value. So to gain acceptance for the paper monies, governments required that the issuers agree to convert these fiat monies into gold at a fixed price; this requirement was supposed to insure against excessive production of the paper money. However, the free convertibility of paper monies into gold constrained the monetary authorities in their attempts to have independent monetary policies.

When the constraints on independent policies became too severe, the monetary authorities began to reduce the role of gold in their domestic monetary systems and central banks stopped converting their domestic monies into gold. In September 1931 the Bank of England stopped pegging sterling to gold; the British authorities wanted the freedom to pursue a more expansive monetary policy to cope with an unemployment rate of 20-plus percent. In 1933 the U.S. government required all U.S. residents to sell their gold to the government; the government wanted to eliminate the pressure on U.S. commercial banks to sell gold.

Central banks held gold as an international money because they believed gold would be a better store of value than other international monies. Each central bank bought gold in the belief that at some future date it would be able to sell the gold to the monetary authorities of other countries. Obviously the argument was circular—central banks bought gold because they believed other central banks would in turn buy gold. This circularity is what confidence in any money, including the various paper monies (such as U.S. Treasury notes), is all about.

Gold's domestic monetary functions have gradually declined. Today, private parties rarely use gold as a medium of payment and almost never as a unit of account; they hold gold as a store of value—as an investment, either as a hedge against inflation, or as a precaution against a political crisis. This change in gold's role is not a result of planning or government decree; it is simply more efficient to use various national monies as a medium of payment and to state prices in terms of national currency units than in terms of gold units.

Similarly, gold's role as an international money has gradually declined, so that it is now used primarily as a store of value. Gold is no longer used as a unit of account for central banks; the parities for most national currencies are stated in terms of some other national currency. Nor has gold had any significant impact on commodity price levels for over sixty years. Central banks use gold infrequently as a means of payment; instead, payments imbalances are financed by transfers of deposits, denominated in the dollar or in the German mark or some other major currency.

That some central banks still prefer gold to dollars or other international monies as a store of value may seem irrational, for gold earns no interest, while these other assets do. One explanation often given is tradition; central banks got used to holding gold during the gold standard era, and their preference remains unchanged, even though the system has changed. But this explanation is not very convincing. What needs to be explained is why central banks hold gold and thus forgo the opportunity to hold their international money in assets yielding 10 or 12 percent. One advantage of gold over these other assets is greater acceptability; gold may be acceptable as money by other central banks when dollars or other international monies are not. Another advantage is gold's underlying value as a commodity; gold has retained its value despite wars, revolutions, and spendthrift sovereigns.

In the short run, other monies have proved more attractive. But gold has remained, while numerous national monies have come and gone. The continuing demand for gold reflects confidence in its future value and the belief that no one sovereign can diminish this value significantly.

For most observers, the idea that gold should again play a central role in the system seems bizarre. Yet the century of the gold standard (1815–1914) was one in which there was modest secular inflation; periods of rising prices were followed by periods of declining prices. Moreover, the year-to-year changes in the price level were modest, much less than in the 1970s. The gold standard delivered price stability, more so than the discretionary monetary management of the last fifteen years.

Gold as an Investment

The market price of gold increased so sharply in the 1970s that the rate of return attached to ownership of gold has exceeded that available on nearly every other widely held asset. During the 1970s, when the gold price went from $35 to $800, the average annual return was 36 percent. With the mid-1982 gold price of $350, the average annual return was 22 percent. In any short-term period, the rate of return from holding gold has been high if the prices rose sharply. But over the long run, the rate of return from holding gold has been below that from holding other types of financial assets.

Saying that the gold standard delivered price stability should not obscure the fact that prices fell briefly and sharply in a series of financial crises. These crises frequently reflected failures of large numbers of banks, and a decline in the money supply. The triggers for these crises differed—in some cases, large agricultural surpluses led to very low prices so that farmers could not repay their bank loans; in other cases, collapses in stock market prices led to bank failures. So whether the long-run price level stability was inherent in the system or an accident remains a matter of debate.

The criticism that the gold standard would not work today might be a statement about economics or a statement about politics; it is important to keep the distinction clear. There appear no inherent reasons why the gold standard wouldn't work in the 1980s if it were tried; what is at issue would be the costs, compared with the costs of recent monetary policies. The dominant objections are political; it is said that the authorities are unlikely to be willing to give up the power inherent in domestic monetary management. The implication is that the public will continue to sacrifice its own interests to the promise of discretionary monetary management, while neglecting the costs of such policies.

The Persistent Gold Shortage

The suspension of gold transactions by the U.S. Treasury in 1971 reflected a shortage of monetary gold which had persisted for most of the previous sixty years. The supply of gold available to central banks was smaller than desired because, while production had grown slowly, the private demand for gold as a commodity—for use in jewelry and industry and especially for hoarding and speculation—had grown rapidly. Monetary demand and private demand competed with each other; when more gold was demanded for one use, the amount available for the other use fell. Thus, when private demand for gold increased, less gold was available to central banks. Similarly, when the central bank demand for gold increased—that is, when the banks agreed to pay a higher price for gold—they bid gold away from private users.

The shortage of monetary gold in much of this century reflected that the commodity price level increased more rapidly than the price of gold in terms of the dollar, sterling, and other national currencies. Between 1914 and 1950 the U.S. wholesale price index increased by 125 percent and the monetary price of gold by 70 percent. From 1950 to 1970 the wholesale price level

---

$35 an Ounce and 3.1416 Are Not the Same Kind of Numbers

The choice of $35 as the parity for the dollar in January 1934 was a historical accident; the price might have been $30 or $40. President Roosevelt had been convinced that the way to move the U.S. economy out of the Great Depression was to greatly increase the gold price. Gold production would be stimulated. More gold would be sold to the U.S. monetary authorities. The U.S. money supply would increase, and so would commodity prices. As a result, business firms would no longer incur losses because of declines in the value of their inventories, and banks would no longer be threatened with insolvency because of the declining value of their assets.

To increase the dollar price of gold, a subsidiary of the government-owned Reconstruction Finance Corporation bought gold in New York. The price of gold in the United States then tended to exceed the price, at the prevailing exchange rates, in London. Arbitragers had an incentive to buy gold in London for sale in the United States. But they had to buy sterling first. And their purchases caused the price of sterling to rise in terms of the dollar and numerous other currencies, weakening the competitive position of British firms in the world market. The British objected. The U.S. authorities stabilized the dollar price of gold when the free market price was near $35. Had the British objection been delayed until the free market price was $40, the U.S. gold parity would have been $40.

---

increased by 35 percent; the monetary price of gold remained unchanged. Through most of the postwar period until the early 1970s, gold producers were squeezed between a much sharper increase in production costs than in their selling price.

The gold shortage first became apparent immediately after World War I, and persisted until the early 1930s. The increase in the dollar price of gold in 1934 was not designed to resolve the world shortage but to stimulate the U.S. economy. As it turned out, the increase in the gold price to $35 an ounce led to a glut, for the amount of gold produced exceeded the amount demanded. Excess gold flowed to central banks, especially in the United States; the United States was subject to a "Golden Avalanche." U.S. gold holdings increased from $7 billion in 1934 (valued at the $35 price) to $20 billion in 1939.

The inflation of World War II rapidly eliminated the gold glut, and so the possibility of a gold shortage reappeared. Wholesale commodity prices doubled during the 1940s. Gold-mining firms were again squeezed between higher production costs and a fixed selling price. The private demand for gold again increased, since gold became progressively cheaper in terms of other commodities.

Postwar concern with the gold shortage first became acute in the late 1950s. Between 1949, when the U.S. Treasury's gold holdings peaked at $24 billion, and 1960, U.S. gold holdings declined by $8 billion. This redistribution of gold among the world's central banks was viewed as necessary to provide the financial basis for the postwar growth in world trade. But by 1960 there was growing recognition that the total supply of gold available for central banks as a group was too small to meet their demand.

The impending gold shortage was an issue during the 1960 presidential election campaign. Nixon tagged Kennedy as an inflationary spender—higher prices were around the corner. The first threat of a dollar devaluation appeared in 1960 when a small number of investors increased their gold purchases in the London market. For several weeks their purchases exceeded the flow from new production. Under such circumstances, the Bank of England would normally have sold gold from its holdings to keep the price from rising above $35; it would then have used its dollar receipts to buy gold from the U.S. Treasury. This time, however, someone in the U.S. Treasury had led some British officials to doubt that the Bank of England could buy gold from the U.S. Treasury to replenish its gold holdings after sales to private parties in the London market. So the Bank of England stopped selling gold. A combination of a nervous demand and the absence of a steadying supply led to a rise in the gold price to about $40, an increase which seemed extremely sharp when it occurred but which pales into insignificance when compared with recent price increases. Eventually, the Bank of England supplied gold to the market and the price fell back to $35. Still, the first signal of an impending gold shortage had appeared.

Two kinds of measures might have resolved the shortage: either the private demand for gold might have been reduced by lowering the commodity price level, or the supply might have been increased by raising the monetary price of gold. The scope for reducing the private demand was small, for governments had neither the will nor the incentive to pursue deflationary financial policies. U.S. gold regulations were changed to prohibit American citizens from buying or holding gold outside the United States (they had been prohibited from holding gold domestically since 1933). Efforts to induce foreign governments to apply similar measures to their residents were rebuffed. And attempting to decrease the demand by reducing the world price level—the classic approach of the gold standard—was ruled out by the cost of a deflation in terms of unemployment, business failures, and lost elections.

By 1965 the private demand for gold had increased above the level of production; central banks sold $50 million of gold from their reserves to hold the price at $35. Uncertainties about the future sterling parity led to yet another surge in the private demand for gold. In 1967 central banks sold $1.6 billion of gold to private parties to prevent the price from rising above $35. And in the first ten weeks of 1968, sales to private parties reached $700 million.

Investors were alarmed lest the experience of the 1930s be repeated: they feared that the devaluation of sterling would force a devaluation of the dollar in terms of gold. They believed that, at a minimum, the dollar price of gold would be doubled. Hence the potential for revaluation gains was attractive. Altogether, private parties bought more than $3 billion of gold from central banks in the 1965–1968 period. Much of their demand was supplied, indirectly, from the U.S. Treasury.

Then, in March 1968, the monetary authorities in Europe and the United States agreed to separate the private gold market from the market in which central banks buy and sell gold to each other. Under this two-tier arrangement, nonmonetary and monetary gold became "separate" commodities; the tie between the private market and the official market was severed. Most newly produced gold was to be supplied to the private market, from which industrial, artistic, and hoarding demands had to be satisfied. Initially, central banks continued to deal in gold with each other at the price of $35 an ounce. In the private market the gold price might rise above $35 or, conceivably, fall below $35.

The adoption of the two-tier system raised two problems—one involved how to market South Africa's $1 billion annual gold output. South Africa naturally sought to get the largest possible revenues from its output; it wanted to sell between one-half and two-thirds of its gold output to private parties, at prices of perhaps $38 or $40 or more, and the rest to official institutions at the $35 price. The European central banks liked the South African proposal, since they could continue to add to their gold holdings. At the same time, their own gold holdings would appear more valuable if the price in the private market climbed over $35.

The U.S. authorities, in contrast, wanted South Africa to sell all its gold in the private market, in the belief that the price would then fall, perhaps to $30 or $32. According to the U.S. scenario, central bank confidence in the future of gold as international money would be shaken. At the same time, the preference for other types of international money (including dollars) would increase, and countries would become more receptive to the need for a new international money.

Eventually, a compromise was reached. Under certain conditions, South Africa was permitted to sell limited amounts of gold at $35 to central banks. But this compromise became irrelevant almost as soon as it was concluded, for the increase in private demand in response to worldwide inflation meant that nearly all of the output could be sold to private parties at about $40.

After the August 1971 U.S. suspension of gold transactions, the price of gold in the private market began to rise; by mid-1972 the price had approached $70. By late 1974, when new legislation permitted U.S. citizens to buy gold, the price reached $200.

Once the price of gold in the private market began to exceed the official price, the second problem became apparent—central banks were reluctant to buy and sell gold with each other at the $35 parity if the market price was higher. So the higher free market price reduced the liquidity of gold holdings.

The Choices Now Available

The objective of the U.S. game plan for gold had been to avoid, largely for political reasons, an increase in the dollar price of gold. Successive U.S. presidents following Eisenhower—Kennedy, Johnson, and then Nixon—had said that the dollar price of gold would be fixed forever. The retention of the $35 gold parity was a U.S. commitment like the Monroe Doctrine and access to Berlin. Altering one U.S. commitment would undermine the credibility of other U.S. commitments.

The adoption of the $38 parity and then the $42 parity by the Nixon administration helped resolve the impasse over exchange rate structure, but it made no dent in the gold problem. Yet this minor change led to an important insight; it demonstrated that while a few economists and government officials were vitally interested in the gold price, the public was bored. The price of gold was not a domino. Increasing the dollar price of gold had no significant adverse reaction, at home or abroad.

The U.S. response to the gold shortage was that gold should be gradually phased out of the international monetary system; if gold were demonetized, it would not appear as if the United States had altered its parity. After the parity was changed, first in the Smithsonian Agreement and again in February 1972, the commitment to phasing out gold was retained, even though the costs of altering the $35 parity had already been incurred.

One of the alternatives to the U.S. response is a return to the gold market arrangements of the 1940s and 1950s, only at a much higher monetary price, one related to the market price. The higher gold price would increase the supply and reduce the private demand. The other basic option involves continued sales of gold from monetary stocks, so that gold's monetary role would progressively diminish.

Now that the price of gold has been changed and the costs of this change already incurred, the costs and benefits of retaining gold as a monetary asset or of keeping gold in limbo can be appreciated. Nearly every country has a vested interest in the monetary price of gold. An increase in the gold price—or gold demonetization—makes some groups better off and others worse off. And those who are worse off—or who feel worse off—would probably blame the United States, since the change in the price would be seen as a U.S. policy. Since the United States produces and consumes minimal amounts of gold, the direct U.S. economic interests are trivial. The central U.S. interest in the monetary role for gold is the functioning of the international monetary system and its consequences for U.S. foreign relations.

Changes in the gold price have an impact on gold producers—on the owners of gold mines and their labor force—and on the producers of competitive monies and commodities. When gold is valued at $300 an ounce, speculators' holdings may approach $75 billion. Should the monetary price of gold rise, the producers of competitive monies would lose. If, on the other hand, gold is demonetized, the pattern of winners and losers is reversed.

The price of gold in the London market since 1972 is shown in figure 5.1. From the 1930s on, the price of gold remained unchanged, and even after the move to the two-tier gold market in 1968 the gold price remained relatively stable. Then, in 1973 and 1974, the price began to increase. The gold price fell to just over $100 in 1976 before beginning to increase again, initially modestly, then sharply.

Several questions remain. One is what will happen to the price if gold is demonetized. A second involves the future monetary price should gold be retained as an international money.

Demonetization would likely represent the gradual realization by central banks that their holdings of gold would be of greater value and utility if they sold gold in the commodity markets. Central bank gold sales in the commodity markets might sharply depress the price because the stock of gold held by central banks, 37,000 metric tons, is exceedingly large relative to the annual production of gold, which is less than 1,000 metric tons. Sales which seem small relative to central bank holdings would be quite large relative to the supply from new production. Once the price began to fall, numerous private holders would sell to take their profits or cut their losses, and the price would fall sharply; how rapidly and how far would depend on the size of central bank sales. Almost immediately the six or eight central banks that are the major holders of gold would seek to establish an agreement limiting their sales in the commodity market.

What would be the international consequences of demonetizing gold? Gold-producing countries and those European countries which hold large amounts of gold as international money would clearly lose, since the value of their holdings would

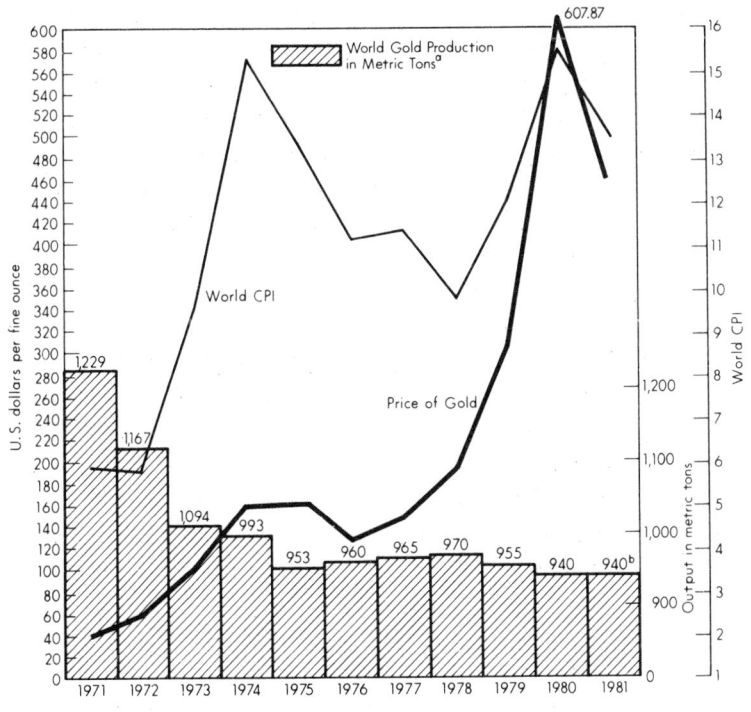

FIGURE 5.1
Gold Price and Gold Production
World Gold Production in Metric Tons[a]

SOURCE: International Monetary Fund, *International Financial Statistics* (Washington, D.C., July 1982); Bank for International Settlements, *Annual Report* (1980–1981).

[a] Excludes USSR, Eastern Europe, mainland China, and North Korea.
[b] Estimated.

93

decline. South Africa would lose since the price of its major export would decline. The Soviet Union would lose. The gainers would include industrial users of gold, since the commodity price would fall. Moreover, to the extent that manpower and materials would no longer be needed to produce a commodity money and could therefore be used to build dams, bridges, and schools, all countries would gain. But this gain would have to be balanced against the cost of having a smaller supply of international money than was formerly deemed optimal.

Gold demonetization would force countries to rethink how they might peg their currencies. Some might continue to peg their currencies to the U.S. dollar; in that case, they too would, in effect, be demonetizing gold. Together with the United States, they would constitute a dollar bloc. Pegged exchange rates would prevail within the bloc.

Assume, on the other hand, that a decision is made to retain gold as an international money; then the price at which gold would be traded among central banks would have to be set. If this price was substantially above the price at which gold had been trading, private parties might be induced to realize their gains, and monetary gold holdings would increase significantly. The authorities would be concerned with a gold glut, much as in the 1930s. If the monetary price were much below the recent market price, then central banks would be reluctant to sell gold to each other, much as in the 1968–1971 period.

Setting the "right" monetary price for gold, which is known as the "reentry problem," would be especially difficult. As long as investors anticipated that the U.S. price level would continue to increase, their demand for gold would remain strong. If the U.S. inflation rate continued to decline, then the gold price would likely continue to fall. And at that time—and only then and not sooner—would the authorities be in a position to consider seriously a new gold parity.

A move to a higher monetary price seems unlikely to occur as a result of a formal international agreement. Rather, the U.S.

government may gradually come to recognize that an important U.S. foreign policy interest would be served by retaining gold in the system. The elements in this decision would include the usefulness of having an international money in the system in addition to the dollar and other national currencies, and the difficulties in having this money produced by an international institution.

The U.S. Treasury would then have to calculate the appropriate price for gold, but it would recognize the chanciness of trying to determine the right price. If the new parity were $200, existing monetary gold holdings would be worth $231 billion and the monetary value of current output would be $8 billion. A higher market price for gold would in the long run stimulate production, so new output might reach $10 billion annually. If private expenditures on gold remained unchanged—the percentage decline in the number of ounces purchased approximating the increase in the market price—monetary gold stocks might increase by $5 or $6 billion annually.

These are rough estimates, not definite projections. Clearly there is a dollar price of gold which would enable both official and private demands to be satisfied adequately, at least for a few years, unless world inflation continues.

The monetary price of gold might be initially set at a level at which the amount supplied exceeded the amount demanded. In that case—if the gold supply were initially excessive—gold would flow into the U.S. Treasury, as happened in the late 1930s. Because of the higher value of the gold output, other countries could satisfy their gold needs without forcing the United States to sell gold.

Some economists have argued that an increase in the gold price would be inflationary: private parties would spend more as a result of their revaluation gains. This concern might be valid if gold were still used as a domestic money; it has much less force now, with gold's monetary role limited to transactions among central banks, and with private gold holdings constituting such a small fraction of private wealth. Some central banks might follow a somewhat more expansive monetary policy as a result of their revaluation gains. Any increase in commodity price levels from an increase in the monetary price of gold would be small relative to increases resulting from other factors such as the desire to finance government deficits.

When Keynes called gold a barbarous relic, he meant that mining gold to produce an international money is unnecessarily expensive. Producing $6 billion of gold uses labor and machinery which might produce $6 billion of other goods. If the IMF or some other international institution produces $6 billion of paper gold, the costs are minimal—the time of some government negotiators and a few clerks to record which central banks owe what to whom. And the labor and machinery otherwise used to mine gold for monetary purposes could then be diverted to producing dams, schools, hospitals, and bombs.

The cost of producing $6 billion of gold falls on those countries which prefer to hold gold in their reserves when they might otherwise hold IMF-produced money, since these countries must earn the gold by exporting goods and services to the gold-mining countries. The European countries with a strong demand for gold would acquire most of the newly produced gold. They would also bear most of the cost.

What about the political consequences of changing the gold price? At one time, it was feared that raising the gold price would give substantial windfall gains to the Soviet Union and South Africa; and that is bad, the argument went, because the former is part of the Sino-Soviet communist conspiracy and the latter practices apartheid. Reducing the gold price inflicts losses on the Soviet Union and South Africa, and that is good. Of course, as long as South Africa manages its gold sales so as to keep the price in the private market high, they have already secured the windfall.

If gold is demonetized, South Africa's ability to maintain the price would indeed decline. But the impact of changes in the gold price on South African apartheid is a complex issue, not to be resolved by armchair sloganeering. If gold is valued at $200 an ounce, South Africa's gold production accounts for 15 percent of its GNP and 50 percent of its exports. At this gold price, the blacks gain in economic welfare; if the gold price were much lower, unemployment among blacks would increase. True, government revenues would also rise from taxes on the profits of gold-mining companies. Even so, it is not obvious that the impact of a higher monetary gold price would change the level and distribution of income in South Africa so as to give the supporters of apartheid greater power. But even if the evidence showed that a gold price increase strengthened apartheid, this cost would have to be weighed against the advantages of resolving the inadequacy of the supply of international money—and the costs and advantages within each country of a higher gold price.

Most European central bankers have a strong preference for increasing the gold price over demonetization—indeed, many prefer a higher gold price to any other approach to revamping the system.

As far as the credibility of U.S. commitments is concerned, an increase in the dollar price of gold is preferable to gold demonetization. If gold is demonetized, then the credibility of the commitments to satisfy the world's demand for international money by producing paper gold would be low. (This issue is more fully discussed in chapter 6.) Raising the gold price would also be more nearly consistent with the structure of the IMF and its Articles of Agreement than would gold demonetization. Gold demonetization would impose substantial losses on those now holding gold, whereas retaining gold by increasing the monetary price imposes losses on no one, although those central banks that hold dollars and other reserve assets might be upset because they would not share in the revaluation gains.

The move toward increasing the gold price might occur after exchange rates were again pegged, or even before. If exchange rates were again pegged, the United States would again need to concern itself with its payments position. Both demonetization and a gold price increase would help reduce any U.S. payments deficit. Demonetization would work because the U.S. authorities would no longer have to worry about the deficit, since foreign official institutions could no longer require the U.S. Treasury to sell gold. And the gold price increase would work because the annual increase in the gold supply would be large enough to enable other countries to satisfy their demand for international money without forcing the United States to incur a payments deficit. Indeed, because of the increase in the value of the annual gold production, every country might add to its gold holdings at the same time.

It is true that reliance on gold is an inefficient way to meet the demand for international money; there are less costly alternatives. The problem, however, is not with gold, but rather with the attitudes and preferences of central banks around the world—and their experience with the credibility of commitments made by foreign governments. The European preference for gold *is* archaic. But it *is* their preference—and they pay the costs of retaining gold in the system.

Ultimately, the choice, as de Gaulle knew, is a U.S. choice. The United States must decide whether the international financial system will function more smoothly and U.S. interests will be better served if the European preferences are satisfied or frustrated. For a decade or more, U.S. authorities focused on trying to wean the European central banks away from their preference for gold. The effort was not notably successful. At some stage, U.S. officials may still seek to build a system around these preferences.

In monetary affairs, the authorities cannot afford to be ambiguous; to do so would point toward profit opportunities open to private investors. So they can never hint that they will change a parity, shift from pegged to floating rates, or favor a change in the monetary gold price. When the timing seems appropriate, however, they can suddenly reverse their policies.

98

They Invented Money So They Could
Have Inflation

One hundred years ago, a mile was a mile, a dollar was a dollar, and a liter of water weighed a kilo. The 1883 kilo is identical to the 1983 kilo. The 1983 dollar is only a pale shadow of its value a century ago. All the national monies in 1983 measure less than they did in 1973, and they were less valuable in 1973 than in 1963.

One hundred years from now, the mile and the kilo will be unchanged as units of distance and weight. It is equally certain that the dollar will have a smaller value, as will the German mark, the Swiss franc, and all other "strong" currencies. While the measurement of the value of money may be less scientific than the measurement of the speed of light or the distance to the moon, the error in the measurement is not in question—the orbit of the earth around the sun also varies within a range. Rather, the question is why, of all the units of account in the world, money is the only one which shrinks in value—gradually but inevitably.

From time to time, the monetary authorities in various countries acknowledge the debasing tendencies of their predecessors—they knock two or three zeros off the monetary units, usually after the bills become too large and the token coins have been melted because their value as commodities has exceeded their value as money. In 1959, General de Gaulle adopted the "heavy franc"; 100 old francs would buy one new franc. In 1983, Argentina adopted a new peso, equal to 1,000 old pesos.

The periods of inflation have been so pervasive recently that previous episodes of sharply declining prices have been forgotten. The U.S. wholesale price index fell 50 percent in 1920–1921; during the same period, the consumer price index fell by more than one-third. Prices fell sharply during the Great Depression of the 1930s. The nineteenth century was one of relative price stability; if the 1800 U.S. wholesale price index is set at 100, the 1900 price index is 64—a decline of .4 percent a year. The opening of new lands—the American West, Canada, Australia, and the Argentine—led to declines in food prices. But the price level doubled during the Civil War.

Two factors distinguish the inflationary record in the twentieth century. One is that the wartime episodes seem more frequent. The second is that prices have not declined for nearly fifty years. The anticipated depression after World War II has not occurred—yet.

Traditionally, shrinkage in the value of money is associated with wartime finance; the sovereign finds it expedient to print money to pay the army. The U.S. consumer price level nearly doubled during the 1915–1920 period; the annual rate of increase averaged 15 percent, about as high as during the Civil War period. From 1940 to 1948, the annual rate of price increase averaged 7 percent. During the Korean War the rate of price increase averaged 5 percent for about two years. From the beginning of major U.S. involvement in Vietnam in 1965 to the climax in 1970, the annual increase in the U.S. consumer price index averaged 4 percent. The progressive decline in the annual rate of price increase over these four wartime episodes suggests that the U.S. government has slowly become more successful in putting wars on a pay-as-you-go basis.

However, increased confidence in the ability of governments to control inflation has been shattered by the world inflation of 1973–1974, virtually unprecedented in peacetime. A new term, "double-digit inflation," hit the newspaper headlines. Prices were increasing nearly as rapidly in peacetime as they had in most previous wars. By almost any peacetime standard, inflation during the four-year interval 1972–1975 was unprecedented: the U.S. consumer price level increased by 36 percent, or nearly 10 percent a year, more rapidly than during World War II.

Yet the inflation rate in the late 1970s was even more rapid than in the first half of the decade. In 1980, the annual inflation rate peaked at 13 percent. And for the six-year period 1977–1982, the increase in the U.S. consumer price level totaled 60 percent.

The world inflation of the 1970s should be distinguished from the Vietnam inflation of the late 1960s. A tight money policy in 1969 pushed the economy into recession. The U.S. commitment in Vietnam and U.S. inflation were winding down together. Whereas during the late 1960s U.S. price levels increased more rapidly than those in other industrialized countries, inflation in the 1970s was worldwide. Price levels abroad were increasing as rapidly as U.S. prices—or more so. Germany and Switzerland were the principal exceptions; prices increased at rates several percentage points below those in the United States.

While inflation has been around as long as money, there remain sharp disagreements about its causes. Is the cause economic, sociological, or psychological? If economic in origin, does inflation reflect supply shortages of a natural or artificial kind, or expansion of demand? The worldwide inflation has been attributed to the growth of the Eurodollar market, to the floating exchange rate system, to the loss of confidence in money, to the sharp increases in the price of oil. Indeed, some experts have gone so far as to say that of the 10 percent increase in U.S. prices, two percentage points represent the increase in oil prices, four percentage points the devaluation of the dollar, and so forth. Some Englishmen talk about a sociological theory of inflation; they mean that strong unions—the railway workers, miners, electrical workers, and other public sector employees—secure large wage increases, and prices are then raised to cover the higher labor costs.

Some Americans wonder whether inflation is inevitable in a democracy. Competition among politicians compels them to promise both more government services and lower tax bills. When the bills come in, the government prints money so its checks will not bounce.

Does the Fed Cause Bank Failures?

Bank failures were commonplace in the nineteenth century. Banks closed their doors when their deposit liabilities exceeded the value of loans, mortgages, and other assets. Once the word got out that a bank might be in difficulty, the depositors rushed to get their money, much more rapidly than if they were to sell a currency about to be devalued. If the bank closed, the depositors might receive 30 or 40 cents on the dollar, depending on how badly the bank had been managed.

In some cases, the run on the bank caused an otherwise good bank to fail. Banks were forced to sell assets to meet their depositors' demand for money. Such sales further weakened the banks position, for inevitably the best assets were sold first. The failure of one bank had a domino effect on the stability of others; bankruptcy became contagious. Credit systems collapsed when the public lost confidence in the banks. Bank failures also meant that the money supply fell, so recessions resulted.

Several institutional innovations were adopted to minimize failure. The National Banking Act of 1863 provided for a comptroller of the currency to protect banks and depositors by ensuring that the assets held by banks were good. Yet there were substantial bank failures in 1883, 1896, and 1907. The Federal Reserve was set up in 1913 to act as a lender of last resort, supplying funds—newly printed money—to banks in distress so they could pay depositors who sought to reduce or close out their accounts. Nevertheless, nearly 6,000 banks failed in the 1920s, 1,352 in

---

1930, 2,294 in 1931, 1,456 in 1932, and 4,000 in 1933. To dampen the snowball effect of deposit withdrawal, in 1933 the U.S. government set up the Federal Deposit Insurance Corporation, Initially, individual deposits were insured to $10,000, then $20,000; in 1975 the ceiling was raised to $40,000, and in April 1980 to $100,000. Banks pay an insurance premium to the FDIC, and it has built up reserves over the years. At the end of 1977, capital accumulated by the FDIC from these insurance premiums totaled $9 billion; the FDIC supposedly has an open credit line at the Treasury if its losses should be larger.

A few banks have failed recently, despite these institutional safeguards. U.S. National Bank in San Diego failed because its managers made high-risk loans to captive firms. Franklin National Bank went under in 1974 because of foreign exchange losses. Security National Bank of Long Island was closed because it had made too many insecure loans. Penn Square Bank of Oklahoma City closed its doors in 1982 because many of its loans to firms involved in oil exploration went sour when the price of oil fell; many of these loans appeared to have been made on the belief that the oil price would go to $50 or $60 a barrel.

The key question is whether a significant number of banks might fail again, and how adequate the safeguards will be. In 1974 and 1975, newspaper reports suggested that the Treasury and the Fed were keeping a close watch on several hundred banks. Some of the business and real estate loans made by these banks went sour during the recession. And the market value of the bonds held by these institutions plummeted with the sharp rise in interest rates. Technically, these institutions were bankrupt; the market value of their assets was less than that of their liabilities. The losses dwarfed the accumulated reserves of the FDIC.

The Fed faced a dilemma. Its tight-money policy had caused the value of bank assets to decline and had forced the banks into technical bankruptcy. The rationale for setting up the Fed was to prevent the failure of banks. But the desire to break the double-digit inflation had driven the banks to the brink of failure. To prevent bank failure, the Fed was obliged to expand the economy—to float off the credit crisis. Monetary expansion could lead to inflation, which would lead to tight money, which would lead to increased bank failures. And so it goes.

Many things happen at the same time in the worlds of business and money. Distinctions must be made between causes and consequences, between causes and associations, between causes and definitions. A frequent pairing of two events sometimes leads to a "scientific truth" or rule, as if causation could be inferred from association. An exception then leads to the statement, "This is the exception that proves the rule." But the statement should read: "This is the exception that proves the rule wrong." It is a fact that the money supply increases with great statistical regularity toward the end of the year, but it would be risky to suggest that increases in the money supply cause Christmas. Casual observation suggests that fire trucks are frequently found near fires, but only a fool would suggest that fire trucks cause fires, or that the fires caused the fire trucks.

To say that inflation is caused by rising prices is like saying that death is caused by the failure of the heart to beat; all deaths are associated with the stoppage of heart movement, but heart failure has not yet put cancer, strokes, and accidents out of business. A definition is not a statement about causation. Brain stoppage measures death, just as rising prices measure inflation; the questions to be answered are why the brain stops functioning and why prices increase.

Whether an alleged example of economic cause and effect is in fact another example of argument by association can sometimes be determined by asking whether the relationship holds over a number of years. While the quadrupling of oil prices in the fall of 1973 may have led to a more rapid increase in world price levels thereafter, it does not explain the rapid increase in prices that had previously occurred—nor does it explain why the prices of sugar, copper, groundnuts, and virtually every other primary product also increased by 200, 300, or even 400 percent. Across-the-board price increases are typical of world booms. The move to floating rates may explain why prices increased more rapidly in some countries than in others—yet the move to floating rates would not have been necessary if prices had not already

104

been increasing more rapidly in the United States than in Germany. Floating exchange rates may have been a result of differential rates of inflation rather than a cause, or at least many Germans believe so. While the growth of the Eurodollar market may have been inflationary, the market grew no more rapidly in 1973 and 1974 than it had in earlier years, when the rate of inflation was much lower.

In the long run, inflation will not occur without an increase in the money supply. But an increase in the commodity price level may occur in response to shortages, even if the money supply is constant. A failure in the corn crop will almost certainly lead to higher corn prices, for the higher price "rations" the reduced supply among competing buyers. Nevertheless, these factors lead to one-shot (or perhaps two-shot) increases in the price level rather than continuing increases.

The question is not what was happening in 1973 and 1974, but rather what happened in 1973 and 1974 that had not happened before. A second question is why rates of price increases differed so sharply among countries. And a third question involves the relation between the severity of the inflation and the severity of the recesson which followed.

Watergate Economics

In the United States, the year immediately preceding presidential elections is likely to be one of expansive financial policies. The party in power wants the economy prosperous when the voters go to the polls. If the economy is sluggish, the ins may soon be the outs. If inflation is soaring, the government may also be in trouble. So it wants to "fine tune" the economy and somehow achieve full employment and stable prices—a neat trick.

Assume the economy is in recession. Initially, measures taken to expand the economy are likely to affect output and employment more than prices and costs as long as there remains substantial spare capacity. Increasingly, as the economy continues to expand, it will bump against more and more supply constraints, and prices will rise to ration scarce goods. At first, price increases will be selective, as scarcities develop in particular goods; then the price increases will become more widespread. Fine tuning suggests that the authorities will try to time the expansion so that the maximum employment effects are felt a week or two before the election; someone else can worry about subsequent price increases after the election.

In 1959 the prospects for a recession in the U.S. economy by November 1960 seemed strong. Arthur F. Burns, formerly chairman of the Council of Economic Advisers and an informal adviser to then Vice-President Nixon, recommended an expansion of the economy to set the stage for a Nixon victory in the 1960 election. Supposedly, President Eisenhower refused to pass on the advice to William McChesney Martin, then chairman of the Federal Reserve. Kennedy won the election on the promise of "Getting the Economy Moving Again." Nixon moved to California.

In 1969, President Nixon appointed Arthur F. Burns as a White House adviser; a year later Burns became chairman of the Federal Reserve Board. After continuing a monetary crunch designed to wring the inflationary excesses out of the U.S. economy in 1970, the Fed began to expand the rate of money supply growth to stimulate the economy in the spring of 1971. In August 1971, one element in Nixon's New Economic Policy was price and wage ceilings, which tilted the effect of increased expenditures toward increases in output and employment rather than increases in prices and wages. The U.S. economy began to boom—industrial production, employment, man-hours per week, and the stock market all went up.

As a recession year, 1971 was unusual. The unemployment rate peaked at about 6 percent, but the consumer price level was still increasing at an annual rate of 3 percent. In previous recessions, in contrast, prices usually increased no more than 1 percent when unemployment peaked—and the unemployment rate peaked lower.

One interpretation is that the structure of the U.S. economy had changed: an increase in the unemployment rate to perhaps 7 or 8 percent for several years would have been necessary to get the rate of price increase down to 1 percent. A second interpretation is that if monetary expansion had not begun in mid-1971, the economy would not have been booming in November 1972. Nixon's margin of votes in the 1972 election was the largest ever.

The 1972 inflation began at a time when prices were already increasing at a rate of 3 percent a year, rather than at the 1 percent rate in the recession years of the 1950s and early 1960s. The public had recently seen the value of the dollar shrink by 30 percent in five years. So when prices resumed their rapid increase, the public began to anticipate further inflation; rather than risk holding money while its value declined, the public began to reduce their money balances. They spent (and prices increased more rapidly than would have been predicted from the money supply changes alone), but spending only transferred money to someone else.

Price increases were inevitable after the election; the uncertainty was the timing. The price ceilings of phase 1, phase 2, and phase N in Nixon's economic policy only delayed the upward movements in prices. Nixon and Burns had a tiger by the tail, and they could not afford to let go—at least not until after the election.

Upward pressures on U.S. prices also resulted from the devaluations of the dollar at the end of 1971 and again in early 1973. In the late 1960s, U.S. consumption increased more rapidly than U.S. production, and imports increased more rapidly than exports. As long as foreign central banks were willing to add to their dollar holdings, it was not necessary for the dollar to be devalued, and the increase in U.S. imports relative to U.S. exports dampened upward pressure on the U.S. price level. The combination of delayed devaluation and price ceilings meant that the price increases, which would have occurred in 1971 and 1972 were instead bunched in a much shorter interval and delayed until after the election. After the devaluation, the incomes of U.S. consumers increased more rapidly than the supply of available goods, so sharp price increases were inevitable to ration the reduced supply. Prior to the devaluation, the increase in imports relative to exports meant that domestic prices increased less rapidly than they otherwise might have; after the devaluation, the reverse was true. In 1973, dollar goods were cheaper to consumers in other industrial countries; U.S. exports soared, and U.S. consumers shifted to domestic goods from more expensive foreign goods. The reduction in the supply of goods because of the decline in the trade deficit, together with the higher price of imports, reinforced the upward pressure on U.S. price levels caused by the Fed's monetary expansion. The effect was delayed by the price ceilings, but these ceilings were removed early in 1973—soon after the 1972 election, long before the 1976 election.

Governments rarely admit their mistakes. If their policies backfire, the problem is that unforeseen—and unforeseeable—events occurred. So the inflation was attributed to supply shortages. The anchovies disappeared from the west coast of Latin America, so there was a deficiency in the world supply of protein. The Russians had a bad wheat crop. These supply shortages contributed to the increase in prices. But the prices of most other commodities were also increasing. In the absence of demand booms, the supply shortfalls would have had a much less severe impact on prices. The U.S. government had sailed too close to the wind; these supply shortfalls would have been far less troublesome if the government had followed a less expansive monetary policy.

Watergate was an exercise in overkill: Nixon would have won the 1972 election even without any possible information that might have been gathered illegally from Democratic national headquarters. Similarly, the Republicans would have won in 1972 even without the rapid monetary expansion of 1971. They chose not to take the risks. The costs fell on the American public.

Carter Economics

Traditionally, Democrats place more emphasis on jobs and less on price stability than the Republicans. Jimmy Carter stuck with tradition. When Carter took the oath as president in January 1977, the unemployment rate was 7.4 percent, and the price level was increasing at a rate of 5.1 percent a year. When Carter returned to Plains, Georgia four years later, the unemployment rate was 7.4, while the price level was increasing at an annual rate of 11.7 percent. Carter's tax and monetary policies clearly got the economy moving again.

Political leaders—at least U.S. political leaders—frequently suggest that if things are not quite perfect at home, at least they are much worse abroad. President Nixon was fond of comparing the rate of U.S. inflation with that of other countries, as long as the U.S. rate was lower.

One of the factors—the Fed's monetary policies—which put upward pressure on U.S. prices during the early 1970s did not directly affect other countries: the Europeans and the Japanese could not vote in the 1972 election. Moreover, if the devaluations of the dollar were supposed to have led to a more rapid increase in U.S. prices, the converse—the revaluations of the yen, the guilder, the Swiss franc, and the mark—should have dampened upward pressure on price levels in these countries. For both reasons, price levels abroad should have increased less rapidly than in the United States. But in fact, prices in most foreign countries increased more rapidly than in the United States (see table 6.1).

The simplest explanation for the differential movements in national price levels is that the market baskets of goods used in the

TABLE 6.1

Inflation Around the World

(Annual rates, fourth quarter)

	1971		1972		1973		1974		1975		1976	
	M[a]	P[b]	M	P	M	P	M	P	M	P	M	P
World	13.0	5.6	14.6	6.2	12.5	12.1	11.5	16.5	14.7	11.7	14.1	10.8
United States	7.0	3.4	8.5	3.4	6.0	8.5	4.1	12.1	4.6	7.3	5.2	5.0
Canada	13.4	4.1	12.6	5.0	9.7	9.1	2.1	12.0	17.2	10.2	1.7	5.9
Great Britain	15.3	9.2	14.8	7.7	5.6	10.4	7.2	18.1	16.2	25.3	13.2	15.0
Germany	13.4	5.6	14.0	6.4	0.3	7.1	10.7	6.4	15.6	5.6	6.1	3.6
France	12.8	5.9	14.9	6.8	7.6	8.2	13.7	15.1	13.1	9.8	10.3	10.0
Switzerland	21.2	6.5	6.3	7.0	0.7	10.7	-2.7	8.8	4.1	4.0	9.0	1.0
Japan	29.9	5.4	23.1	4.5	19.7	16.5	11.1	24.5	10.9	8.5	14.6	9.4

	1977		1978		1979		1980		1981	
	M	P	M	P	M	P	M	P	M	P
World	13.6	10.7	13.8	9.6	13.4	13.5	10.3	15.0	10.5	13.3
United States	8.3	6.7	5.4	8.9	11.7	12.8	6.2	12.5	5.2	9.6
Canada	9.3	9.1	8.9	8.7	2.6	9.5	9.0	11.1	-4.5	12.3
Great Britain	19.5	13.0	15.3	8.1	10.7	17.3	4.2	15.3	9.3	11.9
Germany	10.7	3.5	13.5	2.4	3.7	5.4	4.6	5.3	-1.9	6.5
France	9.0	9.2	11.8	9.5	10.5	11.5	8.2	13.6	15.5	14.1
Switzerland	2.0	1.4	19.2	0.6	-0.4	5.1	-2.2	4.1	.3	7.0
Japan	6.1	6.2	12.3	3.4	5.5	4.9	-1.8	7.9	9.2	4.0

SOURCE: International Monetary Fund, *International Financial Statistics* (Washington, D.C., July 1982).

[a] M refers to money.

[b] P refers to consumer price.

comparison are not identical. Thus, the British price level might be heavily weighted with fish and chips, the American with Big Macs and French fries. This implies that if the components of the indexes are more or less the same, then the indexes should tend to move together. But this explanation is too simple, for while the indexes with similar components may tend to move together, they may not move by the same amount. Within the United States, prices for the same market basket of goods are higher in some cities than in others, and they may increase at a more or less rapid rate. While the goods markets in the various cities are linked by arbitrage, there are enough frictions so that modest differences in price level movements are possible. Similarly, the index in the countries with the most rapid increases in prices might contain relatively more of those goods whose prices are increasing most rapidly. The U.S. Department of State and the United Nations have calculated the cost of living in various national capitals; if New York is 100, then Tokyo is 130, Paris 114, Buenos Aires 67, and Katmandu 75.

The rate of inflation in each country is best measured by the increase in the consumer price index, although the GNP deflator and even the wholesale price indexes are sometimes used. The wholesale price indexes in various countries are more nearly similar to each other than the consumer price indexes, although the wholesale index is much more volatile than the consumer index, because relatively more of the goods included in the wholesale index have their prices set in competitive markets. The movements in the consumer price indexes in several countries may be quite dissimilar, even though the same countries' wholesale price indexes move together.

Two different approaches can be used to explain the differential price movements. The simplest is to assert that prices increase most rapidly in countries that follow the most expansive monetary policies. For years, prices in Argentina, Brazil, and Chile increased more rapidly than those in other countries, and they have been obliged to devalue their currencies; the movements in exchange rates and in price levels should be largely offsetting, or else their goods would become either progressively undervalued or increasingly overvalued. In Europe and Japan, the growth in the money supplies has been more rapid than in the United States, in part because their very large payments surpluses in 1971 led to a sharp increase in the rate of money supply growth. For example, Japan had money supply increases of 30 percent in 1971 and 25 percent in 1972; Germany's were 13 percent and 14 percent, marginally smaller than those for other European countries. Their reluctance to revalue in 1971 had belated price consequences.

Changes in exchange rates generally tend to follow changes in price-level movements. Thus, more rapid price increases have led to devaluations, less rapid price increases to revaluations. The relationship is reciprocal: if a country devalues, its price level is likely to rise, because the domestic price of both imports and exports increases. If it revalues, or if its currency appreciates, its price level should fall relative to those abroad, because imports now cost less, and so there is one less source of upward pressure on the price level.

The way out of the circle is straightforward. To the extent that prices increase more rapidly in Great Britain than in the United States, sterling should depreciate relative to the dollar. To the extent that independent factors, such as capital movements or changes in tastes, induce changes in exchange rates, the changes should affect the price level.

Germany, for example, has generally followed a more restrictive monetary policy than has the United States, although this is not always evident in the differences in money supply growth rates. High German interest rates led investors to acquire mark-denominated assets, so the mark tended to appreciate. Because the mark appreciated, commodity prices increased less rapidly than in the United States. Eventually, because commodtiy prices were rising less rapidly, investors held German monetary assets at interest rates substantially below those in the United States.

Since 1973, prices in France, the Netherlands, and most other European countries have generally risen more rapidly than U.S. prices; at the same time, their currencies have also appreciated. The price-increasing effects of the rapid monetary expansion dominated the price-reducing impact of the appreciation of their currencies.

The Waves Rule Britannia

Great Britain has been an extreme case of graceless economic aging. Britain was the first country to industrialize, and the resulting surge in income provided the economic base for the expansion of the British imperial system. While colonization started in the seventeenth century, it was not until the nineteenth century that the empire flourished. Britannia ruled the waves. London was the world's financial center.

Empires have their own built-in self-destruct systems; they become too large and too rigid to adjust to change. Rome flourished for centuries. In 1914 the sun was never supposed to set on the British empire. In 1975 the sun never appeared to shine on British economic performance. In 1950, British per capita income was twice that in West Germany, but in 1975, German per capita income was twice that in Britain. Moreover, British prices increased more rapidly than those in any other industrial country.

The British self-analysis has been made in terms of the sociological theory of inflation. The workers expected—and demanded—a continual increase in their real standard of living. They expected that their demands could be met by taxing—or soaking—the rich, by redistribution rather than by productivity gains. And by raising the price at which they sold their labor

113

services, they obtained a higher money income; for the most part, the higher wage costs were passed on to consumers as higher prices.

So taxes have been raised, especially on the middle and upper classes, and extensive subsidies have been given to the population at large. Medical services are financed by the government, although patients have to pay token amounts for eyeglasses and drugs. Universities are free. Since some services in the government sector have been priced below their production cost, their losses must somehow be financed. Moreover, as wage costs have increased in the automobile industry, the British-owned private companies have gone bankrupt and have been moved into the public sector.

But because there are so few rich, high taxes on their incomes and wealth have had only a modest impact in raising the living standards of others. The time has long since passed when the living standards of the workers could be significantly raised by further taxing the rich; there are no longer enough rich to go around. Moreover, a thriving cash economy has developed alongside the taxed economy; as plumbers and mechanics moonlight for tax-free income, the tax base grows very slowly. So the country has borrowed abroad. As the ability to borrow abroad declines, the demands of workers can only be satisfied if some workers—or retired workers—take a decline in real income.

The government and its sympathetic supporters suggest that the problem arises because of the aggressive behavior of the unions, not because of British government financial policies. Most sellers recognize that if they increase their prices, demand will fall and eventually they will be left with unsold goods or idle labor. If the government pursues a tight money policy, then the sellers may be cautious about raising their price. In contrast, if the government is concerned that no resources be unemployed, then it in effect surrenders control of the price level to the aggressive unions.

When prices and wages rise 10 to 15 percent a year, it is hard to determine whether wages are pushing up prices or prices are pulling up wages. And it is silly to try to disentangle the two. For regardless of the initial cause, the government is unwilling to bear the costs it believes are associated with measures that would lead to price stability. By exaggerating these costs, the government provides a rationale for doing nothing.

The rate of inflation in Britain was 7 percent in 1972, 9 percent in 1973, 16 percent in 1974, and 25 percent in 1975. In 1975, and to a greater extent in 1976, investors moved out of sterling, and sterling depreciated much more sharply than was suggested by the increases in British prices relative to world prices. British goods became increasingly undervalued. The Parisians tromped to London on Saturdays for their weekend shopping. The rapid depreciation of sterling was in anticipation of continued inflation; the depreciation intensified the price increases.

Then, a combination of events—the decline in the world price level, government success in getting the unions to limit wage demands, and the rapid increase in North Sea oil production—facilitated a reduction in the inflation to just over 15 percent in 1976 and 1977 and to under 10 percent in 1978. That a Labour Government would be willing to accept unemployment of 2 million was very surprising. Few had predicted that the inflation rate could drop so sharply. As the anticipated inflation rate declined, sterling began to recover in the exchange market. In a relatively few months, sterling appreciated from $1.55 to nearly $2.00, even as British prices were rising more rapidly than U.S. prices. Now British goods were becoming too expensive, and the French found shopping in London far less worthwhile. As the exchange rate turned around, the sterling cost of imports fell, and so it became easier to secure reductions in the inflation rate.

By late 1980, sterling was back at $2.40, a result of two factors—the turnabout in Britain's position from being an oil emporter to an oil exporter, and the contractive monetary policy associated with the Conservative government of Margaret

Thatcher. The strengthening of sterling helped contribute to a reduction in the inflation rate, since import prices fell. But sterling became overvalued—and by more than in the late 1920s. As a result, the unemployment rate reached 13 percent—the highest level since the Great Depression of the 1930s. Mrs. Thatcher's standing with the British voters plummeted—until the Argentinians grabbed the Falkland Islands. But the war in the South Atlantic did not make a significant dent in the unemployment rate.

The Tunnel at the End of the Light

What will be the level of U.S. prices in 1990? Will the United States follow the British model of a shrinking empire, an ever-increasing government sector, and more rapid price increases?

Monetary history shows periods of price stability followed by inflationary episodes. The British experience since World War II suggests that inflation may be inherent in the process of aging and slower growth.

Continuation of a succession of rounds of price increases interspersed with periods of price stability means that the value of money will decline, although not at a stable rate. Indeed, the record of the 1965–1975 decade suggests that inflation may get worse before it gets better. Contrast three episodes. In 1965 the economy began to expand after a period of price stability going back to 1959; during the 1959–1964 period the unemployment rate was in the range of 4 to 5 percent. Expansion occurred when the rate of price increase was still around 3 percent and; the unemployment rate had reached 6 percent. Monetary contraction had had substantial business casualties—Penn Central failed, Lockheed teetered on the brink, and many long-established stock brokerage firms—Walston, Glore Forgan, Frances I. Dupont—fell by the wayside.

When the authorities expanded the money supply, the economy boomed; then the 1965–1969 scenario was advanced to 1971–1975. The monetary contraction of 1974 was much more severe than that of 1970; business failures were more acute. Franklin National Bank and Security National Bank were closed, W.T. Grant failed, Pan Am, TWA, and Eastern Airlines were all on the ropes, and numerous real estate investment trusts were far behind in making scheduled payments to their bankers. The years of inflation had weakened the capital structure of numerous firms. The unemployment rate mounted; the automobile industry was shocked by the sharp decline in sales and large increase in imports.

Then, in late 1974, the monetary reins were relaxed and expansion resumed. Yet the rate of price increase was nearly 9 percent. In 1971 the monetary expansion began when prices were increasing at the rate of 3 percent a year; the 1975 expansion began when they were already increasing at nearly 6 percent a year. Yet price increases moderated, and the inflation rate fell to about 6 percent in 1976 and 1977. While the economic expansion tended to have an upward impact on the price level, the combination of excess industrial capacity and good crops led to downward price pressures. By 1978, an excess capacity diminished, prices began to inch upward at a more rapid rate.

Double-digit inflation returned in 1980, and the rate reached 13 percent at the peak. By 1981 the inflation rate was down to 8 percent; by 1982, to 6 percent. Yet the unemployment rate was climbing almost as rapidly as the rate of inflation was falling. At some stage, the unemployment rate would begin to fall—and the key question was what the subsequent change in the price level would be.

One group of seers has the U.S. economy on a roller coaster of accelerating inflation—there may be dips, but the trend is up. The competing story is that politicians eventually respond to the demands of the public, and the public is tired of inflation. While the votes are not all in, the world wide shift to the right suggests some substance to the second view.

Oil and the OPEC Roller Coaster

The quadrupling of the price of crude petroleum in late 1973, from $2.75 a barrel to $12.50 a barrel, led to visions of financial disaster for the West. The World Bank, headed by Robert Mc-Namara, remembered at Ford for the Edsel and at the Pentagon for the McNamara Line in Vietnam, projected that the financial wealth of oil-producing countries would climb to $300 billion by 1980 and $650 billion by 1985. The specter was that the West would transfer much of its money and wealth to the OPEC countries who would stuff dollars into the wells about as fast as they pumped the oil out. Since their wealth would grow more rapidly than world wealth, it was only a matter of time before they would own the world.

The Western industrial countries seemed squeezed; the OPEC countries sat on their lifeline. Prices were higher and employment lower in both the industrial countries and the developing countries as a result of the fourfold price hike. The sharp price increase did not cause the inflation—indeed, the OPEC countries probably could not have increased the oil price sharply in the absence of a world boom. Yet the inflation rate in the Western industrial countries in 1974 was several percentage points higher because of the higher energy prices. While the OPEC action did not cause the recession in the industrial countries, it intensified unemployment, especially in the automobile and supplier industries.

The financial collapse of the West seemed imminent. Italy seemed about to go bankrupt, with the rise in oil prices being the straw that tripped the boot. Japan seemed alone and defenseless, since all of its petroleum and most of its energy were imported. Great Britain was threatened because the OPEC members would eventually shift from holding sterling funds in London to dollar funds in New York and Swiss franc funds in Zurich, so sterling depreciated sharply as a result. Western capitalism was said to be in serious danger, for the OPEC members would buy up the shares of the major industrial companies and run them to suit their own (largely Arab) political aspirations.

Newspaper headlines gave content to the threat. Iran bought 25 percent of Krupp, the major German conglomerate. Kuwait bought a large bloc of shares of Mercedes Benz, one of the most prestigious car firms in the world. Libya bought into Fiat, the major Italian auto firm. The Iranians showed interest in Pan Am and offered to become bankers for Grumman Aircraft. All the major symbols of Western industrial success seemed to be on the auction block. One unidentified group of Arab investors tried to buy a small town in the northwestern United States—George, Washington. The Arabs would buy General Motors, the Bank of America, and the Bank of England.

The view that the OPEC members would eventually own the world depended on extrapolation—the $12.50 a barrel price of crude petroleum was multiplied by 30 million barrels a day of OPEC production and exports. But determining long-term trends by extrapolating from a few short-term observations can be risky.

Take, for example, the case of Charlie Ponzi, who ran a bank in Boston in the early 1920s which paid 30 percent interest a month. Supposedly Ponzi earned the money to pay the interest by buying International Postal Reply coupons with depreciated

European currencies; he would exchange the coupons for U.S. stamps, and then cash the stamps—much as if they were checks—for U.S. currency. He would then buy more sterling, francs, and lira at their depreciated value to buy more International Postal Reply coupons, and so on. In fact, once in business, Ponzi used the money received from February depositors to pay interest to January's depositors; the money received from March depositors was used to pay off February depositors. Many depositors were content to let their funds remain with Ponzi; where else could they get 30 percent a month? So Ponzi could readily meet the cash withdrawals from the inflow of new deposits. Other financiers—Billie Sol Estes, Tino de Angeles—also developed business empires using today's receipts to pay yesterday's interest. Each succeeded—for a while.

Unless financiers are able to attract new funds at a rapid rate, their individual systems falter, for then the inflow of new money is inadequate to meet cash withdrawals. Deposits cannot grow more rapidly than the entire system forever, any more than IBM's sales or profits can forever grow more rapidly than total corporate sales and total profits; if they could, IBM would eventually become larger than the economy. Ponzi and Co. forgot the principle that no element in the system can grow more rapidly than the system itself; the system will eventually restrain the individual element's more rapid growth.

The implication is that OPEC wealth may grow more rapidly than world wealth for a short interval, but thereafter OPEC wealth can grow no more rapidly than world wealth. An economic system has its checks and balances, even if it does not have a written constitution. There are a number of possible checks to the growth in OPEC wealth. The OPEC countries might, for example, become increasingly reluctant lenders as their wealth increases; they might feel that the supply of safe investment is not large enough to justify pumping more oil: better to keep their wealth in the ground than to acquire high-risk investments. Or, the check to the growth of OPEC wealth might arise because the borrowers prove unwilling to increase their debts as rapidly as McNamara suggested they would. Finally, the check might arise because the OPEC countries increase their spending on imports for consumption more rapidly than he predicted.

All countries want the best possible deal in selling their exports, and the OPEC members are no exception. They want the best possible price for their oil; if there had not been a Yom Kippur War, they might have invented one. Nevertheless, most OPEC members face a dilemma. They know that sharp increases in the price of oil today may lead to declines in the price tomorrow because high prices encourage conservation, exploration for more oil, and substitution. Between 1974 and 1978, the price of oil went from $9.76 to about $12.70, but because of an increase in the world price level, the real price of oil fell by nearly 12 percent (see table 7.1). By 1978, the imports of OPEC countries had increased so rapidly that OPEC countries as a group were spending all of their export earnings; they ceased adding to their foreign exchange reserves. Some OPEC members were spending more than their export earnings, financing the difference by

TABLE 7.1
The Price of Oil, Nominal and Real

Year	Nominal Price of Oil[a] (Dollars/Barrel)	World Price Level (1975=100)	Real Price of Oil (1950 Dollars)
1950	$ 1.71	29.3	$1.71
1960	1.50	40.2	1.09
1970	1.30	62.0	.61
1972	1.90	69.4	.80
1974	9.76	87.9	3.25
1976	11.51	110.9	3.04
1978	12.70	134.9	2.76
1980	28.67	174.0	4.83
1981	32.50	197.8	4.81
1982	33.30	222.0	4.40

SOURCE: International Monetary Fund, *International Financial Statistics* (Washington, D.C., 1982).
[a] Saudi Arabia.

spending reserves and by borrowing. And it seemed only a matter of time before OPEC would appear broke.

In 1979 the oil-producing countries increased the price of oil to $18 a barrel; these higher prices held because oil production declined following the departure of the Shah from Iran and the sharp reduction in Iranian oil production and exports. A further increase in the oil price occurred when exports of oil from Iraq declined after the Iraqi attack on Iran. By early 1981, the oil price was nearly $34 a barrel. Projections of OPEC surpluses for 1981 reached $120 to $150 billion. Once again, the seers forecasted that OPEC surpluses would remain a permanent feature of the economic scene. Yet by 1982, OPEC countries as a group were in a payments deficit. The check arose this time from the combination of an increase in their imports, and a reduction in export earnings as both volume and price per barrel declined.

The skeptics were proved correct; by 1978 OPEC wealth had grown far less rapidly than had been anticipated in 1974. Moreover, in terms of 1974 prices, the $180 billion in financial assets of OPEC countries was worth only about $120 billion, much below the earlier forecasts. And by March 1983, the OPEC countries seemed in a desperate situation, for the price of oil had fallen to below $30 a barrel—and appeared headed south.

Recycling Money

If the OPEC members spend less than their export earnings on imports of goods, their financial wealth is lodged in the industrial countries. While they might be able to bury the checkbooks in the desert sands, they cannot bury the money: it remains as deposit balances in the banks of petroleum-importing countries (hereafter PICs). The early common view was that the money paid the sheikhs for oil had to be recycled, or it would somehow disappear from the system. But this view was incorrect: money paid for oil imports is recycled automatically. The oil exporters are paid for oil with checks drawn on the major international banks. They deposit these checks in their banks (which are the fifty or sixty major international banks), and their bank deposit balances increase. Then they can spend the money, give it away, or lend it—and they may simply produce less oil if the investment opportunities do not appear sufficiently attractive. Unless they spend, lend, or give the money away, the banks will be in a position to increase their loans—for example, to importers of oil, to developers of new energy sources, and to numerous other borrowers.

The rich have one problem the poor lack: they must decide how to invest their wealth. OPEC members have the same problem. They have to choose between securities issued by primary borrowers, such as firms and governments, and securities issued by banks and other financial intermediaries; between securities denominated in dollars and those denominated in Swiss francs or German marks or sterling or many other currencies; between fixed-price assets, such as bank deposits and bonds, and variable-price real assets, such as land and equities. And if investments are made in equities, they have to decide whether they want a controlling interest or a minority interest.

There was immediate concern over whether there was a sufficient volume of the "right" securities—securities that would appeal to OPEC members—among the PICs. The fear was that the rapid growth in oil wealth meant that OPEC members could quickly buy all available PIC securities. Then they would reduce their oil production.

In 1973, when OPEC wealth rose sharply, the $50 billion annual projected increase in OPEC financial wealth seemed very large compared with the value of listed equities in the United States, Great Britain, and continental Europe. At the end of 1974, the market value of IBM—the product of its shares outstanding and their price—was $8 billion. The implication was that if OPEC countries invested all of their savings in IBM shares, they could buy the company—lock, stock, and barrel—in two months. Ponzi would have calculated that it would take only ten years for OPEC to buy all U.S. equities, three years to buy all of British equities, and a year to buy all of the equities in continental Europe. But the extrapolators fell into the world Ponzian trap, for the prices of these shares and all other shares would rise as OPEC members bought them. The rumor that the Kuwaitis would buy some IBM shares led to a 10 percent increase in the price of the shares in one day—even before the Kuwaitis had bought a share. Relatively small OPEC purchases of shares would lead to increases in their price, so that the same dollar volume of purchases would buy fewer and fewer shares.

Long before OPEC countries could buy up IBM or Shell, the governments of their countries of origin would apply limits on these purchases; they would be concerned about loss of control. So total foreign ownership of "security sensitive" industries might be limited to 25 percent—or perhaps even less. Such limits would deflect OPEC demand to other assets.

Matching the $50 billion annual increase in OPEC wealth with the increase in the supply of PIC equities, or even with the total supply of equities, is a straw-man argument; equities are a

TABLE 7.2

International Reserve Assets of Selected OPEC Countries
(Total Reserves Minus Gold: Millions of U.S. Dollars)

Year	Saudi Arabia	Iran	Kuwait	Indonesia	Nigeria
1950	0	111	50	147	110
1960	167	53	72	294	343
1970	543	77	117	156	202
1972	2,383	818	269	572	355
1974	14,153	8,223	1,249	1,490	5,602
1976	26,900	8,681	1,702	1,497	5,180
1978	19,200	11,977	2,500	2,676	1,884
1980	23,437	15,478	3,928	5,342	10,235
1981	32,236	N.A.[a]	4,067	5,014	3,894

SOURCE: International Monetary Fund, *International Financial Statistics* (Washington, D.C., 1982).
[a] N.A. = not available.

modest part of total financial wealth. The more effective comparison is between the annual increase in OPEC financial wealth and the annual increase in total financial wealth. The increase in financial wealth covers a wide range of financial instruments—bank deposits, stocks, equities, mortgages, and so on. Total financial wealth in the United States is about $5,000 billion, and the annual increase in U.S. financial wealth is about $200 billion; comparable numbers for all other PICs combined are $7,000 billion and $300 billion. So $50 billion of OPEC purchases is about 10 percent of the annual increase in the supply of financial wealth of $500 billion. The OPEC countries buy more than 10 percent of some assets, relatively less of others. If they develop large appetites for particular types of assets, the prices of these assets would rise, and more of them would be produced.

True, $50 billion a year is a large number, even when compared with $500 billion. But there is a wide array of investment assets available in the PICs—if OPEC has the money to invest, the PICs have the securities to sell.

The asset preferences of OPEC members are similar to those of investors in other countries in one important respect: they like diversification. To the extent that the oil producers prefer assets denominated in a particular PIC currency, the price of this currency will rise in the foreign exchange market. The greater their demand for assets denominated in the Swiss franc, the greater the appreciation of the Swiss franc. Then, as the Swiss franc becomes more expensive relative to the mark, the dollar, and other currencies, Switzerland's ability to export cheese and chocolate bars will decline. However, the Swiss will find it relatively easy to finance their oil imports.

A preference for assets denominated in some currencies means that assets denominated in other currencies are disfavored. Some PICs may not be able to borrow to finance their oil imports. Bangladesh and India are in this group, and for a while, Italy and Britain appeared likely to join them. If these countries cannot borrow, they may have to curtail their imports, if not of oil, then of other raw materials and of various producer goods. The analogy with the household is useful: if John Doe loses his job and cannot borrow to finance his consumption of cars and corn muffins, he must consume less. Charity from the Salvation Army and checks from the unemployment insurance bureau and the welfare department set an upper limit to his consumption. If he consumes only essentials and their prices rise, then he must tighten his belt even further and consume fewer essentials. Similarly, if a country cannot borrow to finance its imports of petroleum and other essentials, the country is obliged to reduce its imports. So OPEC exports will decline.

The OPEC countries might find it in their interest to extend credit to Bangladesh, Ethiopia, and Paraguay; subsidized or cheap credit is a sales supplement for high-priced oil. As long as the effective price of oil exceeds the cost of producing the oil—and it does by a factor of 50 or 100—then such sales are desirable. If the cost of production is 20 cents a barrel, the world price is $30, and the discounted price is $20, the profit from cutting the price for the poorer countries is $19.80—if cutting the price leads to an increase in the volume of sales.

The difference between the $30 world price and the $20 sales price is counted as OPEC foreign aid. OPEC members have sold some oil to the developing countries at reduced prices or at subsidized credit terms; these discounts and credits have been small relative to their total sales to the developing countries. If the OPEC members are not willing to recycle to the least creditworthy borrowers, then the rate at which their foreign investment grows will be smaller than McNamara's estimates. Unless, of course, the World Bank and other international institutions are willing to lend to the borrowers that OPEC will not lend to—so OPEC can continue to sell them expensive oil.

The International Monetary Fund has developed a credit arrangement under which the IMF borrows from OPEC members and in turn lends to its poorer members. Similarly, Saudi Arabia has made funds available to the World Bank. While OPEC members could lend directly to the oil importers, the international institutions provide much more attractive guarantees, and they can still sell their oil at the discounted $20 price. Bangladesh may fail to repay OPEC and not go out of business, but the IMF is not about to fail to repay OPEC.

Every Surplus Requires a Deficit

Half the readers of this book are above average. Booms have meanings only if there are busts. Bulls and bears are a pair. For every surplus there must be a deficit.

The oil price increases were a major shock to the international monetary system, the biggest shock since World War II. From 1974 through 1981, OPEC surpluses summed to $300 billion. Where did the money go—how did they invest the money? Most of these investments were made by government agencies. There were a few purchases of part or all of ongoing businesses—the Kuwaitis bought Santa Fe International, a U.S. oil field service business for more than $2 billion, and 25 percent of Daimler-Benz, producer of Mercedes cars and trucks. Individual businessmen from various oil producing countries bought banks and insurance companies and hotels.

The oil price increase would have had exchange rate impacts even if the OPEC countries spent their export earnings as fast as the money came. There are two sides to these impacts—one involves the impact of the importing countries' increased oil bills on their exchange rates. They must somehow obtain the dollars to pay for the oil, so their export earnings must increase, and their currencies must depreciate. The second side involves the oil exporters' pattern of expenditures; they must spend or invest the funds as rapidly as they come in. To the extent that they buy Swiss goods or securities, the Swiss franc will appreciate, and the non-Swiss currencies will depreciate.

If OPEC members as a group have surpluses of $50 billion a year, then PICs as a group must have deficits of $50 billion a year. Some oil importing countries who have been international lenders may become borrowers; others, who have been small borrowers, may become large borrowers. Unless PICs as a group are willing to borrow $50 billion a year, OPEC cannot lend $50 billion, even if it is willing.

The $50 billion of PIC borrowings must be distributed among the oil-importing countries. Some oil-importing countries increase the amounts they borrow abroad to pay for imports. One approach toward the distribution of $50 billion would be for each PIC to increase its annual borrowing by the increase in its oil import payments, less any increase in its commodity exports to OPEC members. For example, assume the oil import bill for Japan and Germany increases by $10 billion given the volume of their oil imports. To the extent that these countries are able to increase their commodity exports to various OPEC members, their need to borrow would decline. If each PIC increased its exports to OPEC members by its share of the increased payments for oil imports, then the position of one PIC would not change relative to others; its currency would neither appreciate nor depreciate. The difference between the increase in oil import payments and the increase in exports would be borrowed from OPEC countries or, indirectly, from other international lenders.

This approach toward distribution of PIC borrowings leads to a standstill, since the payments position of each PIC does not change relative to any other PIC. If the exchange rates are pegged, then the deficits and surpluses of individual PICs do not change. If currencies float, then the pattern of exchange rates would not be affected by the increase in the oil import bills; PIC currencies neither appreciate nor depreciate. The foreign indebtedness of some PICs—those who are large importers of petroleum—would increase more rapidly than that of others.

The alternative way to distribute the $50 billion among PICs would be for many or most PIC countries to choose to pay for oil on a pay-as-you-go basis, because of their reluctance to incur the international indebtedness by the amounts implied in the standstill approach. These countries would adjust to the increase in the cost of oil imports by allowing their currencies to depreciate in the foreign market; thus, while their exports would increase to help finance the increase in their oil import payments, their non-oil imports would decline. The combination of the increase in export earnings and the reduction of import payments would equal the increase in oil import payments and their sales of domestic assets to foreigners.

At the extreme, the currencies of all PICs except one might depreciate in the foreign exchange market; this country—the Nth—would incur the indebtedness which would mirror the increase in OPEC investments. The Nth country would be the United States. Just as the U.S. payments deficits in the 1950s and early 1960s were determined by the reserve demands of other countries, so the post-OPEC change in U.S. indebtedness would equal the difference between the increase in wealth of OPEC members and the increase in foreign indebtedness of all other PICs. At most, the United States would increase its indebtedness by $50 billion annually. Germany, Japan, and other PICs would increase their exports of autos, steel, and chemicals to the United States to earn the dollars to pay for their oil; their foreign indebtedness would remain unchanged.

Both the standstill and the pay-as-you-go approaches are concepts which represent the ends of a spectrum. And so the question becomes whether the system will move toward one end of the spectrum or the other. If countries follow the standstill approach, then they must take the initiative and borrow abroad. If they are reluctant or unwilling to borrow, their currencies will automatically depreciate, and they will—willy-nilly—move toward the pay-as-you-go end of the spectrum.

The more individual PICs borrow abroad—that is, the more they export their securities—the less their currencies will depreciate. Increased exports of securities are a substitute for increased exports of goods. But there is a difference—if a PIC borrows, then it must repay. To get the foreign exchange necessary to repay the credit, the country must increase its exports in the future—or else borrow in the future to repay its maturing loans.

The choice for the authorities in each PIC is not whether its currency will depreciate to pay for oil, since the currency will depreciate anyway—in the immediate future if the country follows the pay-as-you-go approach, in the distant future if it follows the standstill approach. If the line of least resistance is to do nothing, the automatic and instantaneous depreciation of the currency will ensure that oil imports can be paid for currently without any initiative toward borrowing abroad—provided the country has the ability to increase its exports.

Whenever a PIC permits its currency to depreciate, the domestic price of oil increases and the amount spent on oil imports will decline. Domestic production of coal, petroleum, and other types of energy will be encouraged. Some countries have taken nonmarket measures to limit their oil imports; they have placed ceilings or quotas on these imports. Others have raised tariffs to reduce oil imports. Several have engaged in barter deals with individual OPEC members, exchanging tanks and trucks and atomic plants for oil. Some have placed a ceiling on the rate at which they will allow their foreign indebtedness to increase. Taken together, these various measures determine the upper limit of PIC borrowings—and the OPEC surplus. The increased oil payments by the PICs caused their currencies to depreciate. The increased PIC exports of goods and securities caused their currencies to appreciate. Both depreciation and appreciation were measured relative to the U.S. dollar, because most payments for oil have traditionally been made in terms of the dollar. Whether an indvidual PIC currency appreciated or depreciated depended on whether the increase in its payments for oil was smaller or larger than the increase in its exports of goods and securities.

If PICs are willing to borrow less than OPEC members are prepared to lend, then the indebtedness will increase by the smaller total. Each PIC would then adjust to the reduced availability of petroleum. And OPEC members would allocate the reduction in petroleum exports among themselves.

Shortly after the oil price increased, the common view was that the Western European currencies and the Japanese yen would weaken relative to the dollar, because these countries imported much more of their oil than the United States. Subsequently, however, the European currencies and the yen appreciated, for the increase in their exports of goods, services, and securities to OPEC members dominated the increase in their oil payments. For example, Germany's oil import bill increased by $10 billion as a result of higher oil prices; yet in 1974 the increase in German exports was several billion dollars larger than the increase in German oil imports. And the Germans borrowed several billion dollars abroad. Similarly, the Japanese trade surplus in 1974 decreased by much less than the increase in the Japanese oil import bill. While U.S. payments for imported oil went up by $25 billion, U.S. imports rose by only $10 billion.

Thus, Germany and Japan, two of the three largest countries in the system, followed the pay-as-you-go approach, and for a brief while, the United States leaned in this direction. The major PIC borrowers were Great Britain, Italy, and to a lesser extent, France. More than half of the increase in OPEC financial wealth was associated with the increase in the payments deficits of the developing countries.

Initially, the countries with the weakest economies did much of the borrowing. As they reached the limit in their ability or their willingness to borrow abroad, the deficits were shuttled elsewhere in the system. If OPEC had a surplus, the United States would end up with the counterpart deficit as all other countries eventually moved to the pay-as-you-go approach.

Decline in Oil Imports

Twice in a decade, once in 1973–1974, and again in 1979–1980, sharp increases in the price of OPEC oil shocked international financial arrangements. In both instances, OPEC countries achieved large payments surpluses, peaking at $65 billion in OPEC I (1973–1974) and $120 billion in OPEC II (1979–1980). Yet the OPEC surpluses evaporated almost as rapidly as they appeared. When the oil price went up sharply, the OPEC countries appeared to have unlimited market power; and, again, apparently only their benevolence toward the oil-importing countries restrained them from pushing the oil price even higher then they did. Yet by mid-1980, an oil glut had appeared.

Each producer of oil—and every other raw material—faces the following economic decision: Am I better off if I produce one more barrel of oil and put the money in the bank, or would it be more rewarding to keep the oil in the ground and profit from the increase in its price? If the interest rate that might be earned if the money is put in the bank is higher than the anticipated rate of price increases, then the producer benefits from pumping one more barrel of oil. In contrast, if the interest rate is lower, then the more profitable course is to reduce or delay production.

Some OPEC countries, the Hawks, leaned toward reducing output and charging a higher price; others, primarily the Saudis, wanted to increase production. The Hawks raised their selling prices—and for a while, they could sell all the oil they could produce. But their sales declined as world demand declined. Within a matter of a few months, the Hawks found they were earning less money from oil production than they were spending to pay for imports. For a while, at least, they could pay for imports by drawing down their bank balances and by borrowing abroad. Eventually, to increase their oil exports, they cut prices, partly by discounting, partly by allowing the oil companies more time to pay for the oil. But to increase exports significantly, the

Hawks had to reduce their selling price below that of the Saudis. Even then, however, the companies that had benefited so greatly by being able to obtain Saudi oil at the low price were reluctant to buy more from the Hawks because of past favors from the Saudis. So to increase market share significantly, the Hawks had to set their selling price substantially below that of the Saudis.

The OPEC Hawks believed that they would benefit by raising the current price even more rapidly than they did. Others, however, were concerned that too-sharp increases in the price would prove counterproductive in the long run, both because producers of other types of energy—coal, gas, nuclear, hydro, even biomass and solar—would increase output, while energy users would economize on their consumption of gasoline. Countries like Algeria, Nigeria, and Venezuela, where populations were large relative to oil reserves, were in the first group. In contrast, Saudi Arabia and Kuwait were in the second group; their oil reserves would last for decades, because their relatively small populations required only a limited amount of imports.

The dispute between these two groups of countries became especially sharp in 1980. Then, in the context of the shortage brought about by the Khomeni government in Iran and then the Iran-Iraq war, the first group—the Hawks—raised their selling price to $38 or $40 a barrel, substantially above the OPEC agreed-upon price of $32 a barrel. The oil companies bought as much as they could of the lower-priced oil; then, to meet world demand they filled up at the higher-priced suppliers. The companies able to buy from Saudi Arabia—the former Aramco partners—had a bonanza for they were able to fill up at the low price source and sell at the higher world price.

As demand for petroleum fell, the oil companies reduced the amount of oil they bought from the Hawks. The Saudi's meanwhile increased their output from 9 million to 10.5 million barrels a day as part of the deal to induce the U.S. government to sell AWACs; more production of low price Saudi oil meant less demand for the oil of the Hawks. Subsequently the Saudis cut production to 6.5 million barrels a day to reduce excess supply.

By the spring of 1982, the demand for OPEC oil had fallen to 17 million barrels a day, only slightly more than half of the 30 million barrels that OPEC had produced in 1980. One explanation for the decline was the worldwide recession; the implication was that the market power of OPEC—its ability to raise production and increase exports—would be restored when the recession ended. The other explanations for the decline in OPEC production were less favorable to the restoration of OPEC power; these explanations centered on the substitution of non-OPEC oil— from sources like the North Sea, the North Slope of Alaska, Mexico, and Egypt—for OPEC oil and the substitution of other types of energy for oil. Moreover, demand for energy declined in response to the much higher price; thus the 1983 model cars were twice as efficient as the older cars being scrapped. The 1983 models, however, were designed when the oil price was $18 a barrel; not until 1984 or 1985 will the cars entering the fleet be those designed in response to $30-plus per barrel. As new cars enter the fleet and older models are scrapped, energy demand will continue to decline. Similarly, throughout the 1980s, new aircraft will be introduced which are 50 percent more efficient in terms of passenger seat miles per gallon of fuel than older aircraft. The changeover to a more energy-efficient capital stock in housing and industry and office buildings means that the total amount of energy demanded may decline for ten or more years.

So the OPEC countries found themselves in a quandary as their export earnings fell relative to their import bill. If they raised their selling price in an effort to generate more revenues, they might quicken the reduction in demand for energy and the substitution of non-OPEC energy for OPEC energy. If they reduced the price to maintain market share, other energy producers might follow with price cuts of their own.

Moreover, OPEC's ability to sell at $30 plus was greatly strengthened by the reduction of Iranian and Iraqi oil exports. When hostilities in this war cease, these countries will seek to increase their oil exports, if only to get the foreign exchange to help pay for imports necessary to rebuild their economies—and their military machines. Increased oil exports from these countries will put sharp downward pressure on the oil price unless other OPEC countries reduce their exports by about the same amount. Yet OPEC production is already so low that no other OPEC country can reduce its production without causing its export revenues to fall significantly.

The Dollar and Coca-Cola
Are Both Brand Names

The money-producing industry is like the soda pop industry; a large number of firms make a similar product. Soda pop is basically carbonated colored water. One brand of pop is a good substitute for another. Each pop-producing firm strives to make its brands attractive; the product is available in large, small, and medium-sized packages, and the packages are attractively designed. Coca-Cola has been so successful in its marketing strategy that a gallon of Coke—caramel-colored fizzy water—sells for more than $1, or more than the pretax price of a gallon of gasoline. High profits automatically attract competitive imitators who frequently choose a similar name and in other ways try to infringe on the market position of the brand leader. The market leaders strive to distinguish themselves from their competitors; they protect their brand names by copyrights.

So it is with money. Each national central bank produces its own brand of money. Each of these national monies serves an identical set of functions—as a medium of payment, a store of value, and a unit of account. Each national money is a differentiated product. U.S. dollars and Canadian dollars are not perfect substitutes for each other, and neither are French francs and Swiss francs, or English pounds and Irish pounds. However, one national money may be a good substitute for another as a means of payment, and even a better substitute as a store of value or a unit of account.

The analogy between the soda pop industry and the money industry may seem invalid within the United States, for while the supermarkets carry numerous brands of pop, the banks carry only one brand of money. Nearly all transactions are settled by payments in U.S. dollars. But some U.S. firms and some U.S. residents hold large amounts of money in London, the Bahamas, Zurich, and elsewhere for business convenience, or to avoid U.S. monetary and fiscal regulations (see chapter 9 on the Eurodollar market and chapter 14 on tax avoidance). More importantly, foreign residents have had a much greater incentive to hold dollar assets because of the brand leadership position of the U.S. dollar.

For much of the postwar period, the U.S. dollar was the leading brand name in the money industry. Immediately after World War II, U.S. currency notes circulated extensively in Europe. In Latin America, Europe, and Asia, many firms and individuals held a substantial portion of their money and other financial assets in dollars. And some business firms in Europe and Asia with substantial international business interests kept their books in dollars.

Some central banks have changed the brand name of their own product to "dollar" to increase its attractiveness; this name change is sometimes accompanied by changes in packaging. When Australia, Jamaica, and Malaysia gave up pounds and shillings and decimalized their currencies, they named their standard currency unit the dollar, a tribute to the preeminent standing of the U.S. dollar. But there is only one U.S. dollar; the other central banks are poaching on the established market position of the U.S. producer.

Another favored brand of money, one which appeals to a specialized and small segment of the market (like the Ferrari in automobiles, or Chivas Regal in Scotch whiskey, or Perrier in the bottled water industry), is the Swiss franc.

Central banks, like the soda pop–producing firms, sell their product. The public "pays" for the money produced by the central bank by supplying goods and services. When Brazil's central bank produces more cruzeiros, the Brazilian investors acquire these cruzeiros by selling goods, services, and securities to the central bank and to its owner, the Brazilian government. The larger the public's demand for money in the form of cruzeiros, the larger the volume of goods and services that the Brazilian government can acquire without having to raise taxes. Each central bank, like each firm in the soda pop industry, has a vested interest in increasing the demand for its product.

The production of commemorative postage stamps, Green Stamps, Plaid Stamps, and other trading stamps provides another good analogy to the production of money. Like money, these stamps can be produced at very low cost; the major expense is developing designs and paper that are costly to imitate. The producers of these bits of colored engraved paper want the public to hold more and more of their stamps; they much prefer to have these stamps pasted into collectors' books than onto letters. Liechtenstein would go broke if most of the postage stamps it sells were used to mail letters. Similarly, the producers of Green Stamps and Plaid Stamps want the public to collect their stamps rather than redeem them; therefore they offer high-priced "gifts" in exchange for thirty or forty books of stamps to lengthen the period between the time the stamps are sold and the time they are redeemed. In the meantime, the stamp companies have free use of the stamp-collector's money.

Similarly, the producers of traveler's checks profit handsomely from their sale, for the receipts from the sale of these non-interest bearing checks are used to buy interest-earning assets. So more and more banks and travel companies have begun to produce traveler's checks with their own names, hoping to cash in on the profits of the market leaders.

Each central bank has a marketing strategy to strengthen the demand for its particular brand of money. Just as each of the soda pop firms wants the public to buy more of its pop and less of its competitors', each central bank wants the public to buy, use, and hold more of its money. The greater the demand the more readily the product—the national money—can be sold. The more money that can be sold, the smaller the need to sell interest-bearing bonds or to raise taxes.

Packaging is one element in the marketing strategy—two or three colors may be used in the printing. In the United States, the bank notes carry the portraits of presidents; in Great Britain, the king or queen; in Austria, the composers. Frequently, the central bank provides a money-back guarantee, and offers to repurchase its own money in exchange for a leading foreign money at a guaranteed price, the exchange parity for its currency.

The packaging arrangements in the soda pop industry are a component of pricing policy; the more attractive the package, the higher the price. Brand name products sell at substantially higher prices than virtually identical unbranded goods. In some cases, the firm sells a way of life or a self-image rather than a product.* In much the same way, the packaging arrangements in the money-producing industry are designed to enhance the attractiveness of brand names, and thus to reduce the interest rates on assets which carry those brand labels. Finance ministers and treasury secretaries want low interest rates to minimize their borrowing costs. In Britain, holders of certain treasury securities can participate in a special lottery; the British Treasury sells these securities at a lower interest rate. The lottery prizes cost the government less than the savings in interest costs. Similarly, holders of some U.S. Treasury securities receive special tax ad-

---

* This technique conforms to Michael Aliber's First Theorem: "When you buy baseball cards, you get the gum free."

vantages which are intended to reduce the interest rates necessary to attract lenders. From the U.S. Treasury's point of view, the cost of the tax advantages should be smaller than the reduction in interest payments. Some countries link the interest rates on domestic securities to the price of gold or to the price of the U.S. dollar to increase the attractiveness of these securities. All such devices are marketing gimmicks designed to create investor interest in particular brands—the central bank's counterpart of Green Stamps and baseball cards.

In the money industry, just as in the soda pop industry, overproduction occurs. In the soda pop industry, any firm which increases its output very rapidly may have to cut its prices or else its cans and bottles will pile up on supermarket shelves. When too much money is produced, people may shift from domestic money to goods—or to other brands of money. Central banks can produce more money, but they cannot force people to hold it. So the price of money—the exchange rate—falls until willing customers can be attracted.

Authorities frequently take direct measures to enhance investor demand for the national brand of securities. Most governments stipulate that only the national money is legal tender within their boundaries; the tax collectors refuse to accept payment in foreign monies. Ministers of finance and secretaries of the treasury continually "talk up" the national brand by wrapping their policies in the flag. When the voluntary approach proves inadequate, compulsory measures are often used, and purchases of monies and securities denominated in foreign currencies may be taxed or licensed.

The Market Position of Currency Brands

The contrast between the number of brand names in money—more than 100—and the number available in automobiles and jet aircraft is strong. While every country except the very small ones—the Panamas and the Liechtensteins—has its own currency brand, most countries import their jet aircraft and automobiles from foreign producers. Thus, the German and Canadian airline companies buy U.S.-produced jet aircraft because they are cheaper than domestically produced jets would be. Their national airlines—which compete with Pan Am, TWA, Japan Air Lines, and other foreign airlines in the search for customers and profits—are reluctant to incur the additional cost of buying higher-priced, domestically produced aircraft, for they would then be at a competitive disadvantage in the world market.

One reason nearly every country insists on producing its own money is that there seems to be no cost to having a national money. But for most countries, the decision to have a national money raises the interest rate on its domestic loans. If Denmark, for example, were to give up its own money and adopt the Swedish brand or if Canada adopted the U.S. brand, the interest rates to borrowers in Denmark and Canada would probably decline. Having a national currency clearly puts borrowers in Denmark and Canada at a cost disadvantage in the international marketplace.

Indeed, many Canadian firms, as well as the Canadian provincial governments, come to New York and Chicago and issue U.S. dollar securities to reduce their interest cost below the rates they would pay if they borrowed in Canada. To the extent that the higher interest rates charged Canadians are a result of having a national money, there is a real cost to Canada, for some investment projects which might be undertaken if interest rates were lower are never launched.

Yet governments continue to retain national monies despite their costs; few have decided to abandon their national brands. Countries want the prestige of a national money. Moreover, only with a national money can a country have its own monetary policy. And kings and presidents want their constituents to be proud of their heritage: the prouder they are, the less reluctant they will be, in theory, to pay taxes.

141

The government profits from having a national money, for the cost of producing the money—printing the bank notes or issuing the deposits—is less than its purchasing power in terms of goods and services. These profits are an indirect form of taxation. Indeed, issuing money is often a less costly way of taxing the public, especially if the administrative fiscal apparatus is inadequate or corrupt. Being able to produce money enables government leaders to circumvent parliamentary opposition to higher tax rates and it explains why national price levels increase.

In market economies, the prices of financial assets—or the prices of most of them—vary continuously in response to changes in the supply and demand of securities. Prices adjust to find buyers. If the prices are sufficiently low, buyers can be found even for such risky securities as the bond issues of Penn Central in 1976 and the Czar Bonds of 1912. Within a country, investors continually shuffle the ownership of short-term debts, long-term debts, growth stocks, and public utility stocks as their assessments of the future change. Similarly investors continually compare the attractiveness of monies with different brand names.

All financial assets—bank notes, demand deposits, government bonds, corporate bonds—must have a brand name. The buyers of these assets can choose among twelve kinds of dollars, eight kinds of francs, the cruzeiro, the baht, the kip, and numerous other national currency brands. These investors must calculate whether the currency brands which are most attractive will remain so. Possible changes in the market position of the various brand names—and in their exchange rates—are closely examined.

In part, interest rates on assets denominated in Danish kroner exceed those on assets denominated in Swedish kroner because investors anticipate that the Danish currency will depreciate; they want the additional interest income to offset any loss from holding a depreciating currency. If there were complete confidence in the predictablity of future changes in exchange rates, then investors would shift funds between Danish and Swedish securities until the difference between interest rates on assets denominated in these currencies reflected the anticipated change in the exchange rate. If they expect Danish kroner to depreciate 1 percent a year more rapidly than Swedish kroner, they would buy Swedish assets and sell Danish assets until interest rates on Danish assets were 1 percent a year higher than on Swedish assets. In all likelihood, if the Swedish assets are preferred, then the interest rates on Danish assets will exceed those on comparable Swedish assets by somewhat more than 1 percent a year—a reflection of the preference.

Currency brands can be ranked like songs on a hit parade, with the standings based on the interest rates on assets which are similar except for currency of denomination. Investor preferences for currency and checking account money—assets which usually carry no explicit market yield—can be inferred from their preferences for short-term, interest-bearing assets denominated in the same currencies. For example, if the interest rates on short-term dollar assets are below those on short-term sterling assets, then the dollar stands above sterling on the currency hit parade. Investors would hold assets denominated in sterling only if interest rates were sufficiently high to compensate for the probable fall in the value of sterling relative to the dollar. Higher interest rates are necessary to find buyers for money and other financial assets denominated in sterling—that is, to adjust for the overproduction of sterling. Higher interest rates are the international money market's counterpart to price cutting in the soda pop market.

True, some borrowers seemingly ignore the brand name problem when issuing liabilities, as do some lenders when acquiring assets. Most investors deal in securities denominated in the national brand, the currency of the country in which they live. Similarly, most individuals vote for the same party in election after election. Candidates for office pitch their campaigns to the 10 to 20 percent of the electorate whose changing preferences swing the election results. Brand loyalty is—or once was—strong in cigarettes and beer. Producers within these industries—money, politics, and tobacco—market their products toward the swing voters and the swing buyers. Convenience, ignorance, uncertainty about exchange rates, and exchange controls help explain the preference for the domestic brand of money.

Still, some borrowers calculate the advantages of issuing securities denominated in foreign currencies, just as some lenders calculate the advantages of acquiring such securities. The smaller the country, the more likely that its residents will compare foreign alternatives to domestic monies and securities. Dutch and Swiss investors, for example, are very much aware of assets denominated in foreign currencies; many U.S. dollar securities are listed on the stock exchanges in Amsterdam and Zurich.

For most of the last fifty years, dollar-denominated assets have been at the top of the brand name hit parade. In contrast, currencies which have been more or less subject to continuous devaluations have ranked low; the yields of assets denominated in such currencies have been correspondingly high. Thus, interest rates on assets denominated in sterling, the Canadian dollar, the Japanese yen, and even the German mark have been higher than interest rates on assets denominated in dollars because investors believed that assets denominated in these currencies were riskier.

One exception is Switzerland: interest rates on assets denominated in Swiss francs have been lower than those on dollar assets. Switzerland is attractive to investors for a variety of reasons. Switzerland is politically stable. The Swiss franc has been a very strong currency. And the tax rates on interest income are low. The Swiss authorities are not especially curious about the sources of the suitcase money carried over the Alps to Lugano, or flown in from the United States. The Swiss provide a laundry for money—at a price.

Before World War I, London was the world's principal financial center and sterling was at the top of the currency hit parade. At that time, borrowers from around the world found it cheaper to issue sterling-denominated securities than to borrow in their domestic markets. American firms went to London to borrow; London was the center of the international capital market.

The dollar displaced sterling at the top of the hit parade as a result of financial events associated with World War I. The dollar was the only currency which remained pegged to gold during

TABLE 8.1

Interest Rates, Nominal and Real *(percent)*

	1965	1970	1975	1980	1981
United States					
Interest Rate[a]	4.3	6.9	8.2	11.4	13.7
Inflation Rate[b]	1.3	4.2	6.8	8.9	9.8
Real Interest Rate[c]	3.0	2.7	1.4	2.5	3.9
Canada					
Interest Rate	5.2	7.9	9.0	12.5	15.2
Inflation Rate	1.6	3.9	7.3	8.7	9.7
Real Interest Rate	3.6	4.0	1.7	3.8	5.5
Great Britain					
Interest Rate	6.6	9.2	14.4	13.8	14.7
Inflation Rate	3.3	4.6	13.0	14.4	13.4
Real Interest Rate	3.3	4.6	1.4	−0.6	1.3
Germany					
Interest Rate	7.1	8.3	8.5	8.5	10.4
Inflation Rate	2.7	2.4	6.1	4.1	4.4
Real Interest Rate	4.4	5.9	2.4	4.4	6.0
France					
Interest Rate	5.3	8.1	9.5	13.0	15.7
Inflation Rate	3.7	4.4	8.9	10.4	11.1
Real Interest Rate	1.6	3.7	0.6	2.6	4.6
Switzerland					
Interest Rate	4.0	5.8	6.4	4.8	5.6
Inflation Rate	3.2	3.5	7.7	5.9	3.3
Real Interest Rate	0.8	2.3	−1.3	−1.1	2.3

SOURCE: International Monetary Fund, *International Financial Statistics* (Washington, D.C., 1982).
[a] Interest Rate = long-term government bond rate.
[b] Inflation Rate = inflation over previous five years.
[c] Real Interest Rate = arithmetic differential.

World War I. Moreover, U.S. prices had risen much less during the war than those in various European countries. Overproduction of sterling during the war led to a loss of investor confidence. U.S. financial markets offered investors a wide range of securities, and the United States took on a dominant role in the international economy. Central banks in Europe and elsewhere began to acquire dollar assets as a form of international money.

The question today is whether the successive devaluations of the dollar in terms of gold and the concurrent appreciation of the mark, the yen, and the Swiss franc may lead to a displacement of the dollar from the top spot, much as sterling was displaced earlier.

A Dollar Standard World?

The dollar has been a workhorse currency in the postwar period. It has been the currency used by central banks in their exchange market intervention. Holdings of dollar assets have been the largest component of central bank reserves since 1970. International firms and investors have used the dollar as a vehicle currency; more international trade transactions are denominated in the dollar than in any other currency. These multiple roles reflect the dominant size of the United States in the world economy; what happens in the United States has a substantial impact on economic events abroad. Changes in the U.S. money supply have a major impact on changes in the world money supply.

Changes in the U.S. price level necessarily have a major direct impact on the world price level, and extensive indirect impacts. A change in the U.S. price level has a greater effect on the world price level than is suggested by the U.S. share of world GNP.

Because of the central importance of the United States, the dollar is frequently the numeraire currency, or the unit of account on transactions which do not involve Americans. Thus international airline fares are stated in terms of dollars; the price of a London–New York ticket in Britain is the product of the dollar price and the sterling–dollar exchange rate. The prices of many international commodities—the price of gold in Zurich, of petroleum in the Persian Gulf—are stated in terms of dollars. So it seems that the world is on a dollar standard, much as the world was once on the gold standard.

One meaning of the term dollar standard is that the rest of the world is obliged to hold the U.S.-produced dollars that U.S. residents will not hold. In fact, by almost every measure, the U.S. payments deficit since 1950 has been large. In some years the deficit was only $2 or $3 billion; in 1971 it reached $30 billion.

The cumulative U.S. payments deficit between 1950 and 1970 was between $50 and $70 billion, depending on how it is calculated. In the last decade, the U.S. deficit has exceeded probably within the range of $250 to $300 billion. The deficit or surplus is measured by sales and purchases of gold and liquid dollar assets to and from foreign central banks, commercial banks, and private parties. But economists disagree on whether all sales of dollar assets to foreigners should be included in the calculation of the U.S. payments balance.

Formerly, the U.S. authorities included all purchases and sales of gold and other international monies held by U.S. authorities together with purchases and sales of liquid dollar assets by foreign central banks, foreign commercial banks, and foreign private parties in the computation of the payments balance; this is known as the *net liquidity balance.* This meant that if a large U.S. bank exchanged deposits of $100 million with its London branch, the payments deficit would increase by $100 million. Why? Because the increase in the dollar holdings of the London bank was included in the calculation of the U.S. payments balance, while the increase in the London deposit of the U.S. bank was excluded. In a period in which foreign commercial banks and foreign private parties were adding to their dollar holdings, this measure tended to overstate the U.S. deficit.

A second approach, known as the *official reserves transactions balance,* was then adopted; this approach provides that only the purchases and sales of liquid dollar assets by foreign official institutions are included in the calculation of the payments balance. This definition differs from the net liquidity balance in that changes in the liquid dollar assets of foreign commercial banks and foreign private parties are excluded from the calculation.

The shortcoming of both definitions is that they fail to recognize the unique role of the United States as a producer of international money. The United States exports dollar assets to satisfy the needs of foreigners, just as Germany exports Volkswagens, Ecuador exports bananas, and South Africa exports gold. As long as investors retain confidence in the dollar brand name, the use of the term "deficit" to describe intended and voluntary increases in the dollar holdings of foreigners is misleading. These increases in dollar holdings might easily be excluded from the calculation of the U.S. deficit.

Of course, separating the intended from the unintended increases in foreign holdings of dollars would be difficult. But the errors that might arise in making this distinction operational are likely to be smaller than those resulting from a more misleading concept.

When the deficit became persistent and large, the U.S. authorities stopped reporting the deficit. Reporters with a ten-dollar calculator could readily determine the deficit by adding changes in U.S. reserve holdings and changes in the dollar holdings of various groups of nonresidents. Until 1968 or so, the U.S. balance-of-payments deficit was primarily an accounting phenomenon which reflected the desire of other countries to have payments surpluses; the U.S. deficit was a "system" problem rather than a U.S. problem. No one was really upset about U.S. monetary policies or U.S. price-level performance, and dollars were not being overproduced. In the absence of data on payments balances, no one would have been upset about the performance of the U.S. economy, or about the impact of changes in U.S. policies on foreign economies.

One of the paradoxes of the late 1960s was that just as the U.S. payments deficit began to increase, some analysts asserted that the world was on the dollar standard. The meaning of the term was vague; the implication was that changes in the dollar money supply, like changes in the monetary gold supply sixty and seventy years earlier, determined the world price level. True, the U.S. government's policies for financing the Vietnam war led to sharp increases both in the U.S. price level and in the U.S. payments deficit, and the parallel increases in the payments surpluses of other countries meant that their own money supplies increased sharply, so that prices abroad rose as rapidly as did U.S. prices. The United States was exporting inflation. But the logical implication of the phrase "the world is on the dollar standard" was that foreign central banks had shifted to dependent monetary policies and were unwilling to revalue their currencies.

This dollar standard view of the world was shattered by the decisions of Canada, Germany, and the Netherlands to permit their currencies to float, and by subsequent appreciation of various European currencies and the yen relative to the dollar.

Does the depreciation of the dollar in the 1970s mean it is "Afternoon on the Potomac" for the U.S. currency? The answer involves disentangling two overlapping but distinct relationships. The first concerns the market position of all national currencies—the dollar, sterling, the Swiss franc, the mark—relative to gold. The second concerns the position of the dollar relative to other currencies on the hit parade.

Both relationships can be analyzed in terms of interest rate structures. Interest rates on assets denominated in dollars, sterling, Swiss francs, and other currencies increased substantially in the 1960s and were much higher in the 1960s than in the 1950s. The market position of all national currencies as a group declined relative to that of gold, evident from the increasing shortage of monetary gold and the rise in the price of gold. Throughout the 1960s, currencies were overvalued relative to gold.

The combination of U.S. gold sales and the increase in foreign-owned dollars led many observers to conclude that the dollar was overvalued in relation to the mark, the yen, and the currencies of the other countries with payments surpluses. If a currency which serves as international money is overvalued, then the currencies of some other large countries—perhaps Germany, Japan, and France—must have been undervalued; that is, either the international money holdings of these countries were too large, or they were increasing at too rapid a rate. One test of whether the dollar was overvalued is to ask: What would have happened if the dollar had been devalued in terms of gold by 10 or 15 percent? How many countries would have maintained their exchange rates against the dollar (thus also devaluing their currencies in terms of gold), and how many would have allowed their currencies to appreciate in terms of the dollar?

The answer depends on when the question was asked. During the early 1960s nearly every country, with the possible exception of Germany, the Netherlands, and Switzerland, would have maintained its exchange rate peg against the dollar. In contrast, if the currency of a small country, say Denmark, had been devalued, few if any other countries would have devalued their currencies. Most would have permitted their currencies to appreciate relative to the Danish krone.

Until 1969 the international payment imbalances could more easily be explained in terms of the demand of foreign central banks for international money and the undervaluation of several currencies—primarily the mark—than in terms of an overvalued dollar. The statement that the dollar was overvalued was wrong in the early and mid-1960s. The statement became correct in the late 1960s as the increase in the U.S. inflation rate led to a larger U.S. payments deficit.

The surge in the dollar holdings of foreign central banks in the early 1970s led to great concern about the stability of the international monetary system, for some of these holdings were undesired. Several questions arose. One involved determining how much of the total reserve holdings of foreign central banks was excessive. A second was how much of their dollar holdings was excessive.

The increase in foreign holdings of dollars in the 1970s proved extremely relative to increase in the 1960s. Until the dollar began to float, part of the increase in foreign dollar holdings reflected the weakness of the dollar; foreign monetary authorities were reluctant to take the initiative and revalue their currencies. In the last few years, foreign monetary authorities have acquired dollar assets to limit the rate at which their own currencies appreciated. The paradox is that they apparently acquired assets denominated in a currency deemed weak—to limit the rate at which it would become weaker.

The Dollar on the Hit Parade

The demise of sterling as the world's preeminent currency suggests one possible future scenario for the dollar. When Britain entered World War I, the Bank of England immediately withdrew its money-back guarantee; sterling was no longer convertible into gold. Exchange controls limited imports of goods and of foreign securities. British prices rose rapidly as a result of an inflationary monetary policy. At the end of the war, official sentiment was strongly in favor of a return to the gold standard at the prewar parity. But sterling was then overvalued by at least 10 or 15 percent. Throughout the early 1920s, British economic policy was geared to reattain the 1913 gold parity. This target was reached in 1925; then the problem was to maintain the parity, since sterling was still overvalued. Investors were increasingly apprehensive that a change in British policy would lead to a depreciation of sterling relative to the dollar and gold. But these factors were the result of overproduction of sterling during the war. They should be distinguished from the real factors: the sharp decline in British foreign investments and the sluggish British industrial performance.

The error of the British authorities was that they confused a pegged exchange rate for sterling with a particular rate at which sterling should be pegged. When Britain deemed the time appropriate for again pegging sterling to gold, it should have chosen a parity which left the dollar-sterling exchange rate at $4.00 or $4.20. Interest rates on sterling assets would then have been lower, since there would have been no need to pay a high interest rate to investors concerned about the risk that sterling might be devalued. Business in Britain would have boomed, and foreign capital would have flowed to London.

Whether sterling could have retained its brand leader position with even the most sensible of policies is doubtful; the war hastened a move of the dollar to the top of the hit parade which seemed inevitable in any case. The U.S. economy was growing very rapidly, and U.S. financial markets were developing depth, breadth, and resiliency. Investments in Europe seemed riskier than investments in the United States, partly for political reasons.

Just as sterling was displaced by the dollar, so the dollar can only be displaced from its dominant position by another currency brand. In the past, every country whose currency has been at the top has had attractive financial markets, an economy open to international trade and investment, and relative price stability, and has been the dominant international economic power. Today no country appears to satisfy all these criteria. Switzerland is too small and lacks adequate financial markets. Japan is too peripheral and its economy too closed to foreigners. Germany's long-run record for monetary stability is poor—as is its record for political stability; its remarkable performance in the 1960s and 1970s follows two hyper-inflations earlier in the century. No country other than the United States appears to combine economic size and a record for financial stability. But as the U.S. scorecard on financial stability declines, investors explore the alternatives.

The members of the European Community have planned their own currency; if it comes about, this currency might eventually go to the top of the hit parade. The new Europe would still be smaller in economic size than the United States; and its financial markets, even if integrated, would be considerably smaller than the U.S. market. The European countries must first succeed with the plan to merge their currencies—that is, they must give up monetary sovereignty. Then the new currency will have to establish a record for monetary stability.

Already, long before the new European currency appears, investors are already beginning to acquire relatively more assets denominated in the major European currencies. Some central banks outside Europe have acquired reserves denominated in the mark and the Swiss franc. Firms within Europe—in Scandinavia, the Low Countries, and the Mediterranean countries are increasing the share of assets denominated in the mark in their working balances; the variations in the price of the mark are substantially smaller than those of the dollar in terms of their own currency. Eventually, the central banks in these countries will also begin to acquire reserves denominated in the mark. So the move to another international currency to supplement the dollar is underway.

The position of the dollar on the hit parade has been enhanced by U.S. success in reducing its inflation rate, by changes in the foreign exchange value of the dollar, and by any changes in the monetary role of gold. In the early 1980s, the dollar appreciated sharply in response to the contractive U.S. monetary policies. If the U.S. inflation rate continues to decline, then the likelihood of any significant trend movement in the exchange rate will be low, and the dollar will remain at the top of the hit parade. For a while, its brand leadership position will be shaky, and many investors will seek to diversify, building up their holdings of assets denominated in other currencies.

The future attractiveness of the dollar will be directly affected by decisions about the future role of gold. A decision that gold would again be a reserve asset would remove the uncertainty about the future of gold as a money. The U.S. international monetary position would be stronger, since U.S. gold holdings would increase greatly in relation to foreign holdings of dollars. The U.S. Treasury would be able to sell gold in exchange for any excess dollar holdings of foreign monetary authorities. And for some time thereafter, the United States would no longer need to produce international money in large amounts to satisfy the demands of other countries.

One lesson that can be learned from the experience is that decisive action may be preferable to continued piddling with minor changes in the financial arrangements. The British paid an extremely high price for attempting to avoid or delay changes in the sterling parity that were inevitable. Throughout the 1960s, U.S. authorities followed a similar strategy of trying to avoid what proved inevitable—initially a change in the monetary price of gold, then a change in the exchange rate structure.

Fortunately, the U.S. authorities are no longer hung up on the need to hold the dollar to a fixed value. But the U.S. authorities have no clear view of the unique role of the dollar in international financial arrangements.

The real factors—the size and wealth of the U.S. economy—suggest that the dollar will continue at the top of the hit parade. The monetary factors are uncertain, however. Economic mismanagement in the future could tarnish the dollar's attractiveness to world investors. If the U.S. inflation rate continues to decline, then investors around the world are likely to shift more of their wealth back to dollar brand securities.

Radio Luxembourg and the Eurodollar
Market Are Both Offshore Stations

Radio Luxembourg is a commercial broadcasting station based in Luxembourg whose programs are beamed primarily to two markets, Britain and France. A few years ago, neither country permitted commerical broadcasting; each relied solely on government-owned stations. Programs within each country reflected what the producers—the bureaucrats of the British Broadcasting Corporation and Radiodiffusion Française—felt the public should have.

Perhaps these government officials had correctly gauged the public's wants. Perhaps, but unlikely, for if they had, they would not have needed their monopoly power to limit the choice of programs.

Radio Luxembourg, which produces consumer-oriented programs as a way of selling commercials, was created to fill this gap in the market—and to generate profits. Although the radio signals were produced in Luxembourg and "consumed" in Britain and in France, neither country raised "tariffs" or other barriers to the imports of foreign commercial broadcasts. (Only the Russians and the Albanians jam airwaves.) Transport costs for radio waves are low.

155

Radio Luxembourg prospered. Predictably, numerous competitive stations were established. Radio Caroline, for example, had its transmission facilities parked on a tugboat just outside the three-mile limit of British jurisdiction.

Radio Luxembourg is a classic example of an externalized activity—that is, a good or service produced in one jurisdiction and consumed in another. Another example is the sale of alcohol, tobacco, and other tax-free products at airport shops; these sales are taxed differently from domestic sales, since the product is consumed (or supposed to be consumed) abroad. The traveler does not pay transport costs or customs duty on imports. Similarly, in Washington, D.C., externalized transactions—sales of alcohol and tobacco—take place; residents of Maryland and Virginia buy these products in Washington, where the taxes are lower. Imports of these untaxed products into the adjacent states, while illegal, are not significantly regulated.

Externalized activities occur because governments—national, state, or local—often regulate the same transaction or activity in different ways. Thus, production will often occur in jurisdictions with low taxes or minimal regulation to meet the consumption needs of people in other jurisdictions with higher taxes and more severe regulation. Differential regulation is necessary for an externalized activity to develop, but such activities occur only if the costs of transporting the goods or services from the production area to the consumption area and the barriers to these movements are low.

The External Currency Market

Today the largest, most rapidly growing external transactions involve the production of dollar bank deposits in London, Zurich, and other centers outside the United States; of Swiss franc deposits in London, Amsterdam, and other centers outside Switzerland; and of mark deposits in Luxembourg. The generic term for all these transactions is the "external currency market"; the popular terms are the "Eurodollar" or "Eurocurrency" market. The unique feature of this market is that banks produce deposits denominated in currencies other than those of the country in which the banks are located.

The banks which produce external currency deposits are known as Eurobanks. Thus, banks in London become Eurobanks whenever they issue deposits denominated in dollars or Swiss francs or German marks—or, indeed, in any currency other than sterling. Similarly, banks in Zurich are Eurobanks whenever they sell deposits denominated in currencies other than the Swiss franc. Eurobanks need not be located in Europe. Singapore, for example, is a thriving center for the Asian branch of the Eurodollar market; Panama City performs the same function in Latin America.

Eurobanking is only one activity of a commercial bank. Banks in London which produce dollar deposits also produce sterling deposits. Altogether, there may be 300 to 400 Eurobanks; for most, these Euro-transactions are a sideline to their primary activities as domestic banks. And their standing as domestic banks determines how competitive they will be as Eurobanks.

Today some of the leading Eurobanks are branches of the Bank of America, Citibank, Morgan Guaranty, and other U.S.-based banks in the major European financial centers. Participation in the Eurodollar market is the primary activity of most of the fifty or so London branches of U.S. banks. In the absence of transactions in dollars, most of these banks would not have established London branches. Similarly, participation in the Euromark market is the primary activity of the branches of the German banks in Luxembourg.

That banks in London conduct some of their business in dollars, marks, Swiss francs, and guilders may seem strange. It seems more natural for banks in each country to produce deposits and make loans in the domestic currency—for banks in Switzerland to deal in Swiss francs and banks in the Netherlands to deal in guilders. But dealing only in the domestic currency is a traditional bank practice rather than a legal necessity.

Banks outside the United States issue dollar deposits in response to investor demand. The dollar is a unit of account—one of the yardsticks in the world of money, a measure comparable to the gallon or meter. The "real" meter—the piece of metal about 39-plus inches long, which is one ten-millionth of the distance between the equator and the North Pole—remains in the International Bureau of Weights and Measures near Paris. The French could not prevent Americans or Swiss from using the meter as a measurement even if they wished. Similarly, the U.S. government cannot prevent British, Swiss, German, and Japanese banks from issuing deposits denominated in dollars, since these banks are outside U.S. legal jurisdiction. There are London dollar deposits or Zurich dollar deposits, and perhaps one day even Peking dollar deposits; they are not U.S. dollar deposits. The adjective is important, for dollar deposits in London are subject to British regulation, while dollar deposits in Zurich are subject to Swiss regulation.

Note that banking readily satisfies the requirements for an externalized activity. The transportation costs for money are extremely low. A million dollars, or a billion dollars, can be moved across the Atlantic at the cost of a couple of telegrams or phone calls. Bank regulations differ widely among countries; regulation of banks in the United States, for example, traditionally has been more restrictive than in Britain. In most countries, moreover, deposits denominated in foreign currencies are less extensively regulated than deposits in domestic currency. In London, for example, dollar deposits are not subject to the various requirements applied to sterling deposits. Similarly in Zurich and other major centers for external currency transactions, the interest rate ceilings applicable to deposits in the domestic currency do not apply to deposits denominated in foreign currencies. In the United States, however, foreign as well as domestic currency deposits are subject to Federal Reserve regulations stipulating that commercial banks could not pay interest on demand deposits (the ceiling is zero). Finally, most of the developed countries have been reluctant to apply barriers to the importation of funds from external currency banks located abroad.

Thus, borrowing and lending activities are externalized in the Eurodollar market—that is, shifted from U.S. political jurisdiction to the less severely regulated foreign or offshore markets. Depositors shift funds from dollar deposits in New York to dollar deposits in London and Zurich primarily for higher interest income. U.S. banks and Japanese banks and German banks set up branches in London and Zurich to "intermediate"—to bring borrowers and lenders together—because they are thus able to circumvent federal and state restrictions on geographic expansion of branches.

Where Eurodollars Come From

By the end of 1982, bank deposits denominated in external currencies were about $1,000 billion, compared to only $1 billion in 1961. About 70 percent of external currency deposits are denominated in dollars; the other principal currencies for the denomination of offshore deposits are Swiss francs and German marks. Modest amounts of deposits are also denominated in the Dutch guilder, British sterling, the French franc, and the Japanese yen.

One noteworthy aspect of the growth in external currency deposits is that the proportion of dollar-denominated deposits to total external deposits has declined, but only modestly. The second is that external deposits have grown at an average annual rate of 30 percent, much more rapidly than domestic deposits.

London is the principal financial center for Eurodollar business, followed by Zurich. The volume of foreign currency deposits in the United States is small, not because they are prohibited

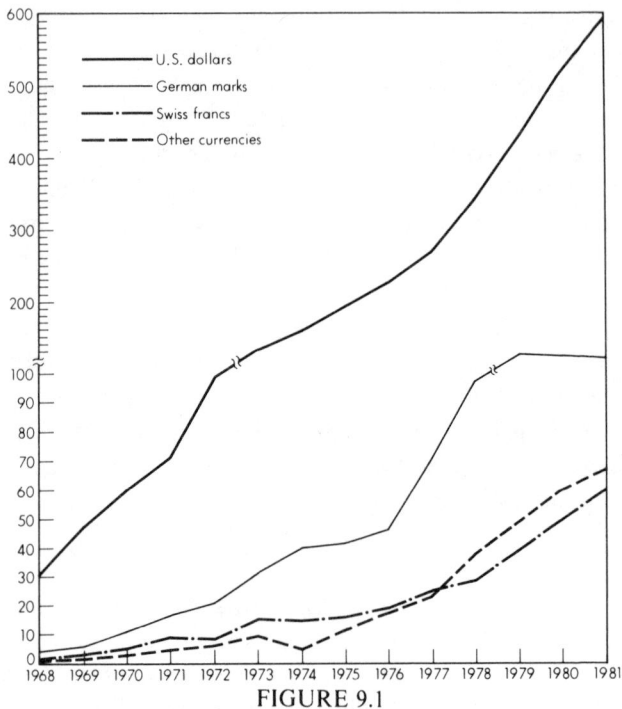

FIGURE 9.1

External Currency Deposits by Currency,
for Eight Reporting European Countries
(Billions of U.S. dollars, end of year)

SOURCE: Bank for International Settlements, *Annual Report* (1982).

but because U.S. regulations make such transactions unprofitable. Such deposits would be subject to reserve requirements.

No mystery attaches to the production of Eurodollar deposits. In principle, the process is the same as when an individual with a deposit on the west side of Fifth Avenue in New York transfers funds to a bank on the east side of the avenue. The only difference is that the Eurobank in London is across the Atlantic Ocean rather than across the street. If an individual with a dollar deposit in New York decides to shift funds to the London branch of the same bank, the bank ends up producing an offshore dollar deposit. The London bank deposits this check in its account in a U.S. bank. The investor now holds a dollar deposit in a bank in London rather than a bank in New York. The total deposits of the banks in the United States are unchanged; however, individual investors hold smaller deposits in the United States, and larger deposits in London. The London bank now has a larger deposit in the United States. The increase in the London bank's deposits in the New York bank is matched by the increase in dollar deposits for the world as a whole: the volume of dollar deposits in New York remains unchanged, while the volume in London increases.

Another initiative leading to the production of Eurodollar deposits occurs when the London bank increases its loans. Assume, for example, that Worldwide International Conglomerate (WIC) seeks to borrow dollars from a bank in London. WIC signs a promissory note or transfers a mortgage on some tankers to the London bank; the London bank "pays" by increasing the size of WIC's deposit in the bank. Note that this process of deposit creation is identical with the process that occurs whenever anyone borrows from a U.S. bank.

The London bank must be concerned about the impact of WIC's payments to various other firms on its own deposit balances. Domestic banks have the same concern. Yet these domestic banks do not worry, for they can take advantage of the law of large numbers: while some depositors will be reducing their balances, others will be increasing theirs. Similarly these offshore banks can readily adjust to a decline in their own deposit balances in banks in the United States by raising the interest rates they pay on deposits.

In the domestic economy, the capacity of banks to expand their deposits is limited by the monetary authorities, who determine both the reserve base of the banking system (the supply of high-powered money) and reserve requirements. In the external currency market, in contrast, there are no reserve requirements. Eurobanks sell additional deposits whenever the interest rates they are willing to pay are high enough to attract new depositors.

Yet the absence of reserve requirements on offshore deposits does not mean that there is the potential for an infinite expansion of deposits and credit, just as, in the absence of reserve requirements domestically, there would not be an infinite expansion of domestic deposits and credit. The growth of offshore deposits is limited by the willingness of investors to acquire such deposits in competition with domestic deposits; this comparison involves the risk and return on offshore deposits and the risk and return on domestic deposits. The Eurobank system in dollars is an offshore extension of the domestic dollar banking system, just as the Eurobank system in marks is an offshore extension of the domestic mark banking system. There are no important Eurobanks which are not offshore branches of the major international banks.

One explanation why U.S. banks have been eager to set up branches in London and Zurich, even though they usually pay higher interest rates on deposits than they do in the United States, is that they wish to grow, and branch expansion abroad is easier than in the United States. Another is that if they do not expand abroad, they may lose dollar deposits to foreign banks and to domestic competitors who have offshore branches; there is a follow-the-leader tendency. A third is that even though the interest rates paid on dollar deposits in London are higher than the interest rates paid on dollar deposits in New York, the other costs may be lower. Most domestic banks are required to hold reserves, usually in the form of a non-interest-bearing deposit in the central bank. This requirement is a "tax" on their earnings, since otherwise the bank would have invested nearly all these funds in income-earning assets. Eurobanks are not subject to this tax. Moreover, the costs of Eurobanks are low because the market is a wholesale market; the minimum deposit size is $50,000, and the average deposit is much larger. Thus, banks are willing to pay a higher interest rate on external deposits than on domestic deposits so long as this additional interest cost is outweighed by the savings.

Finally, the growth of the external currency market enables some non-U.S. banks to enter the market for U.S. dollar deposits at less cost than if they were to establish branches in the United States. U.S. banks have responded to this competitive challenge by setting up branches abroad that are prepared to offer the same terms on such deposits.

What remains to be explained is why some U.S. investors continue to hold domestic dollar deposits when, with minimal effort, they could earn higher interest rates on external dollar deposits. The answer is that dollar deposits in London are subject to risks not encountered on domestic deposits, and these risks deter some depositors from buying offshore deposits. For example, the British authorities might restrict banks in London from fulfilling their commitments on foreign currency deposits. Eurobanks might be told that depositors could withdraw deposits only if they satisfy conditions X, Y, and Z. Or they might subject the external deposits to exchange controls, requiring depositors to sell their deposits to the Bank of England in exchange for sterling. Or the investors might be concerned that U.S. authorities would penalize the repatriation of dollar funds from overseas.

London dollar deposits differ from New York dollar deposits in terms of political risk: they are subject to the whim of a different set of government authorities. Those who continue to hold dollars in New York believe that London dollars are too risky, and that the additional interest income is not justified in terms of the possible loss if a shift of funds back to New York were somehow restricted. The continued growth in external deposits during the 1960s reflected increasing investor confidence that the additional risks attached to external deposits were small. And the risks of holding funds in Europe seemed small, especially when coupled with the increase in interest rates on offshore deposits relative to domestic deposits.

External currency transactions probably go back to the seventeenth century, when one sovereign would counterfeit the gold coins of another. One popular explanation for the growth of the external market in the 1950s is that during the early years of the cold war, the Russians wanted dollar deposits because the dollar was the most useful currency for financing their international transactions. But they were reluctant to hold these deposits in New York because of the threat that the U.S. authorities might "freeze" the deposits. In effect, the Russians believed that the political risk of London dollar deposits was lower than in New York.

While the Russians may have been the cause of the rapid growth of offshore deposits during the 1950s, the remarkable growth in the 1960s reflects three additional factors: the steep climb in interest rates, which made it increasingly profitable to escape national regulation; the expansion of multinational firms; and the great competitive expansion of banks.

Depositors contemplating a shift of funds to the external market must decide whether to acquire external deposits in London, Zurich, Paris, or some other center. Depositors choose among centers on the basis of their estimates of political risk. Moscow and São Paulo seem risky—the heavy hand of bureaucratic regulation is all too evident. Even though there is undoubtedly an interest rate which would induce lenders to acquire Moscow dollar deposits, banks issuing these deposits do not have the investment opportunities to justify paying such high interest rates.

The Links Between External Deposits in Different Currencies

External deposits denominated in dollars, marks, francs, and other currencies are closely linked by the Eurobanks engaged in interest arbitrage. Eurobanks bid for deposits in six or seven currencies, not because they wish to make loans in each of these currencies but because funds received from selling deposits in one currency can be used to buy loans in any other currency. For example, a Eurobank might issue a deposit in Swiss francs. Finding relatively few attractive loan opportunities in Swiss francs, the bank would sell the Swiss francs for marks in the spot exchange market and make a loan in marks. To protect itself against the exchange risk, the bank would buy Swiss francs in the forward exchange market at the same time that it sold Swiss francs in the spot market. Because banks are willing to arbitrage in this way, the interest rates they offer on deposits in various currencies differ by the interest equivalent of the spread between the forward exchange rate and the spot exchange rate.

The external currency market provides a new set of links among the national money markets. Funds flow continuously between the domestic and external markets in response to changes in interest rate differentials and estimates of risk. By increasing the links between national money markets, the growth of the external currency market has further reduced the scope for national monetary independence.

Internationalizing Regulation

Central bankers lie awake at night worrying about the wheelers and dealers trafficking in their currencies in jurisdictions outside their direct control. Dollar deposits in London seem outside U.S. control because they are in London, and outside British concern because they are denominated in dollars. The authorities are worried that much of the growth in Eurodollars has resulted in an expansion of credit, arranged in an inverted pyramid, and the pyramid might collapse. Thus, each transfer of $1 million from New York to bank A in London may lead to a much larger increase in Eurodollar deposits, for bank B in London might borrow dollars from A to lend to bank C, and so on. The borrower from one Eurobank may deposit the proceeds in another Eurobank—or buy goods, services, or securities from a seller who deposits his proceeds in a Eurobank. As a result, total London dollar deposits might increase by much more than the initial transfer from New York to London, as banks lend to each other and customers borrow from one bank and shift the funds to another. The central bankers worry that a shock to the base of the pyramid could have a disastrous impact, bringing the whole credit pyramid down with a crash. The concern increases when the authorities remember that offshore deposits are not subject to reserve requirements, and, even worse, that the offshore banks hold no reserves.

Assume that bank A decides to ask bank B to repay its loan. Where will B get the money? Perhaps from bank C. Ultimately, some bank in the system will ask a nonbank borrower to repay. If the borrower cannot repay, then the ability of all the banks to repay declines. And the weaker the banks appear, the quicker their depositors will be to shift funds to those banks which seem safer.

In 1974, the pyramid began to shake when two banks, Herstatt and Franklin National, closed because of their losses in foreign exchange speculation. Both banks had borrowed extensively from Eurobanks. The fear was that some of these Eurobanks would be unable to repay their depositors; then a run on the Eurobanking system would begin, and Eurobanks would have to call their loans to get the funds to repay their depositors. The cliché image is that of a tumbling house of cards.

The worry is needless; a collapse of the offshore system is no more likely than the collapse of the domestic banking system. Since all Eurobanks are branches of U.S., Swiss, German, and other major banks; as long as the domestic branches remain open, the offshore branches cannot close. The central banks would be likely to step in if they thought a general collapse of credit possible. Nevertheless, central banks might delay their assistance, since they might feel less than completely reponsible for the survival of banks whose raison d'être has been the avoidance of regulation.

The authorities are also concerned that access to the Eurodollar market enables borrowers, lenders, and intermediaries to circumvent domestic monetary control, thus reducing the effectiveness of regulation and creating inequities between banks that participate in market and banks that do not. Someday a clever entrepreneur might establish a Eurobank on a tugboat five or ten miles from New York City in the Atlantic Ocean; this would be the monetary equivalent of Radio Caroline. U.S. residents would shift funds to the Tugboat Bank because it would offer higher interest rates than those available in New York and Chicago; borrowers would seek loans from the Tugboat Bank rather than from banks in New York. The Tugboat Bank would be in a favored competitve position since it would be beyond the scope of U.S. regulation.

So, increasingly and inevitably, the long arm of regulation must reach out to Eurobanks and to external currency transactions. The Bank of England and the Bundesbank control the foreign currency activities of banks within their legal jurisdictions, although the British do so in a very relaxed way. U.S. authorities apply a reserve regulation to funds received by U.S. banks from their foreign branches. These controls have usually been applied only to commercial banks, for only these entities are within the functional jurisdiction of the central banks. Since regulations reduce the profitability of Eurobanking in London and Zurich, the inevitable next step is for Eurobanks to shift to less extensively regulated jurisdictions.

Just as Radio Luxembourg can satisfy its customers because of official reluctance to disrupt its signals, so Eurobanks can flourish in Luxembourg and Nassau—as long as depositors and borrowers are free to do business there. The Eurobanks will flourish as long as U.S. authorities permit the offshore branches of U.S. banks to operate with lower reserve requirements than the domestic offices. The U.S. authorities might begin to unify reserve requirements, raising them on offshore branches of U.S. banks, and reducing them on domestic deposits.

The belated response to the growth of offshore deposits has enabled banks in the United States to establish international banking facilities—deposits in these facilities are not subject to reserve requirements. Thus far only foreigners are eligible to acquire such deposits—the irony is that foreigners can get higher interest rates on dollar deposits in these international banking facilities in the major U.S. cities than U.S. residents can. The authorities are discriminating against the natives!

One day, perhaps, countries will unify their regulations both for radio broadcasting and for commercial banking. Radio Luxembourg will fade away, and the Eurobanks will disappear. That day, however, does not seem imminent. For the central bank authorities have had the choice of harmonizing their regulations to reduce the incentives for Eurocurrency transactions or of attempting to regulate these transactions; they have chosen the latter path. Monetary independence and the central banks' own viability as independent institutions are the issues at stake.

10

Central Bankers Read Election Returns, Not Balance Sheets

For most of the last few years, finance ministers of the world have been pursuing the grail of monetary reform. They have met each other at the annual meetings of the IMF, at the monthly meetings of BIS, at the ad hoc meetings of the OECD, at the Group of Ten and the Committee of Twenty, at UNCTAD (United Nations Committee on Trade and Development) in New York. The finance ministers of the countries in the European Economic Community have met in Brussels, Paris, and Bremen. The Presidents and Prime Ministers of the United States, Germany, Japan, Canada, Britain, France, and Italy have met at Rambouillet, Puerto Rico, London, Bonn, Tokyo, Ottawa, and Versailles at annual summit meetings. There have been scores of meetings on a bilateral basis. The prize remains elusive.

Yet without reform, the system survives. Whatever is, is a system. The push for reform is a push for a System with a capital S—a set of rules which would govern the growth of international money and the exchange rate policies—perhaps even the choice of monetary and fiscal policies—of the system's members.

Reform of the international monetary system could be accomplished with changes in a few key arrangements. A system of pegged rates could be designed to allow for more flexible responses to payments deficits and surpluses, with only a minimal increase in the uncertainty felt by international traders and investors. A system of floating rates could be readily designed with comprehensive rules governing when national authorities might intervene in the exchange market, and when intervention would be proscribed. A mechanism could be found to produce the appropriate amount of international money without forcing the United States to incur payments deficits.

Stated in this way, the reform problem does not sound difficult. Surely it should be possible to obtain the agreement of central bankers and finance ministers to such modest proposals. But this view ignores the politics of the problem. One of the most dramatic solutions to problems raised by the existence of more than 100 national monies would be to adopt a common worldwide money. Since there would be no exchange rates, crises associated with pending changes in parities and with sharp depreciations would disappear. There would be no further need to coordinate the monetary policies of various central banks, for there would be only one central bank and one monetary policy. Nor would there be any need to be concerned with the relationship between the rates of growth of national monies and of international monies, since the distinction between the two would disappear. Indeed, the advantages of a worldwide money appear so overwhelming that one wonders why national monies are retained.

Once there was a common worldwide money—gold. The move away from the gold standard suggests why the idea of a worldwide money is utopian. The twentieth century is a century of nationalism. National governments have given increased priority to domestic objectives. The growth in the power of the state and the increase in attention to domestic objectives are not accidents. At first, monetary policy was manipulated to help finance World War I expenditures. Then, during the Great Depression, national governments geared monetary policy to expand domestic employment. In the final analysis, the attachment to the gold standard faded because governments wanted the advantages of a national money.

The library shelves are lined with books full of plans for reforming the monetary system and reducing its susceptibility to various crises. These books are full of articles, paragraphs, sections, and subsections which spell out, in detail, when a country can change its exchange rate and when it cannot, when it can borrow from other countries or international institutions and when it is obliged to lend to them. In reality, all of these articles, paragraphs, sections, and subsections are proxies for issues that are rarely discussed formally. For what each national government really wants to know is how the proposed arrangements will affect its ability to achieve its own national objectives—full employment, a stable price level, rapid growth, and increased control over its own destiny. The leaders in each government want to know how any plan will affect their ability to keep their constituents sufficiently happy to win the next election or forestall the next coup. When adjustments must be made, national governments want to be sure that the burden and costs fall on other countries. If some event occurs that adversely affects their constituents, they want to be able to show that the event, like the weather, was imported and beyond governmental control.

Many countries are concerned that an international monetary agreement might limit their freedom to set domestic policies, thus making it more difficult to satisfy their domestic constituencies. When the British joined the European Common Market, for example, they worried over what would happen to employment in Birmingham and Coventry once the bureaucrats in Brussels began to set monetary policy. They feared that the Bank of England might lose its independence and eventually become a branch office of a European central bank, much as the Federal Reserve Bank of Atlanta is a branch of the Federal Reserve System in Washington.

Every government would readily sign an agreement for international monetary reform if it were allowed to write the treaty, select the managers for the institution, and formulate its policies. Each would then design the arrangements so as to minimize any external constraint on its choice of domestic policies. In this case, membership would impose no cost on the government generating the proposal. The inevitable costs of adjustment would fall on other countries. Naturally, the proposals of various nations would be inconsistent. What is good for France is not necessarily good for Germany—as the Germans have learned, at some cost to their own taxpayers, at meetings of the European Community in Brussels.

A fact of political life that explains why efforts to establish new rules have not proved very successful is that the interests of residents of different countries frequently conflict. Some produce and export oil, many import oil. Some are interested in price stability, others in full employment. Some believe major economic decisions should be resolved by the decentralized interplay of market forces, while others believe these decisions should be made in accord with a central plan.

Whenever payments imbalances occur, there is sporadic conflict over whether the deficit countries or the surplus countries should take the initiative in making the necessary adjustments. When exchange rates change sharply, the debate is over whether the countries with the appreciating currencies or those with the depreciating currencies should intervene to dampen rate movements. Political leaders talk about the virtues of international cooperation, but domestic factors frequently take priority, especially when the next election may be only months away. Monetary reform has a limited constituency.

The movement toward monetary reform might be advanced if the positions of each of the major countries on the central issues could be predicted: if their proposed arrangements for producing international money and for adjusting to payments imbalances were known in advance. Someplace, somewhere, there may be some systematic knowledge about this question. But in the absence of such knowledge, anecdotal evidence about differing national attitudes toward inflation, bureaucracy, economic openness, and the market must suffice.

Inflation Is No Accident

Consider how the views of Britain and Germany might differ toward reform of the system. Since the late 1940s the dollar price of sterling has fallen by more than half, while the dollar price of the mark has nearly doubled. The changes in the foreign exchange values of the sterling and the mark reflect their price-level performance: prices have risen rapidly in Britain and slowly in Germany. This difference is no accident. In fact, the financial policies pursued by each country during the 1960s and 1970s can be traced to its economic performance during the early 1920s. In the interwar period, Great Britain's unemployment rate reached nearly 20 percent. After World War II, British economic policy sought to maintain full employment, regardless of the impact on domestic prices. Germany, on the other hand, has been almost paranoid about increases in its price level, as a result of German experiences with the hyperinflations of 1922–1923 and 1944–1948, during which its currency and most of its financial assets became worthless. These national experiences fostered attitudes that directly affect national monetary policies and indirectly affect positions on monetary reform.

Countries whose prices rise more rapidly than the average, such as Britain and Denmark, tend to have payments deficits and depreciating currencies; they also have more ambitious approaches toward international monetary rules than do countries with greater price stability, such as Germany and the Netherlands, which tend to have payments surpluses and appreciating currencies. The deficit countries want foreign loans and credits made available on an automatic basis, without strings and lectures about good financial behavior; they want to avoid the need to devalue, and they hope their currencies will not depreciate. If changes in exchange rates are necessary, then they want the surplus countries to take the initiative. If the deficit countries themselves must take the initiative, then they want to be able to restrict their foreign payments without subjecting themselves to the criticism or surveillance of other countries or of international institutions.

Countries with payments surpluses, on the other hand, do not want to commit themselves to extending large credits to deficit countries; they fear that if they do, their payments surpluses will become even larger and they will in effect import inflation. Nor do they want to be put in the position of having to revalue to avoid having to inflate.

Substantial payments imbalances or changes in exchange rates are the result of differences among countries in the rates at which their prices increase and, indirectly, at which their national money supplies grow. Differences among countries in rates of monetary growth are likely to reflect institutional differences in their tax systems or in their union-management relations.

The common explanation of rising prices—too much money chasing too few goods—describes a situation known as demand-pull inflation. Annual price increases of 50 to 100 percent, as in some Latin American countries, are neither mistakes nor accidents; they are the result of government expenditures and credit policies that are not consistent with price stability. Few governments are perpetually ignorant of the financial policies needed to produce price stability. When prices continue to rise, it is because anti-inflationary policies are deemed more expensive than those that permit a continuation of the inflation; the belief is that these policies will lead to reductions of both demand and production and to higher unemployment.

Demand-pull inflation occurs because the government wants the profits from the production of money, either to finance its own expenditures or to divert them to its supporters. Because the government is unwilling to raise its tax rates, expenditures within the public sector are financed with newly produced money. The Vietnam inflation in the United States and the U.S. inflation in Vietnam both reflect increased government spending based on monetary expansion. The Johnson administration believed that it was less costly politically to finance the full costs of an unpopular war through debasement of the money than by raising tax rates.

Similarly, within Vietnam the Thieu government financed its local expenditures and those of U.S. forces by "printing press" money; the money supply grew at rates of 40 and 50 percent a year. Both governments were able to increase their expenditures, just as if they had raised their income and sales tax rates. In both the United States and Vietnam, the holders of money were taxed—the widows and orphans and pensioners who held savings bonds and other fixed-price assets, like cash, savings accounts, and life insurance policies. Even those individuals who did not have to pay taxes nevertheless had to pay the inflation tax.

An alternative explanation for rising prices, especially in countries with well-organized, independent, and militant labor unions, is cost-push inflation. The scenario begins with a strike or the threat of a strike. To obtain labor peace, firms grant large wage increases. Since their labor costs rise, they must raise their prices to avoid sharp declines in their profits or, more likely, to avoid substantial losses.

The national authorities may decide that the solution to the cost-push problem is to wait until the higher prices reduce the demand for the firms' product and the consequent demand for labor. At that point, the higher unemployment rate might be sufficient to dampen further upward pressure on wages, and the power of the unions might be broken. But the unemployed vote. Elections may occur long before the union structure is weakened. So the authorities may adopt an expansive monetary policy to reduce unemployment; the increase in the money supply leads to an increase in demand for goods and for labor, sustaining the higher prices and the higher wages. When the unemployment rate falls, unions will again be in a good position to strike for another wage increase.

In Britain, which has a large number of decentralized unions, local strikes have been frequent. For a long time British employers were prepared to buy labor peace, knowing they could pass on the higher costs by raising prices. Germany, in contrast, can afford its inflation paranoia because its labor force has been relatively docile and has not pressed aggressively for large wage hikes. Moreover, Germany, unlike Britain, has been a willing importer of foreign labor. Germany could not have achieved its relative price stability with a British-type industrial structure. And British prices would have risen much less rapidly if its labor unions had resembled their German counterparts. The economic structures in each country have thus reinforced the importance that each attaches to price stability and to full employment.

If the European Community moves seriously toward a common currency, then either the British or the Germans—and perhaps both—will be in for a shock. There is no one rate of monetary expansion which will leave both happy, and a compromise rate might even leave both unhappy.

National central banks respond to their own fiscal and labor market structures. That is why greater harmonization or unification of the economic structures in various countries may be necessary before a comprehensive international monetary agreement, limiting monetary independence in individual countries, can be negotiated. If a comprehensive reform agreement was negotiated while these economic differences remained substantial, the likelihood is high that the agreement would break down when the national views about the appropriate rate of monetary growth diverged sharply. Institutions must adjust to accommodate national diversity, for national diversity will not adjust to institutions.

Bureaucracy Is a Growth Industry

Change is as inevitable in economic life as it is in biological life. Individuals go through a sequence of stages of growth. At some stages they grow rapidly; then they mature, stabilize, degenerate, and eventually die. Throughout the life cycle, they are subject to shocks of disease and accident, which may alter the growth process.

Economies also go through stages, although the distinction among the stages may be less clear. Moreover, the length of particular stages in the various economies may differ. Finally, economies are subject to shocks—both structural, such as crop failures, or accidental, such as wars. Technological change is a shock to individuals and firms within an economy, since it may result in a decline in the demand for their products.

Adjustments are necessary whenever shocks occur. Few people welcome shocks, and an increasingly large part of governmental activity has involved reducing shocks or minimizing their effects. Frequently, what government does is to reallocate the costs of a shock among various elements in the economy; the costs and the risks of the shock are socialized. Disaster relief is a tax on the general population to subsidize those who have incurred large losses because of floods, fires, or tornadoes. Unemployment compensation is a tax on the employed to subsidize the unemployed. Social security is a tax on the young to subsidize the aged.

Countries differ sharply in the way they respond to similar shocks. Most countries have a traditional economic style, evident from the different roles played by government in determining price, wage, credit, and investment decisions. In Japan (and in France, to a lesser extent) the bureaucracy plays a major role in setting the target growth rates and the investment levels of particular industries and firms. In other countries these decisions reflect market forces. Americans, for example, favor decentralized decision making: the government should be responsible for monetary and fiscal policy, households should make the consumption decisions, and business firms the investment decisions. The mix of goods and services to be produced and who is to produce them are the outcomes of millions of private decisions. A few other countries, such as Germany and Switzerland, share the U.S. perspective. Elsewhere governmental authorities are more fully involved in production and investment decisions.

National attitudes toward government intervention are closely related to the prestige enjoyed by the bureaucracy. In Japan and France the brightest graduates of the most elite universities vie for careers in government service; in these countries bureaucratic intervention in investment and production decisions is readily accepted. A strong central government is deemed desirable, and the bureaucrats are regarded as highly competent.

As a general rule, the more powerful the bureaucracy, the smaller the scope for market-oriented decisions. Governmental intervention is justified on various grounds, from reducing uncertainty associated with free markets to minimizing excessive competitive waste or reducing business conflict. The bureaucracy affects decisions in several ways—for example, through its influence over the allocation of credit, through taxes, and through the issuance of building, investment, and import permits.

The views of most politicians about how the international economy should be managed are an extension of their views about how their domestic economies should be managed. Countries which place a low value on bureaucracy tend to favor an open international economy, with minimal barriers to the free flow of goods and capital internationally. They feel either that exchange rates should be allowed to float freely so as to balance international payments and receipts, or that the supply of international money should be managed so as to satisfy the needs of individual countries. In either case, individuals and firms should be free to choose between domestic and foreign goods on the basis of price, without arbitrary restrictions at the border.

Countries with strong centralized bureaucratic controls over their domestic economies, on the other hand, tend to favor the use of bureaucratic controls to manage international payments. International monetary reform usually has a lower priority for such countries, since their bureaucrats are in a position to correct payments imbalances by tightening or easing controls on purchases of foreign exchange and on imports. Moves toward a more open economy would tend to weaken bureaucratic control and thus threaten the future of the national bureaucracies.

Thus, it is no accident that U.S. government officials are likely to be more favorable to floating exchange rates than their French or Japanese counterparts. Nor is it surprising that U.S. government officials are more intensely concerned with the adequacy of international money than officials in other countries, for the officials in other countries are more willing to make arbitrary decisions regulating international payments at their borders.

Inevitably, government officials in countries outside the United States are concerned about the costs to the national economies of two types of errors: one is too small a supply of reserves, the other, too large a supply. If the supply is too small, as it was in the early 1960s, other countries may still be able to earn payments surpluses by forcing the United States to incur payments deficits. If the supply is too large, as in the late 1960s, these countries import inflation, perhaps from the United States. Foreign bureaucrats believe the cost to their countries of adjusting to too small a supply of reserves is much less than the cost of adjusting to too large a supply. The U.S. authorities, not surprisingly, come to the opposite conclusion.

The New Mercantilists

One of the conflicts in the international economy is over openness: are foreign residents treated on a par with domestic residents, or are they discriminated against in access to markets, jobs, investments, and tax relief? In earlier periods, nationalism was the opposite of openness, and mercantilism was the term for this nationalistic behavior. The mercantilists were interested in acquiring and hoarding gold as a basis for enhancing their country's power. An open international economy would threaten, almost by definition, the advocates of nationalism. Nationalism means that the economic interests of domestic producers are preferred over those of foreign competitors—that domestic residents have preferred access to markets, products, and jobs. Tariffs, quotas, and restrictions on the ownership of domestic assets by foreigners reflect nationalist pressures.

Countries subject to strong nationalist pressures are likely to place substantial barriers in the way of imports of foreign goods and services, as well as the sale of domestic securities to foreigners. Japan has a strong nationalist bias. The Japanese rush toward modernization in the last third of the nineteenth century reflected the fear that foreign imperialists would begin to dismember Japan into colonies or enclaves, as they had China. Thus, Japan became a strong industrial power to resist a perceived external threat. Japanese attitudes toward trade and investment decisions continue to reflect this strong desire to maintain a cultural identity. So Japan resists foreign investments and is reluctant to liberalize its import policies; domestic residents should not be injured or inconvenienced for the sake of international harmony. Rather, U.S. textile workers should lose their jobs so that Japanese textile workers can produce for the U.S. market.

One pervasive worldwide tendency of the last fifty years has been an increase in the government's role in production. Often, when private entrepreneurs find a particular industry increasingly unprofitable, foreign competition further reduces the number of domestic producers. Yet the government, while reluctant to subsidize private entrepreneurs, usually wants to maintain domestic production. So the activity is shifted to the public sector. Many of the "private" firms in Italy are owned by one of three large holding companies: IRI (National Institute for Industrial Reconstruction), ENI (National Hydrocarbon Corporation), and ENEL (National Corporation for Electric Energy), each of which is largely owned by the government. Sometimes national ownership may be justified on grounds of national security. General de Gaulle insisted that France needed a computer industry for national security, and so part of Machines Bull, the largest French computer firm, was absorbed by the government when it would otherwise have been liquidated. Similarly, the Conservative government in Great Britain nationalized Rolls Royce because the immediate unemployment in areas near the company's factories would have been excessively high had the company folded.

As government assumes a bigger role in production, openness to foreign competition declines. Even more than those in the private sector, firms and industries in the public sector demand protection from foreign competition; almost of necessity, the government-owned firms are unprofitable. British Leyland is nationalized; given the productivity of its laborers and their wages, if Leyland prices its cars to cover its costs, not many cars will be sold. If Leyland sells at a lower price, then it will not be able to cover its costs. But government's ability to pay subsidies is limited because the ability to tax is limited. So tariffs and other import barriers are levied to protect domestic producers and to minimize the necessary subsidies for public sector industries. The result is that countries with a large number of government-owned firms in manufacturing are reluctant to reduce barriers to external competition; such moves jeopardize the survival of these domestic firms or raise the cost of the subsidy to the Treasury.

Although other countries may seem more nationalistic than the United States, the difference may be partly an illusion. Its large economic size means that any direct foreign threat to the United States is small; foreign economies have a smaller impact on the level of U.S. business activity than they might on other countries. While Canada and France may worry about U.S. domination of their economies and their national institutions, size alone protects the United States from foreign domination. Foreign ownership of firms—or shares of firms—located in the United States is small. The relatively liberal U.S. position toward foreign ownership would almost certainly change if foreigners tried to acquire a sizeable proportion of major U.S. industries like IBM or General Motors. Shifts in U.S. foreign economic policy in the last ten years to more and higher import barriers—such as quotas on imports of textiles, apparel, steel, beef, and petroleum—suggest that the United States is not immune from nationalist pressures. The threat that various Arab countries might use some of their new-found wealth to buy up various U.S. firms sent a number of congressmen up the wall.

Who Takes the Consensus?

International monetary reform would be a cinch if countries were homogeneous—if each were made in the same image. But most national borders are not arbitrary; rather, they tend to segment economies with differing industrial and institutional structures and electorates with different values. Conflicts in interests are inevitable and complicate monetary reform.

Moreover, the increasing priority given to national interests is a worldwide phenomenon; the pull of nationalism intensifies the growth of bureaucracy and domestic demands for monetary flexibility. In time, perhaps, the strength of these national pulls may diminish. In the meantime, efforts at monetary reform which ignore these pressures are not likely to succeed.

11

Monetary Reform—Where Do the Problems
Go When They Are Assumed Away?

A paradox of the 1960s was the glaring contrast between the problems of the system—the gold and foreign exchange crises and the threat to the dollar—and all the good advice in the editorials of the *New York Times* and the *Economist,* in congressional testimony, in international conferences of economists and bankers, and in university lectures. Salvation was readily available. The system's problems would be solved if only the monetary price of gold were doubled or tripled, or if gold were eliminated altogether from the monetary system, or if the support limits around currency parities were widened, or narrowed, or if currencies were allowed to float, or if a world central bank were established, or if national monetary policies were coordinated, or if national currencies were eliminated. Or if . . .

Each of these proposals had the support of eminent authorities. Nearly every expert left the impression that if only his favorite proposal were adopted, the system's problems soon would disappear, or at least become much less pressing. Since few of the proposals—other than that of floating rates—were adopted, the experts' convictions cannot be readily tested. The wide diversity of the "solutions" is surprising. Some proposals—raise the gold price or demonetize gold, widen the support limits or narrow these limits—were contradictory; some of the authorities were wrong if others were right.

If these proposals were as attractive as their proponents suggested, why were so few adopted? Why was the adoption of floating exchange rates a necessity rather than a move of conviction? The simple answer to the general question is that the politicians around the world were not convinced about the merits of any one proposal. But if not, why not? Perhaps the national political leaders were unable to understand the proposals. Perhaps vested interests in the various countries prevented their adoption. Or perhaps the proposals were ahead of their time—whatever that means.

One feature common to each of these diverse proposals was the belief that changes in the institutional framework of the international monetary system would somehow resolve the problems associated with payments imbalances. Old problems, however, unlike old soldiers, do not always fade away. Changes in the institutional framework may help countries reconcile some conflicts between their domestic and their external objectives and between their national economic objectives and those of other countries. But some conflicts are inevitable as long as there are separate countries, each with its own economic structure, its own set of economic priorities, and its own national constituency. Changing the institutional arrangements for the exchange market or for producing international money may make it easier to resolve some conflicts. But such arrangements, by themselves, do not eliminate the conflicts of interest; rather, they alter the framework within which the conflict appears.

A country, after all, is at most a group of individuals with similar aspirations and values. Some countries, such as Belgium, Canada, Malaysia, Switzerland, and Yugoslavia, contain two or three such groups. Some countries in Africa have twenty or thirty tribes. In a few cases the country is smaller than the group; this is especially true of a few English Commonwealth countries. In most cases, the country is larger than the group.

The Flat-Earthers

Before Columbus, many people believed the earth was flat; it stood to reason that if it were not, everyone on the underside would fall off. The flat-earthers prospered until Columbus sailed to the Indies in 1492 and Newton defined gravity in the *Principia* in 1687. The conclusions of the flat-earthers in other areas—business, language, and money—may be as incomplete as they were in geography and physics; the commonsense, intuitive approach does not always produce the right answer.

In business and economic life, it stands to reason that there would be savings in the costs of doing business if systems of weights and measures used in various countries were the same. It is inane that half the world uses gallons, miles, and inches while the other half uses liters, kilometers, and kilos—and that a U.S. gallon is one quart smaller than a Canadian gallon. It stands to reason that savings would be achieved by the standardization on one system of weights and measures, road signs, electrical voltages, bottle sizes, and liquor proofs.

Less than 100 years ago, each local area in the United States was free to set its own time and to decide when noon occurred. In the 1880s, Congress legislated that the country be divided into four standard time zones. About the same time, international convention segmented the world into twenty-four time zones. Some areas were obliged to move the hands on their clocks ahead, but no area had to change its time-measuring devices or the units. There are inconveniences and costs in having London six or seven hours ahead of Chicago and in trying to remember whether one loses or gains a day when crossing the international date line when flying from San Francisco to Tokyo.

The flat-earthers favor one world time zone; thus, when it is 12:00 in Washington, it would be 12:00 in London and Moscow. But because bedtimes and milking hours would have to be rescheduled in much of the world, the change is not imminent, since

---

185

countries appear unlikely to agree on who incurs the costs and the inconveniences of rescheduling.

Money is a unit of measure or account. Each of the members of the International Monetary Fund has its own money; most other nonmember countries do also. Multiple monies incur costs of foreign exchange transactions, which is the monetary equivalent of language translations. Moreover, the exchange of national monies leads to one problem that is not encountered in language translation, for future values are not known; the price of the yen or the mark a year from now—or even next week—is uncertain, largely because national central banks manage their own monetary policies to achieve domestic employment, growth, and financial objectives.

The flat-earthers favor one world money, just as they favor one world time, one world language, one set of measures; it stands to reason that the costs incurred in foreign exchange transactions would be saved if there were only one money. But money differs from distance, time, and language in that it is managed as an instrument of economic policy. The move to a worldwide money means that the flexibility inherent in national monies would be lost.

Within each country, there are sharp conflicts of interests; this is what political parties, elections, revolutions, and coups are all about. Differences in views and interests and values must be accommodated. If the existing rules seem inadequate to accommodate the desired changes, some groups may have a tea party and set up a new set of rules. And to the extent that the existing rules are designed to obstruct peaceful changes in the structure of the rules, the higher the likelihood of a tea party. For international conflicts, too, there are numerous parties to be heard from when a new set of rules is devised.

The major features of the new set of rules for international financial relations will almost inevitably be drawn from proposals that are already on the shelf. Most of these proposals can be placed in one of several categories. One set of proposals would have countries submerge their national interests and act as if they shared identical interests—even though they do not. Proposals for a common international currency, a world central bank, monetary unification, and even for the coordination and the harmonization of national policies fall into this category. In contrast, a second set of proposals suggests that countries should concentrate on maximizing their domestic interests; exchange markets should be organized so that any tendency toward payments imbalances would be adjusted by anonymous market forces. The floating exchange rate system would be retained and legitimatized, although rules might have to be adopted to prevent national authorities from fiddling in the foreign exchange market. Someplace between these two groups is a third, which recognizes the conflict among domestic interests in various countries and seeks to find some optimum path between the desires for national monetary independence and the competing desires for a free and open international economy.

In the 1970s, confidence that the problems of the system could be readily resolved by adopting an institutional talisman diminished. A few observers still felt that if their advice had been accepted in the 1960s, the Bretton Woods system might have been retained, with modest changes, and the world inflation, the recession, and the pressures toward protectionism triggered by sharp movements in exchange rates might have been avoided. The Bretton Woods system was shelved because the monetary authorities were unable to adjust exchange parities to cope with the inflationary pressures. When the pegged exchange rate arrangement became obsolete, the system lost its only effective set of rules, and so there were significantly fewer constraints on the measures that individual countries might take to improve their own national economic welfare, despite the costs that might be imposed on their trading partners.

Politicizing Economic Conflict:
An International Money

A frequent observation is that national monies are redundant, since the price of wine in terms of wheat is pretty much the same in each country, after conversion at the prevailing exchange rate. So the argument goes that since relative prices are similar across countries, no economic function is served by having separate national currencies. In fact, the observation is incorrect—or, more politely, insufficiently exact.

The cost of virtually identical Holiday Inn rooms may vary from $25 to $90, depending on whether the room is in a small town in Alabama or in New York City. The United Nations calculates that with the costs for a particular standard of living set at an average of 100 for all the capital cities of the world, the specific cost may range from a low of 50 in Manila to 200 in Tokyo and Paris. The cost of producing the standard Volkswagen "Rabbit" also differs sharply between New Stanton, Pennsylvania, and Wolfsburg, Germany even though the selling price is the same. The prices of internationally traded goods are similar, more so than their costs of production. The prices of goods and services which are less readily traded—haircuts are the standard example—may differ across countries by substantially more than the prices of tradable goods.

Those who believe that national currencies are redundant also sometimes argue that changes in exchange rates are ineffective, since relative prices do not change. Perhaps. But there seems considerable evidence that changes in exchange rates are effective, for the relation between the prices of traded and nontraded goods changes.

Most—but not all—changes in exchange rates result from differences in national rates of inflation. It might be argued that inflations change only absolute prices, not relative prices. But if that were the case, no one would be concerned with inflation, except for the minor inconveniences of having to carry more money around. In fact, inflations change relative prices, at least for a while—*which is why they occur.* In the early stages of inflation, farmers become better off and city folk less well off; borrowers may do well and lenders poorly. In a deflation, or even when the rate of inflation declines, the tables are turned; lenders gain and borrowers lose.

The demand for separate national monies has an analogy in the need for national armies. During most years, most countries are at peace. If a country is at peace, it might seem that it has no need for military forces; indeed, its army might be disbanded. But military forces are needed when peaceful means of settling disputes between nations are not deemed satisfactory by at least one party. So, too, a separate national currency may be needed to attain national price-level and employment targets.

Proposals for a common international money as a substitute for separate national monies are attractive. Exchange crises would disappear. There would no longer be a need to debate whether a country with a payments surplus should lend international money or its own currency to deficit countries, for there would be no measurable payments imbalances and no more bickering over which countries should take the initiative in adjusting to payments imbalances. There would no longer be a concern with whether a currency was overvalued or undervalued; the words would no longer have meaning or relevance.

But a common international money would not eliminate the problems of the existing system; it would simply shift their location. Problems of accommodating divergent national interests would become centralized in the management of the international money-producing institution. This institution would have a set of directors who would be ultimately responsive to the political authorities of the member countries. The institution's directors would have to determine how its managers were to be selected, how rapidly the institution should produce money, and when countries might control payments to foreign areas.

The participating countries would also have to agree on the voting strength of each member country. Would the United States, the Netherlands, and Brazil each have the same number of votes, as in the General Assembly of the United Nations and most other international institutions? If not, what criteria should be used to determine the voting strength of each member country? Would the largest countries have veto power over any decisions of the institution's managers, or would they be obliged to follow their mandate? The United Nations principle of one country, one vote would mean that the United States, a nation of 230 million, could readily be outvoted by Trinidad, Jamaica, and other Caribbean countries whose total population is less than that of Chicago. The costs of adjustment to payments imbalances might be shifted to the United States. At the other extreme, if votes of each country were in proportion to its population (on the principle of one person, one vote), then China and India together would come close to having a voting majority for the world.

Clearly, some accommodation is necessary between these extremes. But what formula would be acceptable to countries with large and small populations, with high and low per capita incomes? Until this issue can be resolved, an agreement is virtually impossible. Some countries would be more willing than others to compromise, not because the agreement fully satisfied their needs but because they would know that if the costs of abiding by the agreement were too high, they could ignore their commitments; they could adopt exchange controls or refuse to lend their currencies to other countries. Some countries are substantially more cynical than others when signing international treaties.

Almost as soon as the international authority was established, a decision would have to be made about how fast the supply of the common international money should grow. Each country would have its own views: some might favor a growth rate of 5 percent a year, others 10 or 15 percent. This disagreement would reflect differences in national economic structures and priorities.

190

Some countries grow more rapidly than others, perhaps because they have higher savings and investment rates, or because their labor forces expand rapidly or because they adapt better to the new technologies. Labor unions are much more militant in some countries than in others; these countries may favor a more rapid growth in money supplies to permit sustained full employment. Moreover, some countries are more tolerant about inflation and would be willing to risk more rapid price increases in the belief that they might thus reduce their unemployment rates.

Thus, countries which formerly permitted their national money supplies to grow at a 15 percent annual rate probably would want the supply of common international currency to grow at a similar rate. Countries that had previously favored a slower growth for their own national money would probably also want the international money to grow at a slower rate. Japan, for example, would want a rapid rate of monetary growth, while Germany would want a slower growth rate. But Japan and Germany cannot each have its way if there is only one money in the world.

Perhaps the directors from different countries could be shown that the differences among them regarding the appropriate rate of money supply growth are unimportant. If so, the rate of money supply growth could be determined by a more or less random process. Then each country could quickly adjust to the new rate, and the costs and inconvenience of forgoing the preferred rate for the community rate would be small. Perhaps. But it is unlikely.

The debates among directors from different countries about the preferred rates of money supply growth would be vigorous, just as they frequently are within individual countries. Countries with similar interests would form caucuses and vote as a bloc. The small countries would be concerned that their interests might be steamrollered by the large countries. Large industrial countries, on the other hand, would worry about being outvoted by coalitions of the many small countries.

Some countries might devise numerous ad hoc means to limit

their international payments—even in defiance of the rules. A few might threaten to secede from the common currency union rather than accept a monetary policy deemed inappropriate to their needs. As long as there is substantial diversity among nations, a common international money and a unified monetary policy are a contradiction in terms. Those who advocate such a union either blithely ignore the real problem or else harbor secret knowledge about how diversity among nations can be readily reconciled—knowledge that is not generally available.

As long as basic structural differences in national economies remain, and countries retain sovereignty, there is little chance that a common international currency might be adopted—and even less that it would work if it were. Control over the production of national money is a large part of what sovereignty is all about. It is not an accident that member countries of the European Community were able to eliminate tariffs on internal trade, accept a common tariff on imports from outside the EC, harmonize their tax policies, and yet still find it difficult to unify their currencies. That countries would give up the flexibility of a national money—and the associated domestic political advantages—to avoid the costs and the newspaper headlines of exchange crises seems unlikely. Perhaps more importantly, such a move would be questionable on the grounds that as long as national economic structures and values differ, countries as a group may gain if this diversity of interests is recognized and accommodated rather than suppressed.

In time, the differences in the national interests of participating countries may diminish and be eliminated. Eventually, business cycles will be in phase across countries, and rates of productivity growth—even attitudes toward inflation and the inflation-unemployment tradeoff—might be more nearly similar. The nation state as an efficient political unit will then be obsolete. However, the date at which interests will become so similar that the nation state can be shelved as an effective decision-making unit does not seem imminent.

National monies have been around for about as long as there have been nations. One implication—the most likely if not the only one—is that national monies will disappear only as the distinctions among nations lose their economic significance. This process is likely to occur on the basis of regional groupings, as countries with similar characteristics merge their currencies. The European Community is one such group; other potential groups are in Southeast Asia, East Africa, Central America, and the Spanish-speaking countries of South America.

The fact is that a move to a common worldwide currency is an extreme solution and a straw man, and relatively few experts favor the idea. Yet the political problems associated with less ambitious reform proposals are similar to those encountered in this more extreme solution. The smaller the scope that individual countries have in setting their own monetary policies and their own exchange rates, the larger the energies they will inevitably direct to how the international monetary system is managed. The politicians in each country are understandably reluctant to permit international civil servants to undertake measures whose costs they must bear; the civil servants are not obliged to run for office.

A less ambitious approach involves adoption of one international money and the retention of national monies. The U.S. suspension of gold transactions in August 1971 led to proposals for a new international monetary system to be built around Special Drawing Rights (SDRs) as the only international money; the international roles of the dollar and of gold would be phased out. National monies would be retained, and each national currency would have a parity in terms of SDR. Each country could devalue its currency in terms of SDR if it had a large payments deficit, or it could revalue its currency—perhaps even be obliged to do so—if it had a large payments surplus.

The SDR-producing institution would become an international central bank. Member countries would jointly decide how many SDRs to produce each year and how many newly produced

SDRs to allocate to each country. Each country's view about these decisions almost certainly would reflect its view of how best to advance its own interests. The rate at which the supply of SDRs would grow would not satisfy all of the participating countries, any more than all would be satisfied if there were a common international currency which grew at the rate of 3, 5, or 8 percent a year.

Proposing an SDR system, either by that name or by some other, is easier than getting it accepted, for countries are naturally concerned with the future value of SDR. Gold was acceptable as an international money because of its underlying commodity value. Central banks held gold believing that if it were demonetized their losses would be minimal, since they could sell gold in the commodity market. Similarly, dollar assets and sterling assets were acceptable as international money because it seemed—once—that these monies could be used to buy gold from the U.S. Treasury and the Bank of England, or at least to buy American or British goods.

Every central bank recognizes that SDRs are useful only if they can be converted into a national currency. Central banks in a few countries must worry that some other central banks might prove reluctant to sell their currencies for SDRs.

U.S. participation is essential to the success of the SDR system, for holders of SDRs would want assurance that they could convert SDRs into dollars to make payments for the purchase of U.S. goods or securities. The United States has the world's largest market in goods and the most comprehensive set of financial markets. Participation in the SDR arrangement by Argentina and Zambia is insufficient for its success if the United States does not participate. Without U.S. involvement, the SDR arrangement would flounder, whereas it makes little difference if Argentina and Zambia do not participate. The reason is that the supplies of goods available in those two countries are not so large that the various central banks would want to hold the Argentinian peso or the Zambian kwacha as international money.

As it is, many countries would probably prefer U.S. dollars to SDRs as international money, for the dollar has greater "moneyness." Foreign central banks would hold SDRs because they could be used to buy dollars. Some countries would fear that the United States might at some future date stop selling dollars in exchange for SDRs. In that case, holdings of SDRs would become much less valuable than the dollar. Few countries would accept SDRs if they were not acceptable at the U.S. Treasury. To minimize this concern, the United States could pledge to remain attached to the SDR standard. But this pledge could be broken. The United States could give a super-pledge; but the super-pledge could be broken, as was the U.S. commitment, and a succession of super-commitments, to maintain the $35 gold parity. Many countries would remain reluctant to hold a substantial part of their reserve assets as SDRs, as long as they doubted the commitment of the U.S. authorities—currently and in the indefinite future—to buy SDRs in exchange for dollars.

A paper money or paper gold proposal can only succeed if countries have confidence in the money—that is, in its future purchasing power in terms of goods. This confidence requirement is not likely to be satisfied simply because the members agree to a treaty. For any member might, when it suits its pressing national needs, walk away from the treaty. And every other member recognizes this reality.

The Nonpolitical Market Solution

A system of pegged exchange rates is much like a fair-weather friend—as long as the major countries are able to achieve reasonable price stability, the system is workable. If the exchange rates were free to float, movements in the rates would be modest. However, if there are substantial differences among major countries in their price-level targets or even in the strengths of their commitments to realize these targets, floating rates are inevitable, if only because exchange rate movements are inevitable. Investors shift funds to profit from anticipated appreciations and to avoid losses from anticipated depreciations.

Proposals for floating exchange rates recognize the divergent pulls of independent national monetary policies. The central bank in each country could produce the amount of money deemed appropriate for its domestic needs. In Japan the money supply could grow at 20 percent a year; in Belgium, at 10 percent. Each country would choose the rate of money supply growth that might enable it to achieve its principal economic objectives—high levels of employment and reasonable price stability. If errors occur (which is likely), no country would have to worry about its balance of payments, since market forces would ensure that the country's payments would always be in balance, even if it did not succeed in achieving relative price stability. Exchange rates would change continuously and smoothly, without the volatile movements associated with parity changes.

Developments in the last decade tested these claims. Contrary to predictions, movements in exchange rates have been volatile. Countries have worried acutely about their trade positions and about whether their currencies were appreciating or depreciating. The central banks in many countries have had to intervene in the exchange markets. Paradoxically, the payments imbalances have been substantially larger under the floating-rate system than they ever were under the pegged-rate system. Some of these imbalances were attributable to the surpluses of the OPEC countries. But the sum of the surpluses of all countries as a group was in some years more than twice as large as those of oil exporters. Some countries have sought to achieve a payments surplus as a basis for growth in their own money supplies; not every country has wanted to follow an independent monetary policy. Others have found depreciating their currency the most convenient way to stimulate exports and increase employment; their central banks have bought dollars in the exchange market to limit appreciation of their currencies so as to keep their goods competitive in world markets. Indeed, for some countries, export-led growth may be the preferred way to stimulate the economy. Some countries have a mercantilist preference for exporting goods and importing international money.

The assumption made by proponents of floating exchange rates—that once the rate was free to move in response to market forces, central banks would no longer be interested in the level of the exchange rate—has been proved invalid since 1973. Once the exchange rate is no longer subject to international rules, many governments are likely to manage or manipulate the rate as a useful instrument of policy and as a supplement to their monetary and fiscal policies.

To the extent that central banks do intervene in the exchange market, most buy and sell U.S. dollars. For example, the Bank of Japan might permit a depreciation of the yen to increase exports to the United States. But Germany and France would not welcome this move, since their competitive position in the U.S. market, the Japanese market, and their own domestic markets would be threatened. So they might respond by permitting *their* currencies to depreciate in terms of the dollar; the Japanese threat to German and French exports would be neutralized. One result would be the flooding of the U.S. market with Japanese, German, and French goods. U.S. exporters, in turn, would find themselves at an increasing competitive disadvantage in the foreign markets. And so, U.S. authorities would be under domestic pressure to depreciate the dollar.

The original objective behind the IMF rules of fixed exchange rates had been to prevent individual members from adopting such "beggar thy neighbor" policies. During the 1960s, when most countries were relatively successful in achieving full employment, this problem appeared unimportant. But it became significant in the worldwide recession of 1970 and 1971, when countries sought to import jobs. There is considerable evidence for the proposition that whenever countries find it difficult to attain domestic targets by changes in domestic financial policies, they will manipulate their international transactions.

In 1974 many countries allowed their currencies to become undervalued; they did not take the initiative to borrow the amounts necessary to finance the increase in their net oil imports. Instead, they financed their oil imports on a pay-as-you-go basis, which meant their currencies depreciated—in effect, they increased their exports to earn the dollars to pay for their oil imports. The lesson of the last decade is that few, if any, currencies float freely; most float subject to considerable intervention. Central bankers are not about to rely exclusively on market forces; most want to nudge such forces. The temperament of central bankers—and of their constituents—makes them reluctant to accept the market's verdict about what the appropriate exchange rate is, and how rapidly it should change.

In both 1977 and 1978, the U.S. payments deficits were so large—$30 to $40 billion—that any prediction of their magnitude four or five years before would have been considered lunacy. The explanation was straightforward. The United States was recovering more rapidly from the world recession than its trading partners, and so the U.S. demand for imports—and the foreign supply of exports—were increasing sharply. The dollar tended to depreciate. Yet, most other industrial countries were reluctant to accept the appreciation of their currencies because of the adverse impacts on prices and employment in their export- and import-competing industries.

In 1981 and 1982 by contrast, the U.S. dollar appreciated sharply, to levels of the early 1970s. Whereas in the late 1970s the European complaint to Washington was that the dollar was too weak, in the early 1980s the complaint was that the dollar was too strong. From the U.S. point of view, it began to seem that no U.S. policies could satisfy the Europeans—although the continual complaints may have instead reflected European apprehensiveness about their dependence on the United States. The experience demonstrates that the floating exchange rate system failed to live up to its advertisements.

Most of the minority of economists who favor pegged rates over floating rates would agree that a floating-rate system is workable and feasible, except perhaps in the relatively few periods when individual countries are subject to highly intense uncertainty about their political and economic futures. But the choice of exchange rate system is made by central bankers and government officials, not by economists. And judging by their behavior, most officials favor pegged exchange rates, with only a few exceptions; the experience with floating rates has been chastening. It is not an accident that the financial officials who favor floating rates are in the larger countries, while those in the smaller countries favor pegged rates.

Rules might be negotiated to prevent or limit central bank intervention under a floating-rate system. The problem, however, is complex—and complex international rules tend not to be workable. Like the U.S. commitment to a $35 gold parity, adherence to such rules would cease when the national interest was deemed overriding.

Before a great deal of progress can be made in devising a new set of rules, the disturbances including the changes in monetary policy, which have led to the sharp movements in the exchange rates, must be attenuated. Inflation rates will have to be reduced further, if not to the range of the 2 to 3 percent a year of the 1960s, at least to less than 5 percent a year.

Whither the System?

Several themes stand out among the events following the suspension of gold transactions among central banks in the last decades. First, central banks around the world want to stay in business; few central bankers are interested in phasing out their institutions in favor of an international central bank. Second, most central bankers, with the exception of those in Canada and Germany, abhor the uncertainties and the vagaries of floating exchange rates, except as an interim measure. They believe floating rates have worked far less smoothly than their academic proponents predicted. Third, recent events have reduced confidence in national government commitments which are necessary in any type of international system—an international central bank, an SDR arrangement, even floating rates. Fourth, within many countries bureaucratic regulation of international payments is now accepted as a means of balancing international payments and receipts. Bureaucrats tend to distrust the uncertainties of the market.

These factors limit the scope of reform. The difference between ambitious and modest proposals for reform centers on two variables. One is the size of payments imbalances that could occur before exchange rates changed or were changed, or before controls on international payments were altered to restore equilibrium or at least reduce imbalances. The size of imbalances is limited by the ability of deficit countries to finance them and by the willingness of surplus countries to export goods in exchange for international money. The second variable is how the inevitable changes in the exchange rates would occur: would they involve explicit changes in the rate, or would the changes be implicit, as bureaucrats tighten and loosen controls on international payments?

The unfavorable outcome, from the point of view of an integrated or open international economy, is a system with small scope for payments imbalances, with international payments balanced by variations in controls on international payments rather than by changes in the exchange rate, and with countries competing with each other to secure export and payments surpluses. One cost of this outcome would be that possible gains in economic efficiency from further integration of markets would diminish because of investors' uncertainties about how the system would evolve. A less measurable concern is that the "beggar thy neighbor" trade policies would produce political discord; economic problems are too central to be segmented from political relationships.

Economic Expertise Cannot Solve Political Problems

Each of the systems discussed—an exclusive international money, floating exchange rates, pegged rates, and controls—involves the tug of the international market against the pull of national constituencies. Most politicians win or lose elections on domestic issues or on broad foreign policy issues, not on whether exchange rates float or the price of gold is raised. The first two sets of proposals involve a change in the way countries establish their policies and exchange rates; the third, in contrast, revamps the arrangements to accommodate the pressing needs of individual countries. The fourth approach is less ambitious, although it might be more successful because it acknowledges the diverse interests and preferences of individual countries.

The international money problem reflects the fact that while communications technologies have unified the world of national monies, national economic structures and national values remain diverse. Changes in institutions may provide a more or a less favorable framework for reconciling these national differences, but they cannot eliminate the conflict posed by divergent national interests. The problem appears again and again in determining the rate of growth of international money, in setting appropriate exchange rates, and in determining the allocation and use of international money. The diversity of interests among countries is real. As long as some national monetary authorities have monopoly power, domestic political forces will compel them to exploit this power. Crises result when the established rules of the game limit domestic choices.

The historical record suggests that there will be a move back toward pegged exchange rates once inflation rates in the industrial countries decline and converge. This conclusion is reinforced by the extensive intervention of various central banks when currencies have been free to float.

The move toward pegged rates is likely to more nearly resemble pegging under the gold standard than under the Bretton Woods system. Individual countries will peg their currencies when movements in the exchange rates are small; pegging may be the climax of increasing intervention to limit large swings in the rates. Some countries are likely to peg sooner than others. Moreover, countries are likely to differ in the width of the support limits around their parities or central rates. After currencies are pegged, an international agreement might be negotiated formalizing the exchange market arrangements as they exist, rather than forcing sharp changes from the practices then prevailing.

Similarly, arrangements about the future international monetary role of gold will be negotiated after central banks begin to trade gold with each other at or near the market price. Rules will then be developed to formalize the practices. These practices will result from the give-and-take of trading monies and gold.

PART II

Living with the System

Bargains and the Money Game

One useful model of the world is that of the bazaar or market-place. People, firms, and even governments continually buy and sell, wheel and deal, seeking profits, wealth, and more elusive objectives, like power, esteem, and prestige. The chapters in Part I considered the evolution and operation of the international system and the costs and benefits of a national currency. The chapters in Part II, in contrast, consider some of the consequences of the segmentation of the world into multiple-currency areas. Some of the consequences are direct and result from a firm's advantage in being based in a country whose currency is at the top of the hit parade. Others are indirect and result from the division of the world into numerous currency areas, roughly congruent with the jurisdictions for the collection of taxes and the regulation of business and banking.

A recent phenomenon has been the growth of the Underground economy in the United States, the Black economy in Great Britain, and the Moonlight economy in Germany. There's an extensive Black economy in Moscow run by individuals with access to goods in short supply, including essential goods and consumer goods like Levi's and disco albums of Donna Summer and Michael Jackson. The terms differ, but the meanings are the same—one part of the economy develops outside the legal tax and regulatory framework. The significance of the worldwide growth of these "market economies" for the effectiveness of government policy is discussed in the next chapter.

Differences in national tax structures are frequently said to be unfair; firms in nearly every country believe they are at a competitive disadvantage in the international marketplace because their tax burdens are higher than those of their foreign counterparts. Taxes, like wages and rents, are a cost, and unless they are avoided or evaded, firms pay the cost and seek to raise selling prices accordingly. Firms establish subsidiaries in low-tax jurisdictions to avoid the costs of taxes; where possible, they shift profits to these jurisdictions. As a result, the tax payments of these firms are reduced and their after-tax profits are higher. But most taxes are paid: government expenditures must be financed. Whether the differences in the tax burdens imposed on firms and individuals might explain why German and Japanese firms have had such strong competitive positions in the international marketplace is discussed in chapter 14.

The impact of impending changes in the technology of the money payments process on the competitive position of commercial banks in different countries is discussed in chapter 15. Banking is a regulated industry in every country. Each country has its own set of regulations for commercial banks; these regulations are more extensive and detailed in some countries than in others. These regulations all have one common result: they raise the costs incurred by banks. Almost inevitably, the banks in the countries with the most extensive regulations are at a disadvantage in the international marketplace; if the transport costs of money are high, then this adverse cost differential has a negligible impact on their competitive positions. As costs of transporting money internationally decline, banks based in various countries can compete over a wider market area, so the cost differential will become more important. The buyers of the commercial banks' services will seek out low-cost producers of money, even if they are abroad. So the question of whether U.S., British, or Swiss banks are likely to have a competitive advantage as the market for bank services expands is of central importance.

As the economic costs of distance between countries decline, ideas and concepts developed in one country move rapidly to other countries. New ideas and concepts in finance are frequently developed in the United States before they are developed abroad. Some entrepreneurs, colloquially known as "import transformers," take ideas developed in the United States and convert them for use abroad. Bernie Cornfeld adapted the hard-sell U.S. mutual fund to the needs of savers in Europe and elsewhere to protect their fortunes against inflation. Cornfeld's idea succeeded brilliantly—for three or four years. His failure was triggered by the tight U.S. money policies and the worldwide drop in the demand for his product. Both Cornfeld's success and his failure (see chapter 16) were linked to the relationship between European financial markets and those in the United States.

The expansionary pressures of dynamic business firms, static national boundaries, and the reduction in costs of economic distance have facilitated the growth of multinational corporations—large, diversified firms with operating subsidiaries in many different countries. Production in these subsidiaries is often integrated across national borders; each plant produces components for its domestic market and for numerous foreign markets as well. In the late 1960s most multinational firms appeared to be U.S.-based; many Europeans and Canadians feared an eventual American domination of their domestic economies. Yet by the late 1970s, firms headquartered in Western Europe and Japan became very aggressive in the United States; British firms bought Howard Johnson's and Marshall Field & Co.; a German firm acquired A&P, while Japanese firms acquired various U.S. electronic firms. Why the pattern changed is discussed in chapter 17. The consequences of the growth of multinational companies on economic well-being are also considered.

The major economic success story of the last fifteen years has been Japan. At the end of the fifties, questions remained whether Japan would be able to overcome the handicaps of geographic isolation, the absence of raw materials, discrimination in foreign markets, and its own penchant for exclusiveness, including its reluctance to lower barriers to trade and investment. By the early 1970s, Japan was realizing trade and payments surpluses that threatened the stability of the Bretton Woods system. One pundit predicted that the Japanese economy would continue to grow at annual rates of 10 percent to 12 percent, so that in a decade or two, per capita incomes in Japan would be substantially higher than in the United States and other Western industrial countries like Sweden and Switzerland. A large number of competing explanations have been offered for the remarkable economic performance of Japan. These competing models of the Japanese economy are discussed in chapter 18.

Much of the discussion in previous chapters implicitly assumed that the world consists of market-oriented economies which have reasonably similar per capita incomes. But not all countries fall in this group. A substantial part of the economic world relies on planning rather than market forces for answers to basic economic questions; the Soviet Union, Poland, Rumania, and other Eastern European countries are in this group. These countries participate in the international economy—they trade extensively both with each other and with the market economies. Since private firms cannot import and export for profit as in the market economies, other institutional mechanisms are necessary for arranging trade.

The financial relations between the planned economies of Eastern Europe and the market-oriented Western economies, as well as the relations between the Soviet and other Eastern European countries, are discussed in chapter 19. Business is done and bargains are struck. Imbalances in trade are settled by payments of money, frequently dollars. Exchange rates are inevitable, although they are not used, as in the West, as a mechanism for balancing receipts and payments. Nevertheless, the question is whether the exchange rate is a fair price. In trade among Western countries, the fair price is the free market price or the official parity. But since there are no free markets within Communist countries, some other mechanism is needed to determine domestic prices, export and import prices, and the exchange rates. And some Eastern European countries believe that the prices used in their trade with the Soviet Union are not in their own best interests.

Most members of the United Nations are developing countries with per capita incomes which range from $100 to $800 to $1,000 or more a year. These countries are highly diverse. But with the exception of a few oil-producing countries, most of these countries have been substantial importers of capital from the developed countries; their foreign debts have escalated.

The financial relationships between the market-oriented industrial countries and the developing countries are discussed in chapter 20. Private foreign investment within the developing countries has been growing, and receipts of the developing countries from various forms of foreign aid—grants, technical assistance, export credits, and long-term development loans—have grown even more rapidly. These countries' debts to government agencies in the industrial countries and to international institutions have been growing at the rate of 15 percent a year, or about three to four times faster than their exports and national incomes. Annual payments of interest and loan reduction principal have already exceeded the repayment ability of many countries. However, none has gone bankrupt; instead, new loans are issued so that countries can repay the older debts. This pattern may continue indefinitely, for default would be costly to the lenders.

Several themes run through the chapters of Part II. The costs of economic distance are declining; market areas are expanding beyond national boundaries. Differences in business frameworks that were insignificant when the costs of distance were high are now becoming much more significant and are likely to be a cause of friction among nations. While pressures for harmonization and coordination will develop, counterpressures for retaining the advantages of the costs of distance will also rise.

13

The Underground Economies and
the Bureaucratic Imperative

One way to get the trains to run on time is to straighten the tracks. Another is to use more powerful, or more reliable locomotives. A less costly way—indeed the cheapest way—is to lengthen the time allowed for the journey. In the 1920s the Chicago–New York trip on the Twentieth Century Limited took fifteen hours; passengers got rebates if the train was late, with the payments scaled to the length of the delay. In 1982, on Amtrak, the same journey took twenty-two hours—if you're lucky. The mileage between Chicago and New York is a constant, more or less. If the trains can't adjust to the timetables, then the timetables must adjust to the trains. Mussolini's last claim to fame was that he got the trains to run on time; but mostly what he did was lengthen the timetables.

Improvements in transport technology almost certainly should have led to a decline in the time required for most trips over the last half-century. Fifty years ago, air travel between Chicago and New York took two days with an overnight in Cleveland. The same trip today takes ninety minutes, or less, unless you're stacked over O'Hare. Even with the 55-miles-per-hour speed limit, the driving time, New York to Chicago, is about fifteen hours. Forty years ago, the trip took eighteen to twenty hours.

Japan has its Bullet Trains between Tokyo and Osaka, while France has the TVG between Paris and Lyon. Even Britain has some very new, very fast trains—although not as fast as the TVG. Yet even where the trains run faster, they usually run at a loss—and when they run slower, they almost certainly do. Amtrak costs the average American taxpayer about $25 a year.

One of the paradoxes of the last several decades is the increase in the size of government in most countries and the apparent decline in the government's efficiency in delivering services. The U.S. Immigration and Naturalization Service finds it difficult to prevent illegal entry into the United States. The estimates are that there are from three to seven million "illegals" in the United States; because they don't have the right papers, no one knows. Some estimates place the number at twenty million—equivalent to the population of California or Canada. The Internal Revenue Service finds it difficult to collect taxes; tax revenues would be $50 billion more—or 10 percent higher—if there were 100 percent compliance. There are horror stories of the John Smiths who continue to collect Social Security ten years after they've passed away or the John Does who can't manage to collect their unemployment compensation checks because the system has lost their employment records. The Food Stamp program was established to reduce government-owned surplus food stocks and at the same time to provide better nourishment for the poor; now food stamps are a second currency and often a source of considerable fraud. Government-owned firms—the airlines and railroads and steel mills—frequently incur losses year after year after year; there's pressure to provide jobs and employment security, and besides, the annual operating deficits can be buried in government budgets.

There are similar horror stories about the shortcomings of large organizations in the private sector; they're not unique to government. Patients get lost in hospitals; once a year, the appendix is removed from a person in the hospital waiting for a tonsillectomy. The power companies turn off the electricity at the wrong house. Deliveries are made to the wrong apartment. Yet governmental inefficiency may still be unique for several reasons—the governments are usually much larger than these private groups, government agencies are responsive to political factors rather than to profit motives, and employees in most government agencies have more job security than those in private firms.

The growth in the size of government is a worldwide phenomenon. The expansion of government activities is associated with noble purposes—providing medical care and housing and education and roads and income support. And everyone wants more of these programs, for the value of services exceeds the price paid for them—but not the cost of production. Yet these expenditures must be financed. And there are only a couple of ways to get the money to pay for these expenditures—either taxes must be raised, or governments must borrow and pay interest to the lenders. Few people want to pay higher taxes. Because "needs" are so large relative to taxes, the governments frequently borrow. Some governments borrow to get the money to pay the interest on the amounts they borrowed last year and the year before. Yet there are limits to the ability to borrow just as there are limits to the ability to tax—as New York City learned to its great dismay in 1975.

Governments are also unique in that very few taxes are directly related to the value of services provided. In the private sector individuals and firms set prices to cover production costs. If prices are below costs, bankruptcy may be inevitable. And if prices are above costs, then new firms enter the industry. With governments, taxes paid and services provided with the funds from these taxes are disconnected. So there's an incentive on the part of J. Q. Public to reach for the services and skip the taxes. And that's also true on the part of the politicians—there are more votes out there providing more and better services to the public—and higher wages and salaries to the teachers and po-licemen and army officers and civil servants—than in raising taxes to pay for these goodies.

As taxes have increased, the incentives to avoid, evade, ignore, side-step, forget, escape, and noncomply have increased. One measure of the reduced effectiveness of government is the growth of Underground economies in the United States, Great Britain, France, Germany, and most of the other industrial na-tions. The story is pervasive. Government taxes income so it's worthwhile to avoid or evade the taxes. Individuals engage in barter in the belief that these transactions aren't income—or at least they don't leave a trail of paper that provides revenue col-lectors with evidence that would satisfy the courts. Government rules restrict or prohibit profitable activities, so the rules are evaded or avoided; sometimes it's the production of—sometimes the provision of—moonshine.

The Underground economy includes three different types of transactions. Firms and individuals have undeclared legal in-come. Much of this undeclared legal income is in cash. But occa-sionally, some of this taxable income may be in kind, a form of barter. Some of the income may be taxable income, some may not. The optometrist swaps a set of contact lenses with his car mechanic for a motor overhaul. Doctors, dentists, and pharma-cists treat each other to professional discounts. Cooks and wait-resses may get several free meals per day along with their money incomes. The parish provides the minister with a house. Univer-sities provide scholarships for faculty. In some types of firms and in some countries, employees have "rights" to fiddles or perks; it's recognized that they will use the company's samples, or its stamps, or its phones, for their personal use. Such goods are part of their pay. But it's undeclared, illegal income. Finally, there's the (illegal) income associated with illegal activities—transac-tions in heroin and marijuana and other drugs, prostitution, pro-duction and sale of "white lightning" and other alcoholic beverages.

The size of the Underground economies in the United States and other countries is important, if only because a rapid growth in these various types of transactions might partially offset the slow measured growth in the legitimate or aboveground economy. Moreover, to the extent that participants in the Underground economy don't pay their taxes, the overall tax burdens are higher.

Estimates vary extensively on the size of these economies, as do the approaches toward estimating the size. Governments usually have an incentive to provide low estimates. Underground transactions are more pervasive where individuals traditionally deal in cash—in rural areas and in low-income areas in central cities. And where the activity is illegal, the transactions are mostly in cash. Some estimate that illegal drugs are a $20 to $30 billion a year business in the United States—or about one percent of GNP. Marijuana is said to be the third largest cash crop in the U.S. economy, after soybeans and wheat. Gambling is about half as large. Prostitution is valued as a $1 to $2 billion a year activity; those making the estimates probably multiply the number of participants by the average wage. These estimates are significantly smaller than those for undeclared legal incomes—the amount of tax evasion. But even if estimates of illegal incomes are half or a third of their "true value," the total is still small in terms of the aboveboard economy. And even if these transactions have increased very rapidly, the amounts involved are so small that the impact on the aggregate level of activity is negligible.

The growth of the Underground economies reflects the decline in the effectiveness of government regulation—and in respect for the rules. Bracket creep has increased with inflation; the tax bites have increased more rapidly than the increases in income. The smaller the effectiveness of a government in implementing its own rules and collecting its taxes, the larger the likelihood that firms and individuals will enter the Underground economy. The counterpart to the reduced ability to collect taxes is the reduced effectiveness in the allocation of expenditures. When government awards money, there are more and more instances of fraud. Each major city has its "Welfare Queen," who manages to collect twelve or fourteen checks a month under fourteen different names.

Why Don't the Trains Run on Time?

Consider some of the other elements in the decline in the effectiveness of government management. The quality of government-produced services has decreased. In Britain, individuals have opted out of the socialized medical system and bought private services either to reduce waiting time or to acquire a service that they believe to be of higher quality. Within the United States, the concern about the decline in the level of public education has led to an increase in expenditure on private education, especially in cities and especially at the elementary and secondary school level. Similarly, with regard to the expenditures on police and security, stores and universities and colleges and churches and businesses have developed their own police forces—which frequently include many part-timers whose primary employment is with a public police force. These individuals are "moonlighting"—working at a second job.

A second element is the decline in the quality of the public infrastructure. Libraries are closed because the governments cannot pay for both books and salaries. There are more potholes; the quality of roads and sewers decline because government is caught between the limited ability to tax and the demands of government employees for higher salaries. Safety on the New York subway and the Chicago El has declined. The paradox is that the salaries in the public sector increase, even as the quality of the services provided declines. While wages in the government sectors are increasing, they increase even more rapidly in the private sector. There appears to be a cost-push element in the public sector wages; the public sector is well organized. So relatively more qualified employees are often shifted to the private sector.

Fiscal deficits are associated with inflation, which leads to overvalued currencies. Overvalued currencies require exchange controls—barriers or tariffs or other controls which separate the domestic market for goods and services from the world market. Such controls enable the governments—and their friends—to buy foreign exchange on terms more favorable than those for business firms and individuals. Lots of countries have used these controls—Great Britain, the United States, and a large number of developing countries. But these measures are effective only to the extent that earners of foreign exchange are not tempted to jump the fence and sell their export earnings at the higher price available in the free market. Hence a pegged exchange rate is rather like a tax on the earnings of foreign exchange. If the currency is overvalued, of course, countries with floating currencies might also use these taxes to increase their own earnings.

The governments with the largest expenditures tend to be borrowers. And for a while at least, they tend to borrow internationally as well as domestically. Thus, when the United States has a large fiscal deficit and the dollar tends to be weak in the foreign exchange market, foreign governments lend to the United States, if only because they intervene to limit the depreciation of the dollar. Their intervention means the U.S. trade deficit is larger than it otherwise might have been, with the consequence that this deficit has to be financed.

One link between the Underground economy and international money flows is the movement of suitcase money. Individuals move currency from high-tax jurisdictions to low-tax jurisdictions; this movement shifting money out of the country makes it much more difficult for the tax collector to prove individuals have underreported income. Or they move currency in suitcases to circumvent domestic exchange controls; they want to get the funds into some other currency area. There are other links—one is that the Underground economies flourish in countries with high tax rates, because these countries have high levels of government expenditures. But the authorities find it easier to increase expenditures than tax revenues. So they borrow. Both taxing and borrowing take money from the public—although taxing is more directly coercive than borrowing.

14

International Tax Avoidance—
A Game for the Rich

Superstar Miss X is a mobile factor of production who has engaged in tax avoidance. She lived in Switzerland and worked elsewhere—Mexico, London, Rome, or Budapest. Her dramatic abilities yielded a magnificent income, nearly all from sources outside Switzerland. Swiss taxes on her income were much lower than U.S. taxes would be if she lived in Hollywood, or than British taxes would be if she lived in London.

Miss X and the Swiss struck a bargain. The Swiss sold Miss X tax-avoidance services—the right to live in a low-tax jurisdiction. Miss X bought this service because she liked the higher after-tax income; better to live where taxes are low than where they are high. The Swiss profit from the transaction, for the taxes paid by Miss X greatly exceeded her demand on local public services. In effect, she subsidized the Swiss. Had she lived in London, Swiss tax revenues would have been lower, and the Swiss would have had to tax themselves more heavily to provide themselves with the same level of public services.

Switzerland is also a tax haven for other mobile factors of production, for Swiss taxes are substantially lower than taxes in most other developed countries. But Switzerland is only one among many tax havens. Liechtenstein, Panama, the Bahamas, the Netherlands Antilles, and the Cayman Islands offer similar services. Tax havens are established to attract income from foreign sources. Competition among tax havens keeps the tax rates on foreign-source income low; if the rates in one haven are higher than those in other havens, relatively little foreign-source income will be attracted.

Tax havens are only one example of tax avoidance. England's richest lords leave London for low-tax jurisdictions to avoid the very high British death duties. U.S. and German firms issue bonds in Luxembourg because interest income there is not subject to withholding tax; buyers of the bonds want to avoid the tax, or the bother of getting a refund on the tax collected at the source. U.S. professors teach in Canada for two years and avoid both U.S. and Canadian income taxes; residence outside the United States for more than eighteen months means they are not subject to U.S. taxes, and Canada does not tax foreign professors on their Canadian income during the first two years of residence. Most individuals, however, cannot move to low-tax jurisdictions without suffering a serious loss in income; their occupations tie them to a particular city or county. Only when the possible tax savings are large relative to the costs of shifting residences do individuals move.

One alternative to moving to a low-tax jurisdiction is to shift income there. Some London-based professors have their royalty and consulting incomes paid to bank accounts in Zurich or Liechtenstein. When a firm uses an Antillian or a Zugian (Zug is a Swiss canton near Zurich, one of the busiest havens in Europe) tax haven, the transfer price—the price at which its affiliates in several countries buy and sell goods and services from each other—may be managed to shift income to a tax haven. For example, a U.S. firm may export goods to its German affiliate through a sales subsidiary in the Bahamas. The parent charges the subsidiary an unusually low price, thereby shifting income from the U.S. parent to the Bahamian subsidiary. The subsidiary charges a high price to the German affiliate, thereby shifting income from Germany to the Bahamas. So the firm's taxable income in the Bahamas increases, while its taxable incomes in the United States and Germany decline. The goods never get to the Bahamas; indeed, neither the documents nor money go there.

Both the U.S. tax collector and the German tax collector know about tax havens. They scan the prices used in transactions between the Bahamian subsidiaries and the domestic offices of the firm to forestall flagrant attempts to avoid taxes. But many intrafirm transactions have no readily available commercial counterparts and no ready-reference market prices, so firms must necessarily be arbitrary in their pricing. Similarly, firms must be arbitrary in their allocation of common overhead costs among their branches and subsidiaries in various countries.

Tax havens are profitable despite the ever-watchful eyes of the tax collector; sales subsidiaries based in tax havens are not usually created unless the probable savings in taxes more than compensates for the legal fees charged by high-priced lawyers (lawyers, incidentally, who frequently received their most valuable legal education about taxation on foreign income while working for the tax collector). But if the use—or abuse—of tax havens were so extensive that governments felt a serious loss from runaway income and forgone taxes, transfer pricing would be examined more closely.

Even without tax havens, differences among national tax systems might be important for the pattern of international transactions. All governments tax, but in different ways and at different rates. They tax income, both personal and corporate, and assets, including real property like houses, land, machinery, and clothing. They tax interest, dividends, and capital gains on land and houses and financial assets. They tax transactions—sales, purchases, imports and exports, births and deaths. Most governments have a virtually unlimited need for tax revenues; more revenues mean larger expenditures, and larger expenditures enhance political support.

But taxes have a cost, for they diminish political support. So each government seeks to increase its tax revenue at minimal cost in terms of political support. Ideally, governments would like to tax foreigners to subsidize domestic residents, which is what tax havens are all about.

Not unexpectedly, the tax rates and the tax base—the types of incomes and transactions which are taxed—differ sharply among countries. These differences are frequently offered as an explanation as to why some nations grow slowly and others grow rapidly, why the exports of some countries grow more rapidly than those of others, or why money flows from some countries to others. In nearly every country, businessmen allege that they are at a disadvantage in international trade because they are taxed more heavily than their foreign competitors. This is another way of saying that they would be better off if their tax burdens were smaller. Like wages, interest rates, and the cost of electricity, taxes obviously have some economic impact, and firms seek to raise their selling prices to cover these costs. The question is whether differences among countries in tax structures and tax rates have a significant economic impact.

Do Differences in Taxes Make a Difference?

The revenue needs of nations differ because the sizes of their public sectors differ. Where the government's role is extensive, tax rates are necessarily high. The larger a nation's fiscal needs, the higher its tax rates and the larger the range of incomes and transactions which are taxed to generate the required revenue.

Everyone agrees that taxes should be fair. Fairness, after all, is like motherhood. The disagreement arises over what is fair—

over whether the government should or should not be involved in particular activities, and how these activities, as well as the total cost of all government activities, should be financed.

Governments differ from private businesses in one important aspect: governments generally offer certain goods and services (except alcohol) below their cost of production. Many of these goods and services are given away; some are sold, but at prices substantially below cost. But while particular goods and services can be sold below cost, the total supply of goods and services cannot be sold below production costs, unless a country can borrow abroad indefinitely. To the extent that some goods and services are available below cost, the prices of other goods and services must exceed their costs of production, and the subsidy to the first group and the tax on the second group must more or less match.

An individual can get a free lunch; society as a whole cannot. Someone pays for the activities of the government. Not surprisingly, one reason for having government provide certain goods and services is that it may be possible to get someone else to pay most or all of the cost. A free lunch at school is cheaper than a cash lunch; attractive as a free lunch may be, however, *someone* has to pay for it.

A sales tax or a value-added tax has a direct impact on raising the final selling price. Similarly, a corporate income tax almost certainly leads firms to raise the prices at which they sell their output. Even personal income taxes might be considered taxes on the sale of labor; the after-tax income of the individual is below the pretax income. Many individuals are primarily interested in their after-tax income; if the tax bite is too large, they may work less, or not at all, or fiddle with their tax returns.

The size of government is a good measure of the amount of goods and services that individuals have chosen to consume collectively. In Western societies, the amount of goods and services supplied by the government ranges from 20 to 60 percent of the total goods and services produced in the economy.

223

The cliché has it that the amount of goods and services supplied by the government is a response to the demands of the society. But the cliché is too easy; some part of government output reflects the ability of various producers to get support for increased output. Most of the benefits of government-produced goods and services go to selected groups—farmers receive agricultural extension services, students get free milk for school lunches, and professors receive research stipends from organizations like the National Science Foundation—while the costs fall broadly on the taxpayers. Each small group sees its own interests advanced by seeking additional benefits; the value of these benefits will almost certainly exceed their share of costs. For as long as the choice is biased and the production of additional government goods and services is dissociated from their costs, advantages may accrue to the government and to those members of the bureaucracy associated with the extension of new services.

A glance at the data in table 14.1 suggests that U.S. corpora-

TABLE 14.1

Comparative National Taxation, 1979

	Percentage of Total Taxes from:				5 Taxes as Percentage of GNP	6 Corporate Taxes as Percentage of GNP
	1 Corporations	2 Households	3 Sales and Other Indirect	4 Social Security		
United States[a]	12.3	32.7	31.2	23.8	32.6	4.0
Canada	12.1	28.4	50.2	9.3	36.0	4.4
Great Britain	7.8	27.5	49.3	15.4	39.5	3.1
Germany	5.4	24.0	38.1	32.5	42.7	2.3
France	3.7	14.5	41.4	40.4	43.4	1.6
Japan	17.7	19.9	34.8	27.6	32.1	5.7
Sweden	1.9	37.8	36.5	23.8	57.7	1.1
Switzerland	7.1	34.8	29.7	28.4	33.3	2.4

SOURCE: Organization for Economic Cooperation and Development, *National Accounts of OECD Countries,* 1979 ed. (Paris, 1981).
[a] Figures for the United States are from 1978. Figures for all other countries are from 1979.

tions are subject to a heavier tax burden than are most foreign firms, since corporate taxes constitute a higher proportion of total taxes (column 1) in the United States than in most other countries, except Japan. Similarly, taxes on households (column 2) account for a higher percentage of total taxes in the United States than elsewhere, except Sweden and Switzerland. But it would be a mistake to infer that the burden on U.S. corporate and personal taxpayers is greater than that on taxpayers in Great Britain, Germany, and the Netherlands. Conclusions about tax rates on corporate income and personal income cannot be drawn from the share of government receipts from each type of tax.

One reason why the ratio of tax receipts to GNP is lower in the United States than abroad is that foreign governments spend a higher proportion of their national incomes than does the United States (column 5). Their revenue needs are greater. A second is that corporate incomes—the tax base—are lower abroad than in the United States. If, for example, corporate tax rates were identical in each country, then revenues generated by the corporate profits tax would be smaller abroad than in the United States because the corporate sectors are smaller abroad. Many of the types of firms that are in the private sector in the United States, including utilities, transportation companies, and even some manufacturing companies, are in the government sector abroad. Moreover, corporate profits may be lower abroad. Similarly, the tax base for personal incomes is smaller abroad; a much larger proportion of taxpayers have incomes so low that they are exempted from personal income taxes. Thus, tax rates on personal incomes are much higher in Great Britain than in the United States, but because personal incomes are lower, taxes on personal income constitute a smaller share of GNP.

Comparison of national tax rates is a necessary first step in determining the impact of taxes on the competitive position of a country. The U.S. corporate tax rates, like those in most other developed countries, are in the 40 to 50 percent range. Italy has

TABLE 14.2

Corporate Tax Rates (*percentages*)

	United States	Great Britain	Germany	France	Japan
Effective Corporate Taxes	28.6	34.2	19.2	15.8	29.8
Posted Tax Rate	46	52	56[a]	50	40[a]
			36[b]		30[b]

SOURCE: Ernest and Whinney (January 1981).
[a] Undistributed.
[b] Distributed.

a lower rate, and Switzerland has a much lower rate. However, definitions of taxable income differ, largely because some countries permit their firms to depreciate their plant and equipment more rapidly than others. When depreciation is more rapid, expenses are higher, profits are smaller, and tax liability and tax payments are lower—even if the tax rates are the same. Moreover, countries differ in the scope of investment tax credits extended to business firms; such credits reduce the effective tax rates. The impact of these devices is to reduce the effective tax rate significantly below the posted rate.

Taxes can be avoided, evaded, or paid. Avoidance is legal, although there are costs. Subsidiaries in tax havens have to be established, and lawyers can be expensive. Evasion of taxes, which is not legal, incurs costs and risks; in some countries, payments to the tax collectors in their personal capacity may obviate the need for much larger payments to the collectors in their official capacity. Still, evaders are caught, fined or jailed, and ostracized.

Despite the variations in corporate tax rates, only individuals pay taxes. Corporations may have an infinite life, but they do not feel, suffer, breed, or smile; only people do. Corporations do not "pay" taxes—they collect funds to pay these taxes from their customers, their shareholders, their employees, or their suppliers. The burden may fall, not on the corporation's owners (as a decline in their after-tax incomes), but on the customers, who pay higher prices, or on the suppliers, who receive lower prices. Thus General Motors pays a tax of 46 percent on its corporate profits; until 1971 it also paid a sales tax of 7 percent on its sales of automobiles. Ostensibly, the corporate tax falls on the profits, while the excise tax falls on the consumer. But GM probably has raised its selling prices to obtain funds to pay these taxes. Similarly, firms do not "pay" social security taxes—they collect them from their employees. Social security taxes and sales taxes are alternative—and additional—ways of taxing individuals.

The large variety of taxes befuddles the taxpayers: if they were aware that 20 or 30 or even 40 percent of their income was taxed, they might be more cautious about further increases in government expenditures. And if all of their taxes were collected by a straightforward income tax or consumption tax or value-added tax, they would have greater incentive to calculate the payoffs from avoidance or evasion.

Thus the legal form of these taxes should be distinguished from their economic impact. The corporate tax and sales tax fall directly on the consumer if the demand for the product is sufficiently strong. Thus consider the impact of a possible increase in the corporate tax rate: GM would probably raise its selling prices to offset higher corporate taxes, so that the after-tax return to GM stockholders would remain pretty much the same in the long run if not immediately. Similarly, the depletion allowance, which allowed oil companies to reduce their tax payments, almost certainly meant a lower price for gasoline; when the allowance was reduced in 1975, the gasoline price went up modestly.

However, a simple example demonstrates that taxes on corporate profits are not likely to have a major impact on selling prices. Assume that the profits for firm X are 10 percent of its sales. Suddenly the government levies a corporate tax of 50 percent; previously there had been no corporate tax. If all the tax is passed forward to consumers, then the pretax profits-to-sales ratio must rise to 20 percent to cover the tax liability; the firm's selling price will increase by 10 percent. If, instead, the profits-to-sales ratio is 20 percent, then the selling price rises by 20 percent; if the ratio is 5 percent, then the selling price rises by 5 percent. And so on. Note that the imposition of a high corporate tax has only a modest impact on the selling price, except when the profits-to-sales ratio is high. The profits-to-sales ratios vary by industry; within the United States, the average for many industries falls within the range of 2 to 6 percent. For firms with a 4 percent ratio, the impact of the introduction of a 50 percent tax would raise the selling price (again assuming all of the tax is passed forward to the consumer) by 4 percent.

Changing the corporate income tax rate is thus likely to have an effect—probably modest—on the competitive position of firms in different industries. Assume another extreme example—the corporate income tax rate goes to zero. Eventually, after a period of adjustment, firms would reduce the price at which they sell their products, so after-tax profits would be the same after the tax is eliminated as before. One consequence would be that price reductions in industries with high profits-to-sales ratios would be larger than those in industries in which these ratios are low, so the first group of industries would probably expand relative to the second. A second consequence is that the ability of the most profitable firms in an industry to cut prices would be enhanced relative to the ability of the less profitable firms, and the failure rate for the marginal firms in each industry would probably increase. Paradoxically, the corporate tax rewards the inefficient, for their tax bills are much lower, relative to their sales, than is the case for their more successful competitors.

But taxes are only part of the story. Governments tax in order to spend. And while taxes raise costs to firms, government expenditures (or at least some of them) may lower those costs. Public expenditures can reduce the need for private expenditures, reducing a firm's costs. Thus, government expenditures on roads lower transportation costs for manufacturers. Expenditures on fire departments reduce the need to purchase similar protection privately, while expenditures on education reduce the need for firms to train their own employees. If government expenditures finance the deficits of nationalized corporations, their selling prices are lower and their customers are subsidized.

Thus, the impact of tax changes on the prices of goods produced by corporations depends on how much of the tax is passed on in the form of higher prices and on whether there is any cost-reducing impact of associated government expenditures. Most economists believe that most or all of the corporate tax is shifted forward to consumers, except for a brief interval after the tax rate is changed. Few economists have attempted to analyze the impact of government expenditures on selling prices.

Corporate tax rates are likely to have a significant impact on international trade only if the tax rates are much higher in some countries than in others. The differences in corporate tax rates among industrial countries are generally smaller than 10 percentage points. For most industries, differences in tax rates can explain only a very small part of the differences in selling prices among countries, except for a few industries in which the profits-to-sales ratio is much higher than average.

Much of the pattern of international trade and investment reflects differences in real costs: bananas can be produced in Ecuador at a lower cost than in Chicago because nature has been more generous with the requisite climate and soil in Ecuador. But steel can be produced at a lower cost in Chicago, since the iron ore is at one end of Lake Michigan and the coal is near the other. The differentials in real cost attributable to the uneven beneficence of nature and the variations in capital accumulation are much more significant in explaining price differentials than the differences in national tax systems.

An increase in taxes in a country, like an increase in wages, may affect its international competitive position in the short run; its economic position in the long run will be unaffected, for the exchange rate will change to offset the price-raising impact of higher taxes on the demand for domestic products. The competitive positions of some firms may improve and those of other firms may worsen, but the overall impact on the country is not likely to be economically significant.

True, if national cost structures become more nearly similar, then differences among the national tax systems will become increasingly important. The reduction of any barrier to mobility of goods and capital would make the differences in tax systems more significant. Then the search for low-tax jurisdictions would increase. And increased attention would undoubtedly be given to tax harmonization and tax coordination among governments, so as to minimize shifts in productive activities among jurisdictions. Inevitably, international arrangements would be established to harmonize national tax structures and to prevent competitive tax practices.

Taxes on Foreign Income

Tax collectors have a voracious appetite. They are continually hunting for new sources of revenue. So they tax firms and individuals on a wide range of their domestic activities. In some countries, they even tax firms and individuals on their foreign income.

Here it is useful to distinguish among three different kinds of taxes: those levied on the domestic incomes of nonresident firms and individuals by the domestic government, those levied on the foreign incomes of nonresident firms and individuals by the domestic government, and those levied on the foreign incomes of domestic firms and individuals. The U.S. government taxes the U.S. income of foreign firms and individuals as if they were domestic residents. Most foreign governments follow the same approach; occasionally governments, especially in the developing countries, may give tax concessions so that foreign investors are spared from paying taxes for five or ten years. No government attempts to tax the foreign income of nonresidents, except insofar as they buy domestically produced products and pay the tax component that is implicit in the price.

Governments differ significantly in the way they tax the foreign income of residents—income which has almost certainly been taxed in the country in which it was earned. The U.S. government taxes the foreign income of U.S. residents as if it were domestic income. The taxpayer calculates his tax liability to Uncle Sam using the U.S. definition of income and the U.S. tax rate. He can then receive a credit against his U.S. tax liability for foreign income taxes paid, as long as the foreign tax rate is not above the U.S. tax rate.

If a foreign affiliate is organized as a branch, the tax payments due the U.S. Treasury must be paid when the income is earned; if the affiliate is organized as a subsidiary—that is, if it is incorporated abroad—U.S. taxes are due when the income is repatriated. The opportunity to delay the tax payments on foreign income, known as tax deferral, is like an interest-free loan; in effect, the right to delay the tax payment means that the effective tax rate on foreign income is below the posted tax rate. At an interest rate of 10 percent, a tax liability of $100 has a value of $50 if the payment can be delayed eight years.

Tax deferrals and tax havens provide firms with attractive and flexible opportunities. Thus, the profitable foreign subsidiaries of a U.S. firm might be tiered—organized as the subsidiaries of a Swiss or Bahamian subsidiary. Profits in high-tax countries could be diverted to the tax haven, and the funds could in turn be invested in another subsidiary which is rapidly growing and needs additional funds from the parent. Transfer pricing can be used to divert profits to the tax haven; the taxes on these profits are then deferred.

A perennial issue is how to tax domestic residents with foreign income relative to domestic residents with domestic income. The equity approach is that domestic taxpayers should be taxed on the same basis, regardless of the source or type of their income. Domestic income and foreign income, earned income and unearned income, interest income on state and local securities and corporate dividends would all be taxed at the same rate.

It is hard to disagree with the general equity principle. But practical problems arise when the taxable foreign income must be defined. Is it foreign income before taxes are paid the foreign tax collector, or is it after-tax income? If it is foreign income after taxes, what recognition should be given to foreign income taxes paid? The current approach is to give a domestic taxpayer a credit against domestic tax liability for foreign income taxes paid: foreign tax payments reduce domestic payments on a dollar-for-dollar basis. An alternative is to treat foreign taxes paid as a deduction or cost in computing domestic tax liability: foreign tax payments of a dollar would reduce domestic tax liability by about 50 cents. In this case, the total taxes paid to the two tax authorities would be higher than if the credit approach were used. Foreign investment would thus be discouraged for two reasons. First, income on foreign investments would be taxed more heavily than income on domestic investments; and second, income earned by U.S. investors in various foreign countries would be taxed more heavily than if the same incomes were earned by a foreigner.

From the U.S. point of view, it might seem desirable to discourage foreign investment, since the income accrues to the United States—both to the owners of the investment and to the U.S. tax authorities—only after taxes have been paid abroad. In some cases the after-tax return to the United States might be larger than if the same funds had been earned in the United States; in most cases, however, the reverse must be true.

The U.S. firms that invest overseas are not impressed with this logic; their own interests are best served by maximizing their profits. From their point of view, if you have seen one tax collector, you have seen them all. Given that they must pay a given amount of tax, they are largely indifferent to whether they pay taxes to Uncle Sam or to his foreign competitors. So the firms engage in a marketing campaign, stressing the favorable effect of their foreign investments on the U.S. balance of payments and U.S. foreign policy.

Thus, there is an inevitable conflict in the design of tax policy, depending on whose interest is to be served. The cosmopolitan or world economic welfare is served if investment funds are allocated between domestic and foreign alternatives on the basis of their pretax rates of return; the implication is that taxes on foreign income should be the same as those on domestic income. The national economic welfare is served only if the rates of return to the economy on foreign investment, after payment of foreign taxes, exceeds the pretax return on domestic investment. From the firm's point of view, it should be sufficient that it pays taxes to the countries in which it operates; there should be no residual tax liability to U.S. authorities. From the point of view of U.S. taxpayers, the taxes on foreign income should be the same as on domestic income; if foreign tax rates are lower than U.S. rates, then an additional tax is due the U.S. Treasury.

Taxes on Money

Medieval kings had a simple technique for raising money. They filled a leather bag with gold coins and shook the bag vigorously. The edges of the coins began to wear away, and gold dust began to collect in the bag. The gold dust was then sent to the mint for manufacture into new coins—and the coins which had been in the bag continued to circulate at their face value. In effect, the king was taxing the holders of gold coins by shaving their commodity value. Sovereigns have been taxing the holders of money ever since.

Currently, sovereigns are more sophisticated in their approach to taxing banks: they provide banks with a monopoly position by limiting entry into the banking business, and then they tax the monopoly profits. (See chapter 15 for a discussion of competition among banks.) As a consequence, borrowers pay higher interest rates on their loans than if competition were more extensive. Similarly, depositors receive lower interest rates and a smaller supply of "free" services than if banks competed more aggressively for deposits. Bank profits are higher than they would be if banking were a competitive industry with unimpeded entry of new firms.

The "excess" profits resulting from barriers to entry are "taxed" by requirements that banks hold certain assets, usually government securities or deposits, at the central bank. For example, U.S. commercial banks must hold from 3 to 18 percent of their assets as deposits in the Federal Reserve System; they earn no interest on these deposits. Without such a requirement, these commercial banks would have more income-earning assets, and the banks' revenues would be greater. And higher revenues would permit the bank to pay higher interest rates on deposits. So the banks would gain in the first instance, but most of these gains would then be competed away.

The significance of this implicit tax on banks' earnings depends on the proportion of bank assets invested in non-interest-bearing funds and on the interest rates available on other assets. For example, assume central bank A requires that its domestic banks hold 14 percent of their assets in non-interest-bearing reserves or deposits while central bank B has a similar requirement of 4 percent; assume also that the average interest rate on bank assets in countries A and B is 10 percent. The revenues of commercial banks in B are 10 percent higher than those in A—so the interest rates paid depositors might be 10 percent higher. If banks in A pay an average interest rate of 6 percent to their depositors, those in B can pay 6.60 percent and still be no worse off.

If commercial banks hold non-interest-paying deposits in the central bank, the central bank in effect receives a loan from these banks on which it pays no interest. And so the central bank can then lend to the government at a low interest rate, since it has no need for interest income.

The system has some of the characteristics of a Rube Goldberg device. Restrictions on entry into banking produce monopoly profits for the commercial banks; the central bank then taxes these producers of money. In the United States, commercial banks increase their reserves or deposits at the Federal Reserve by selling U.S. government securities. And the Federal Reserve in effect buys these securities. So the interest paid by the Treasury on the U.S. government securities owned by the Federal Reserve is subsequently returned by the Fed to the U.S. government.

Differences among countries in the way banks are taxed might have a significant impact on the competitive strength of banks in different countries. What remains to be determined is their impact in intensifying or neutralizing the competitive advantages of banks in different countries in the international marketplace.

15

Banking on the Wire

Q. Why are Swiss bankers rich?
A. They compete against Swiss bankers.

A revolution is hitting commercial banks. The technology of money payments is changing; movement of pieces of paper is being replaced by transmission of electronic impulses and computer tapes. The geographic scope of banking markets is increasing; the number of protected natural and regional markets is declining. The effectiveness of national cartels in limiting competition among banks is declining. In the 1960s, U.S. banks expanded rapidly abroad; in the 1970s, foreign banks became extremely aggressive in the U.S. markets for deposits and loans.

Traditionally, banks have competed within their domestic markets, which were protected from foreigners by the high costs of establishing and managing overseas branches. Moreover, the difficulty of operating in foreign currencies deterred expansion abroad. And regulation, informal as well as formal, has limited development of overseas offices.

Banking is a highly regulated industry. Commercial banks are required to hold reserves in the central banks. Ceilings are placed on the interest rates they can pay on deposits. Banks are required to hold certain types of assets and are prohibited from holding other assets. Their loans to any one customer are limited to a small fraction of their capital; their loans to all customers are limited to a given multiple of their capital.

Regulation is intended to protect the small savers from losses that might occur if the banks in which they hold deposits were to fail, and to protect the economy from the collapse of the banking system. Measures adopted to limit bank failure constrain competition. So regulation has helped the inefficient banks to be more profitable than they otherwise would have been. The efficient banks are probably also more profitable, even though regulation constrains their growth and the increase in their market share.

Competition among banks based in different countries takes several forms. More than fifty U.S. banks have set up branches in London, primarily to sell dollar deposits and buy dollar loans. Few of these London-based banks do a significant business in sterling in competition with British banks. Indeed, if regulations were changed so that dollar transactions in London were forbidden, probably thirty-five or forty U.S. banks would close their London offices. Ten or fifteen would remain to make loans in sterling.

Similarly, if U.S. banks were prohibited from selling dollar deposits and making dollar loans outside the United States, the number of branches of U.S. banks in Luxembourg, the Bahamas, Singapore, Panama, and other offshore centers would decline. Three U.S. banks would retain large numbers of overseas branches; a few more would have branches in the major foreign financial centers.

British and Swiss banks have opened offices in New York, Chicago, and San Francisco. Lloyd's Bank bought First Western Bank & Trust in California. European American Bank, owned by a consortium of six banks in six European countries, acquired the remains of Franklin National Bank. National Westminster Bank has bought National Bank of North America in New York. Hongkong & Shanghai Banking has acquired Marine Midland in New York. The branch system of Bankers Trust in New York was sold to the Bank of Montreal, Bank Leumi (Israel), and Barclays of New York.

U.S. banks have also purchased shares in foreign banks. And when the establishment of branch offices or the purchase of shares in banks abroad has been prohibited or constrained, foreign customers have been invited to do business in the bank's home office or in a convenient regional office. Thus Canadian nationalism has constrained U.S. banks from developing branches in Canada, but those Canadian individuals and firms who desire less costly banking services than are available in Montreal and Toronto have been welcome in New York and Chicago.

Entry into foreign markets by branching or acquisition enables aggressive banks to circumvent the regulations of the national authorities that limit their growth. Many commercial banks have sought to grow rapidly, for they believe their profits increase with size. Every central bank, however, directly limits the expansion of commercial bank liabilities denominated in its currency—and hence the growth in commercial bank assets—to prevent inflation. The upper limit to monetary expansion may be 6, 10, or 20 percent a year, but at each moment every central bank *has* a limit. So individual banks within a country can grow more rapidly than banks as a whole only if they can increase their share of the domestic market, which must be at the expense of some other banks. Aggressive banks can expand into new or ancillary businesses—travel, insurance, leasing, and computer services. Or they can seek to penetrate the domestic banking market in some foreign countries, either by setting up branches near the foreign customers or by attracting customers to their home offices. Large aggressive banks are almost certain to expand abroad, for the costs of obtaining customers in a market which they have not previously entered are likely to be smaller than the costs of increasing their share of the domestic market.

Changes in the technology of banking are almost certain to affect the structure of the banking industry, just as the shift from propeller craft to jets altered the structure of the airline industry. Expanding into foreign markets is becoming progressively easier as changes in the technology of the payments process reduce the economic distance between the banking offices and their customers. In the future, more and more payments will be made by electronic funds transfer. The market areas in which banks compete will be enlarged because the transport costs for money are falling sharply. To the extent banks in some countries are more efficient or have other competitive advantages, they are likely to increase their share of the world market.

What Banks Are All About

Most firms have a highly visible product—General Motors produces Cadillacs and Chevrolets, AT&T produces telephone services, IBM produces computers. But confusion surrounds what banks actually produce, partly because the product is not visible and partly because the banks, when they sell their products, "pay" their customers in toasters, TV sets, and interest income.

Basically, commercial banks produce money in the form of demand and time deposits; they "sell" deposits. The receipts from the sale of these deposits enable them to buy loans, mortgages, bonds, securities, and other assets, each of which carries an interest income. Banks also have numerous other activities for which they receive fixed-fee payments: they rent safe-deposit boxes, sell lottery tickets, and manage trusts. But the bread-and-butter activity of banking—and much of the jam—involves selling demand and time deposits and buying loans.

Banks deal with two groups of customers, depositors and borrowers. (Note that the terms depositors and lenders are interchangeable.) While these roles overlap—most borrowers are also depositors, and some depositors are also borrowers—in practice the roles are sharply different. Business firms tend to be predominantly borrowers. Households tend to be primarily depositors. Banks are intermediaries or brokers between the depositors who want a safe, secure, and convenient place to store some of their wealth, and borrowers, who want to expand their current production or consumption more rapidly than they can on the basis of current wealth and income. The spread or markup between the interest rates that banks pay lenders or depositors and the interest rates they charge borrowers covers their costs and is the source of their profits.

Profits in banking depend on three factors: marketing skills in selling deposits, investment skills in buying loans, and management skills. Since selling deposits by paying higher interest rates—that is, through price competition—is usually limited by the authorities or by a cartel arrangement among the banks, banks compete by offering "free" fountain pens and frying pans and automatic tellers and pretty checks and by giving assurances about their safety and stability. Their skill in selling deposits determines how rapidly they can grow.

Investment skills involve matching the yields on loans, mortgages, and other assets with their risks. Within each economy, riskier loans carry higher yields. Banks—at least the successful ones—seek those assets which offer the highest return for the risk. The banks that are best able to determine which assets are underpriced relative to their risks earn the highest returns. And the banks that earn the highest returns are better able to increase the interest rates they pay on deposits, so they can grow more rapidly.

In many ways, commercial banks are like other financial intermediaries—mutual savings banks, savings and loan associations, even life insurance companies. Each sells its liabilities to the public and uses the money obtained from the public to buy loans, securities, and other income-earning assets. From the point of view of households, owning these liabilities is one way to store wealth. A life insurance policy, a pension, or a passbook deposit are the symbolic forms of wealth; the wealth is the claim on the institution. Thus, the loss of the policy or passbook does not lead to any loss in wealth, for the institution will issue a replacement policy or passbook.

Commercial banks differ from other financial intermediaries in one important way, however: their demand deposit or checking account liabilities are used as money. Money—by definition—is transferred to pay for goods and services, and to settle debts. As a group, banks operate the payments mechanism, which provides for the transfer of money. Checks are messages or signals from depositors to their banks to transfer ownership of bank liabilities to whoever's name follows the phrase "Pay to the order of." The check is the symbolic form of money, but not the money itself; the money is the bank liability. Banks generally pay much higher interest rates on time deposits than on demand deposits. Selling demand deposits thus would appear to be more profitable than selling time deposits, since interest rates are lower. In fact, however, banks incur substantially higher costs in managing their demand deposit business, for they must process billions of checks and shift money from the payers' to the payees' banks; these costs are so high that the sale of demand deposits is only marginally more profitable than the sale of time deposits.

The Payments Mechanism

In the early nineteenth century, the major product of banks was bank notes—promises to pay the bearer in lawful money. Each bank produced its own distinctive notes; the countryside was full of competing bits of paper. Industrial states chartered banks to finance the building of roads, canals, railroads, and other desired improvements. The payments process involved the transfer of bank notes by hand-to-hand circulation. The market area for each bank was limited to its immediate vicinity, largely because individuals lacked confidence in the value of notes issued by banks in distant locations. If the banks failed, the notes issued by the banks would become worthless. Firms and individuals in Chicago were reluctant to accept New York bank notes, because they were wary about the credit standing of banks 700 miles away. Banks in New York were even more reluctant to accept notes issued by Chicago banks. Indeed, bank notes frequently sold below their face value in distant cities; thus, a $1 note issued by a New York bank might sell for 95 cents in the Chicago market, while $1 bank notes issued by banks in Chicago might sell for only 80 or 90 cents in New York. Since the transport costs of money were relatively high, the price of the notes was likely to vary inversely with the distance from the issuing institution. The discount below the face value reflected the risk that buyers were taking on both the legitimacy of the note and the financial standing of the bank that issued it.

The size of the market area of each bank was limited by the costs that potential borrowers and lenders incurred in dealing with a bank: the time and financial inconvenience of dealing with a bank located in a distant city was higher than those in dealing with a nearby bank. Some banks, especially in the smaller cities and country towns, had a neighborhood monopoly: no other bank was within convenient walking—or horseback riding—distance.

When checks began to replace bank notes as a means of payment in the latter part of the nineteenth century, the market area of banks expanded. Checks had a number of advantages over bank notes. One piece of paper could be used for large payments and for payments of odd amounts. The money transfer process was less risky; the theft of checks, unlike the theft of notes, involved little risk, for payment on the check could be stopped. Checks could be safely sent through the mail. Thus, the transport costs for checks were lower than for bank notes and the use of checks facilitated transactions between buyers and sellers separated by great distances. The increased use of checks coincided with the development of a comprehensive railroad system and improvements in the postal system. The fall in transport costs associated with the expansion of the railroad system also enlarged the size of the market area for goods, so individuals had more occasions to pay firms and individuals located at greater distances.

By bringing depositors and borrowers from various locales into the expanding market area of a large number of more distant banks, the change in the technology of payments reduced the monopoly position of neighborhood banks. The size of the market was limited by the speed and efficiency of the check transfer process and by the costs of acquiring information about distant banks. Of course, borrowers still found personal contact with their banks a necessity, for loans had to be negotiated in person, and so bankers found it convenient to stay in their offices to meet borrowers. But even then, the loan negotiations could occur elsewhere—in the borrower's office or on the golf course.

Banks began to develop branches as checks replaced notes. Large banks are more efficient than small banks in that there are economies of scale in the basic functions—selling deposits, managing assets, and operating the payments mechanism. Processing the flow of checks within one institution is less costly than moving these checks among numerous institutions. And branching enables banks to marry offices located in residential and suburban areas, which primarily serve depositors, with those in downtown areas, which primarily serve borrowers. As business firms expanded rapidly and became concentrated in fewer and fewer cities, the demand for large loans from banks increased sharply. In the growing industrial centers, business firms wanted to borrow much more money than the banks in the vicinity of their offices could lend on the basis of local deposits. Banks located near these firms found that the business demand for loans exceeded their lending capacity. Households, in contrast, were spread over a larger residential area. Banks within the residential areas frequently found that they were receiving more money in deposits from households than they could readily lend in their local area. A mechanism was needed so that the deposits of banks in residential neighborhoods could be available for loans in the business areas. Banks in the residential areas could simply lend to banks in the business areas, or banks from each area might merge in order to internalize the transfer of funds within one firm. The growth of branch banks suggests that internalization was more efficient.

The move to electronic banking means that checks—and paper—will no longer be used in the money transfer process. With the electronic transfer of funds, when Joe Doe wishes to pay his electric utility bill or his taxes, he will signal his bank by inserting a coded card in a small device attached to his telephone. This device will have a few keys, like those on push-button phones or handheld calculators. Doe will push the keys accordingly, entering his social security number, his bank account number, a secret number to prevent the misuse of his account by someone else (the coded number serves the same function as the signature on a check); a number that represents the account of the electric utility, and the amount to be paid. The signal will then go to the computer in Doe's bank and from there to the computer in the utility's bank; these computers would be linked electronically.

Much of this system is already in place. The larger banks already have machine tellers that accept deposits and distribute cash; a plastic card and a four- or six- or n-digit code enables one to obtain cash in the evening and on weekends and at other times when the bank is closed. When the bank is open, the automatic tellers are like an express line at the supermarket; customers with simple transactions can be quickly processed. Cash can readily be drawn against the overdraft limits on Mastercard and Visa. These consoles are now usually located at the doorstep of the bank—and increasingly they are being placed in supermarkets.

The electronic banking system has several advantages. Postage costs are avoided. The transfer process is instantaneous; there is no delay between sending and receiving the funds. The monthly or weekly balancing of checkbooks is redundant; the Does can determine their balances whenever they wish, simply by pushing a predetermined key. And there is no equivalent of a bad check; if Doe wants to pay Roe $100 and has only $50 in his account, the computer balks. The printing, transfer, and identification of billions of pieces of paper becomes outmoded.

Wire transfers mean that many traditional credit cards will become obsolete. When John Doe fills up his car at the corner gas station or checks out of his motel room, he will type a message to his computer bank; payment will be made immediately, regardless of the time of day or the day of the week. Bankers may work from nine to three, but computers work around the clock.

Individuals who make relatively few payments will continue to use checks. And notes and coin will still be used for small payments. But those who make a large number of payments are almost certain to find the electronic system less costly and more convenient.

Electronic banking will further enlarge the market area for deposits beyond national boundaries. The distance between the customer and the bank will be irrelevant. The neighborhood becomes the world. Chicago banks will advertise in Frankfurt for mark deposits and loans, while Frankfurt banks will compete for Chicago deposits and loans. Banks will be able to attract foreign customers without the cost of establishing offices abroad. Canadians will be able to bank as easily in Chicago or New York as in Toronto.

International Banking Competition

Banking has been an international industry for centuries. The Rothschilds and the Fuggers were extended families with banking offices spread across countries; however, they were essentially investors rather than producers of money. In the latter part of the nineteenth century, British banks established foreign branches to help finance the overseas trade and investment of firms based in London and Liverpool. But these branches were largely limited to areas in the outpost of the empire which were poorly served by domestic banks. Thus, relatively few branches were set up in the United States, for British firms could use established U.S. banks. Similarly, U.S. banks, when they began to go overseas in the early years of this century, followed U.S. business largely to areas that were not adequately served by existing banks.

In recent years, the motive for overseas expansion has shifted. Initially, relatively few New York and San Francisco banks followed U.S. firms to Europe, competing for these firms' foreign business in the hope of gaining more of their U.S. business. The expansion of the overseas branch networks of the three largest U.S. banks—Bank of America, Citibank, and Chase Manhattan—has been especially rapid. The sudden increase in the number of U.S. banks with branches abroad was partly a defensive response to those first U.S. banks that went overseas; the Chicago banks moved abroad to protect their established relationships from the competitive threat posed by the New York banks already operating abroad. In 1960 about 8 U.S. banks had 130 foreign branches. By 1980, 126 U.S. banks had nearly 1,000 foreign branches.

Over the same period, more than fifty foreign banks set up branches in the United States, nearly all in New York. These banks wanted to participate directly in the largest financial market in the world; their direct interest was in retaining the U.S. business of their domestic customers—and in attracting some U.S. customers.

U.S. banks operating abroad and foreign banks operating in the United States share a common problem: they lack the deposit base essential to providing them with the funds to make loans. They can borrow these funds from their home offices, they can borrow in the interbank money market, and they can borrow from the external currency market. And they do all three. If they have the deposits, they can make the loans. In the loan market, both borrowers and banks are mobile; major U.S. banks, limited by legislation against branching in other states, have set up loan production offices in major cities across the country.

Many countries are reluctant to admit foreign competitors. Thus, Norway and Denmark do not permit foreign banks to establish branches. Peru and Chile have closed the local branches of foreign banks. Venezuela applies discriminatory legislation to foreign banks. U.S. banks find it impossible to establish branches in Mexico. Even when a U.S. bank establishes a branch abroad, the price is often a commitment that the bank will not compete actively for domestic business.

Such attempts by governments to protect their own banks from having to compete with the local branches of foreign banks will become increasingly irrelevant. The move to electronic banking, by reducing the importance of national boundaries as a limit to the size of the market, will diminish the need to establish foreign branches. With electronic banking, instructions to make payments can be handled over the wire. Thus, banks outside Switzerland, for example, can deal in Swiss francs on the same terms as banks inside Switzerland—perhaps on even more favorable terms.

Money havens will follow the tax havens. The computers may be placed in the Cayman Islands or Bermuda, or some other safe banking center; the terminals attached to this computer will be next to the phone. If a face-to-face contact between the bank and the customer is necessary, the local office can concentrate on generating loan and deposit business and information for the home office; this office need not deal in money. As the effective size of the market increases, some banks whose domestic sanctuaries had been protected will find themselves subject to intense pressure from foreign banks. Competitive skills will become increasingly important in the enlarged market area.

The Competitive Edge

The speed of the shift to electronic banking on an international scale is unpredictable. Assume, however, that the system will be in place next Monday morning and that banks will compete vigorously to maintain or enhance their share of the world market for deposits and loans. Some banks will succeed in increasing market share. Others will lose market share. Whether particular banks are in one group or the other will depend partly on how efficient and competitive they have been in the domestic context.

In this new international market, U.S. banks will have three advantages: size, efficiency, and association with a major international currency at the top of the hit parade. Not only is size important in making very large loans, but it also confers a competitive marketing advantage, for depositors often equate safety with size. In the credit crunch of 1974 and again in 1982, the competitive positions of the largest U.S. banks improved relative to those of smaller ones; investors reasoned that the Federal Reserve might permit the twentieth-largest U.S. bank to fail, but it was quite unlikely that the Fed would permit the largest U.S. banks to go bankrupt. And the largest U.S. banks are generally bigger than their foreign competitors. Two of the five largest banks in the world are based in the United States, and so are three of the top twenty and seven of the top fifty. The assets of the largest U.S. banks are substantially larger than those of their major foreign competitors.

Changes in the ranking of banks in the size hit parade frequently reflect mergers. Banks in Europe and, to a lesser extent, Japan have merged in response to the competitive threat posed by the size of U.S. banks. In Great Britain, Barclays, the largest bank, merged with Martin's Bank, while Westminster and National Provincial combined into National Westminster. In Belgium, Banque Lambert, the fourth in size, merged with Banque de Bruxelles, the second largest. In the Netherlands, the number-two and number-three banks have merged. Yet, by international standards, the largest banks in many European countries are still quite small; the largest Swiss bank, for example, is no bigger than the fourteenth-largest U.S. bank, and the largest Swedish, Dutch, and Belgian banks are only one-fifth the size of the largest U.S. bank. The entire Belgian banking system is smaller than Citibank.

If, therefore, European banks want to be as large as one of the three or four leading U.S. banks, they will almost certainly have to merge across national borders. But national differences in the ownership and regulatory structures will make this difficult. French banks, for example, are owned by the government, those in Italy are indirectly government-owned, and those in other European countries are largely private. One alternative to a merger is an association: Crédit Lyonnais, the second largest French bank, Banco di Roma, the fourth largest Italian bank, and Commerzbank, the fourth largest German bank, have formed an association, as have Société Générale de Banque in Brussels, Amsterdam-Rotterdam Bank of the Netherlands, Midland Bank of England, and the Deutsche Bank of Germany. The banks partic-

TABLE 15.1

The Ranking of International Banks, 1969 and 1981

(Billions of dollars of assets, current exchange rates)

1969		1981	
1. Bank America Corp.	$25.6	1. Bank America Corp.	$115.6
2. First National City Corp.	23.1	2. Citicorp	112.7
3. Chase Manhattan Corp.	22.2	3. Banque Nationale de Paris	106.7
4. Barclays Bank	15.1	4. Crédit Agricole	97.8
5. Manufacturers Hanover Corp.	11.9	5. Crédit Lyonnais	93.7
6. Morgan Guaranty Trust Co.	11.5	6. Barclays	93.0
7. National Westminster Bank	10.6	7. Société Générale	87.0
8. United California Bank	10.6	8. Dai-Ichi Kangyo	85.5
9. Banca Nazionale del Lavoro	10.2	9. Deutsche Bank	84.5
10. Chemical New York Group	9.7	10. National Westminster	82.6

SOURCE: The Financial Times Limited, *The Banker* (London, June 1970 and June 1982).

ipating in these associations have agreed to coordinate the world-wide activities of their subsidiaries, to assist each other in providing funds to meet customer needs, and to cooperate in reducing costs and improving their services.

TABLE 15.2

The Distribution of Major Banks by Country 1969 and 1982

	1969			1982		
	Top 10	Top 20	Top 50	Top 10	Top 20	Top 50
Country						
United States	7	8	15	2	3	7
Japan	—	4	10	1	6	13
Germany	—	1	4	1	2	7
Great Britain	2	3	5	2	3	4
Canada	—	2	4	—	1	4
France	—	1	3	4	4	5
Netherlands	—	—	—	—	—	3
Switzerland	—	—	1	—	—	3
Italy	1	1	6	—	—	2
Brazil	—	—	1	—	1	1
Australia	—	—	1	—	—	—
Hong Kong	—	—	—	—	—	1
	10	20	50	10	20	50

SOURCE: The Financial Times Limited, *The Banker* (London, June 1970 and June 1982).

U.S. banks are probably more efficient than those in most foreign countries—a result of the greater competition in the banking markets in the United States. More banks compete for deposits and loans. There are 4,000 banks in the United States, more than in the rest of the world combined. The very large number of U.S. banks reflects the nineteenth-century populist fear of centralized money trusts, which led to prohibitions against branching across state lines, branching across county lines in Indiana, and branching across the street in Chicago. The reason U.S. banks are both more numerous and larger is that the U.S. economy is such a large part of the financial world. There are more financial assets in the

United States per capita than in any other country. Demand deposits in Chicago exceed those in all of France.

Since restrictions on branching constrain U.S. banks from expanding geographically and setting up branches in other states, other means must be used to attract customers. The contrast between the relatively uninhibited growth of U.S. business, both nationally and internationally, and the severe restrictions on the domestic expansion of U.S. banks has forced the banks to become innovative and adaptive. Many of the large U.S. banks attract deposits from, and make loans to, firms in cities 3,000 miles away. As a consequence, the market loans and deposits in New York include more than those in the New York banks; banks with home offices in Newark, Boston, Philadelphia, and Chicago participate actively in this market. Similarly, New York banks participate in the Chicago market. Competition has prevailed, despite the regulations against interstate banking.

The result is that U.S. banks in the major cities have been more fully subject to competitive pressures than banks based abroad. One measure of bank efficiency is provided by the spread between the average price the banks pay on their deposit liabilities and the average price they receive on their loans—that is, by the markup between the interest rates the banks pay on deposits and the interest rates they receive on loans. Within a country, competition ensures that spreads among banks are similar; differences in markups are not sustainable. Otherwise, the banks with larger spreads would lose deposits or loans, and their share of the market, to more efficient banks. Among countries, however, spreads tend to differ: they tend to be larger, in some cases substantially larger, in continental Europe than in the United States. The differences among countries are sustainable only as long as national markets are largely protected from external competition; gradually, banks in the countries with the higher markups will lose their share of the market.

In the new worldwide market, banks based in countries where

larger spreads prevail will be under greater competitive pressure. If, in order to hold deposits, they offer higher interest rates to depositors while their spread remains unchanged, their minimal lending rate will be so high that the least risky domestic borrowers will seek funds at foreign banks, which will be charging lower interest rates. If instead they set rates on loans competitive with those charged by foreign banks, then their deposit rates will fall below those paid by banks that can operate with smaller spreads. They may try to reduce their spreads, but to do so they must pay lower wages, induce their employees to work harder, or find some magical approach to become more efficient.

Some banks will attempt to discriminate by charging a different set of interest rates to those customers who have more attractive opportunities abroad. But such price shading can only be a partial response to the problems raised by the apparently higher costs in European banks. In the final analysis, either costs will be cut or the less efficient banks will lose market share.

The second advantage of U.S. banks in the new international market is that their domestic currency, the dollar, is likely to remain the preferred currency brand name. Indeed, the share of banking business denominated in dollars may increase relative to other currencies. This currency preference provides U.S. banks with a competitive advantage, for if depositors prefer dollar-denominated deposits, they will also prefer that these deposits be issued by U.S. banks. Combined with their lower costs, this suggests that U.S.-owned banks are likely to end up with a larger share of the world market for deposits.

Banking is generally viewed as a sensitive industry, because banks both produce financial wealth and operate the money payments mechanism. Governments are wary of allowing a substantial part of the banking services demanded by their residents to be supplied by foreign banks. If banks in a country are largely foreign-owned, or even if the larger customers of the banks have ready access to foreign banks, then the effectiveness of national regulation and of national monetary policies is threatened.

Some countries may nationalize their banking industry outright, rather than allow foreign firms to supply most of their banking needs. Others will pay to keep the domestic banks' prices competitive, perhaps through various types of subsidies to these banks. Efforts will be made to limit the access of foreign banks to domestic borrowers and lenders, measures which will counter the thrust toward an open international economy.

16

The Rise of the House of Cornfeld—
And the Fall

Bernie Cornfeld provides a contemporary twist to the traditional immigrant saga. Many poor Jewish boys traveled from Europe to Brooklyn in search of riches; Cornfeld went from the United States to Europe and made $100 million—for a while. The Cornfeld saga begins in 1955, when Cornfeld, then a social worker in Philadelphia, went to Paris for a vacation. To stay in Paris, he began to sell U.S. mutual funds, both to U.S. troops in Germany and France and to the expatriate American professional community—diplomats and oil drillers. Then, in 1958, he shifted his operations to Geneva. He prospered, and in 1960 he set up Investors Overseas Services, Ltd., his own investment fund. Then he broadened his clientele to include Europeans, Latin Americans—indeed, anyone with money to invest.

At the peak of his success in 1969, Cornfeld had the largest financial sales organization in the world, an empire of selling offices in 50 countries, a sales force in 100 countries, 30,000 employees, and more than a third of a million shareholders. The assets of the IOS empire were $2.5 billion. In 1968, sales of new shares in IOS funds totaled $800 million.

At first, the European financial establishment looked upon Cornfeld as a hard-sell con artist from Brooklyn. But as IOS grew and Cornfeld acquired hundreds of millions of dollars to invest each year, the establishment became respectful. Cornfeld was hailed, for a while at least, as "the greatest force in Western capitalism"—probably by his public relations flack.

His success was no fluke. Cornfeld capitalized on a shortcoming in the financial markets and institutions of Europe; he developed the right product at the right time. Savers in Europe wanted attractive investments that would provide protection against inflation and devaluation and would also be readily convertible into cash. Offshore mutual funds were the answer.

Mutual funds collect money from savers and invest the proceeds in a diversified group of securities, thereby spreading the market risks of the individual companies. In their most popular form, mutual funds are open-ended—that is, the numbers of shares and shareholders are variable and change in response to investor demand. Any would-be investor can buy into an open-ended fund by paying the net asset value and a sales charge, usually in the range of 4 to 8 percent; the net asset value is computed once or twice a day by dividing the total assets owned by the fund by the number of its shares outstanding at that moment. In addition, any shareholder can sell the shares back to the fund and be immediately repaid on the basis of the net asset value.

The essential feature of offshore funds is that they invest in the companies and real estate of developed countries, principally in U.S. companies and U.S. real estate, while their buyers are located outside the United States. Most are incorporated in low-tax, minimal-regulation jurisdictions like the Bahamas, Panama, and the Cayman Islands.

Buyers of shares in offshore funds are attracted by the concept of having the underlying value of their investments located in the politically secure and wealthy United States. That the mutual funds are designed to minimize taxes on both incomes and capital gains provides sales appeal. In some instances, the funds help their shareholders circumvent exchange controls.

The promoters of offshore funds are not running a charity. They receive income from the buyers of funds in several ways, some direct, some indirect. First, when the funds are sold, there are the sales commissions. The funds require a variety of technical services; these are provided by a management company, owned by the promoters, which receives investment fees for managing the assets and brokerage fees for buying the assets for the funds. The management company can buy these assets from their friends in the brokerage business, and so share in the commission income. The management company might own a bank and provide financial services to a fund or its shareholders—for a fee. The lists of shareowners are salable to other promoters. And as the profits of the management company grow rapidly, the promoters capitalize anticipated profits by selling shares in the management company to the public.

Under these arrangements, the profits of the management company vary directly with the number of shares outstanding, which in turn depends on how hard the funds are sold. Mutual funds are sold, not bought—and the energy given to selling depends on the profit and income orientation of the sales force. Many IOS salesmen sold contractual savings plans; the buyers became committed to a series of periodic payments, monthly or quarterly, over a ten- or fifteen-year period, much as if they were buying life insurance policies. Most of the salesman's commission was taken out of the payments made by the buyer in the first year. The salesman received income immediately against payments that the buyer was committed to make over a ten- or fifteen-year future. The buyer might withdraw from his plan, but the sales commission was nonrefundable.

Certain aspects of IOS activities provoked a hostile reaction, especially among national authorities. Some authorities objected to the hard-selling effort, others to the self-serving investment practices. Many objected to the tax avoidance and violations of exchange controls. The Swiss had strict rules about work permits for nonresidents: IOS evaded the rules by having its foreign employees register as students at the University of Geneva. The Bank of England had strict controls regulating the purchase of dollar securities by British residents; the British subsidiary of IOS adhered to the letter of the regulation while avoiding its spirit. British residents were sold insurance policies through the IOS-owned Dover Plan, and premiums were siphoned into an IOS subsidiary in Luxembourg. The U.S. Securities and Exchange Commission (SEC) required that funds furnish lists of their shareholders; IOS refused. While the financial establishment around the world became more respectful as IOS prospered, the government bureaucrats became more hostile.

By the middle of 1970, Cornfeld's empire was broken, but not because of the hostile reaction of national governments. There were, instead, two principal causes. First, tight money in the United States led to a collapse in U.S. equity prices, so selling shares became much more difficult. Cornfeld and Co. got caught in a bear market triggered by contractive monetary policies. Second, the funds had been extravagantly managed, and the accelerating costs eventually came home to roost. The assets of IOS-managed funds declined rapidly. Shareholders in the management company sold their stock; initially offered at $10 a share, the stock sold for less than $1 in the early 1970s after having reached a peak of $19 in 1969.

Then, when IOS was down and the support of the financial establishment had dried up, the governments began to step in. The Swiss government forbade sales of IOS funds, the Italian government forced the sale of the Italian subsidiary of IOS to a government subsidiary. In Germany the sales force fell by two-thirds. IOS and other offshore funds were subject to heavy withdrawals as shareholders bailed out. Several funds were forced to cease redeeming their shares for cash. Finally, Cornfeld was canned—removed from all responsibility for IOS.

Several morals, usually variants on the Puritan ethic, have

been drawn from Cornfeld's rise and fall—but they often miss the point. His unqualified success highlighted the inadequacies of Europe's financial markets. And his downfall indicated the curious dependence of these markets on U.S. financial developments.

The Elements of Cornfeld's Success

Making $1 million in a tough, competitive world is an achievement; making $100 million is a heroic accomplishment. Cornfeld's success invited imitation. The result was the offshore fund industry, with assets that reached a total of $6 billion in 1969. For several years, the European editions of *Time* and *Newsweek* appeared to be largely supported by the advertisements of Cornfeld and his imitators.

Three factors contributed to Cornfeld's success. One was the inability of European financial markets to supply savers with the types of assets they preferred. The second was Cornfeld's personal ability to motivate salesmen. The third was the economic miracle in Germany. All three elements were necessary to the phenomenal growth of IOS.

Cornfeld's genius was to perceive that the European middle class wanted liquid financial assets that would offer protection against domestic inflation, which was precisely what a mutual fund with a portfolio of dollar-denominated shares was supposed to provide. In the mid-1960s, most European investors had few attractive financial investment opportunities in their own currencies; basically, they could put the money in the bank or buy land. But interest rates on bank deposits were kept deliberately low, partly because banks were inefficient and partly because the banking systems were managed to subsidize borrowers, including the government, at the expense of lenders. In some countries, the interest rates were below the annual increase in the price level, so the real value, the purchasing power, of savings deposits declined over time. Land is a highly illiquid investment; besides, land ownership attracts tax authorities. Land ownership, moreover, is like musical chairs; X can buy land only if Y sells land, and then Y must invest the proceeds. Everyone cannot buy land at the same time.

The European investor could also look to the European stock markets. But the volume of shares in most European countries was then much smaller than in the United States, for nationalization of the utilities, steel, and other industries had reduced the supply of equities; so had the takeovers of European firms by U.S. firms. In every European country, equities were a lower percentage of GNP than in the United States (see table 16.1). Buying shares in European companies, moreover, was frequently like blindman's bluff, because the correct factual information released by many companies was small. Moreover, there were no equivalents of the SEC. Besides, shares in European companies were riskier than shares in U.S. companies, for the day-to-day and week-to-week movements in equity prices were more volatile.

In the long run, share ownership in one country is probably

TABLE 16.1

Market Value of Listed Domestic Equities

(Billions of dollars, current exchange rates, end of year)

	1970	1972	1974	1976	1978	1980	1980 Percent of GNP
United States	$636	$864	$510	$856	$817	$1240	47
Japan	43	152	116	179	327	357	31
Great Britain	76	140	38	65	118	190	45
Germany	28	43	45	54	83	71	9
Canada	48	57	44	52	67	113	46
France	23	31	26	28	45	53	9
Switzerland	10	17	13	22	41	46	46
Italy	11	14	12	9	10	7	7
Sweden	5	8	8	10	10	12	10

SOURCE: Capital International, *Perspective* (Geneva, Switzerland, January 1982).

not much better or worse than in most other countries. Certain proportional relationships dominate financial variables. Thus, stock prices in every country grow about as rapidly as its national income, largely because profits within every country grow about as rapidly as national income. Otherwise, the share of profits in national income would become very large or very small, and the price that investors would pay for corporate profits would become very high or very low. Moreover, in the long run, national income in most developed countries tends to grow at roughly the same rate. (Differences in per capita income among countries reflect that industrialization began earlier in some countries than in others.) Consequently, the price of European shares should grow about as rapidly as the price of U.S. shares.

Of course, in short-run periods of two or three years, share prices grow at different rates in various countries. And Cornfeld benefited greatly from just such a short-run discrepancy between the changes in U.S. and in European stock prices. The European financial establishment was as familiar as Cornfeld with the advantages of dollar equities. But it was largely geared to satisfying the needs of the wealthy, sophisticated European investor who might otherwise deal with a U.S. broker; the middle-class investors in Europe were ignored.

Dollar mutual funds were very attractive in the early 1960s, and their value appeared to be constantly increasing. During the 1950s, their performance had been impressive because stock prices in the United States had risen rapidly—more rapidly than GNP and corporate profits—and mutual funds reflected this gain. In the 1940s, U.S. stock prices were unusually low by historical standards; their rapid rise in the 1950s represented a belated adjustment of the very low level of stock prices set in the Great Depression and to wartime pessimism about the future of capitalism.

In contrast, in the early 1960s, European stock prices were declining or more or less unchanged, even though GNP was rising. Paradoxically, the unimpressive performance of European shares in the early 1960s reflected the legacy of the belated "discovery" of Europe by U.S. securities analysts, the growth of the Common Market, and the German boom in the late 1950s. As the U.S. multinationals began to invest extensively in Europe, U.S. investors bought European equities, and their prices reached peak values in 1961. But this passion for European stocks quickly faded, and their prices then fell almost as rapidly as they had risen. In Germany stock prices more or less fell between 1961 and 1967; only in 1969 did they again reach 1961 levels. Similarly, stock prices in Italy fell during most years after 1961, as they did in the Netherlands. A similar pattern was observable in France, with the difference that prices peaked in 1962. In contrast, U.S. stock price indexes were generally rising during this period; the 1968 values were 50 percent higher than the 1960 values.

In some respects, the mutual fund industry is like the soda pop, soap, breakfast cereal, and cigarette industries; there are a large number of products which are barely distinguishable from each other. While there are some differences in the products, most of these differences are created to facilitate sales. Firms compete in figuring out what the consumer really wants and then design the product accordingly. There are several types of mutual funds: some funds are designed for high income, others for rapid appreciation, and some for a combination of income and appreciation. But there is one important difference between funds and soaps. Each fund has a performance record which indicates year-by-year changes in its net asset value. Investors seek those funds with the most successful investment skills. Certainly the investment performance of IOS cannot explain why it grew so much more rapidly than its competitors; the Salvation Army had a more swinging portfolio.

The personal element in Cornfeld's success was his marketing genius. He established the Fund of Funds. The name had resonance—and the concept was magnificent. Since the basic idea of a mutual fund is to offer an investor greater diversification in his assets than he could obtain by direct purchases of shares of various companies, a fund which owns other funds appears even better diversified—and therefore less risky—than one which only owns shares. In fact, once a fund has forty or fifty different securities whose returns are randomly related to each other, there is no significant reduction in risk through further diversification. The real advantage of layering the funds was that Cornfeld and Co. did not need to engage in investment research about individual securities; they could simply choose funds on the basis of their performance. The managers of the funds whose shares might be purchased provided research and other valuable services, since the purchases enhanced their incomes. Moreover, some of the funds purchased by the Fund of Funds would also be IOS-managed funds, so the IOS management companies obtained two sales commissions.

Cornfeld also had a special genius for motivating salesmen. Sales commissions increased as annual sales increased. Large annual sales qualified a salesman to become a super-salesman, or the boss of other salesmen; a super-salesman got a share of the commissions on the sales of those under his supervision. If the sales of the super-salesman and the group of salesmen under his supervision were sufficiently large, the super-salesman qualified to become a superduper-salesman. And *his* salesmen became super-salesmen, who could in turn hire salesmen if the sales volume of the superduper-salesman's sales force was sufficiently large, and so forth. Moreover, as the salesman advanced higher in the hierarchy, he qualified to buy shares in the IOS management companies at below market prices. The prices of these shares were expected to rise forever. And he could borrow from an IOS bank on favorable terms to buy the shares.

The primary motivation for energetic selling by most salesmen was not current income but the prospect of future income from both the commissions generated by salesmen in the lower stages of the hierarchy and from capital gains on holdings of stock in the management company.

Cornfeld had a money machine. The sales of IOS funds were like a pyramid club or chain letter, where an individual receives a letter with five names and addresses and is told to send a dollar to the name at the top of the list, add his name to the bottom of the list, and mail the list to five friends. Each individual is promised that if he follows the instructions and everyone else does too, then he will receive $625 in fifteen days—provided the mail is delivered on time. Chain letters work well for those who are initially at the top of the list. But eventually the supply of would-be participants is exhausted. (A chain letter with twelve successive stages, for example, would involve nearly 200 million people.)

Whether Cornfeld and Co. recognized that what they were involved in was essentially like a chain letter is irrelevant, although most people in IOS presumably did not. What is relevant is that the forces which led to strong sales motivation were bound to weaken, and any weakening would in turn have a multiplier effect in dampening the drive of the sales force.

Finally, Cornfeld's success was helped enormously by Germany's economic miracle. The base of the IOS empire, especially in the latter part of the 1960s, was in Germany at a time when its savers were becoming richer. But memories of the German financial collapses in 1923, 1930, and 1948 induced prudent investors to seek safety in foreign investments. Germany was a virtually unregulated economy—the largest market economy in Europe—so there was far less regulation of IOS activities in Germany than elsewhere. Moreover, the German government was continually embarrassed by its large balance-of-payments surpluses and therefore it initially welcomed Cornfeld's venture in the hope that importing dollar securities would reduce these surpluses.

These three factors in combination—the inadequacy of European financial markets, Cornfeld's ability to motivate salesmen, and the German boom—developed a momentum of their own. As long as U.S. stock prices were rising, selling dollar shares in IOS funds was relatively easy. As long as sales were easy, recruiting and motivating the sales force was easy. As long as Germany had a large balance-of-payments surplus, Germans appreciated the efforts of Bernie's army of salesmen.

Cornfeld's success in selling mutual funds was so striking that relatively little attention was paid to the high administrative costs of IOS, its lackluster investment record, or the hanky-panky of its management. Continued rapid growth meant that these factors were irrelevant; rising net asset values paid for these shortcomings. The shareholders were happy.

The withdrawal of one of these elements would inevitably dampen the momentum. Once U.S. stock prices stopped rising— or fell—selling shares would be hard. The profits of the management company would falter, and the incentives for the sales force would decline. And so would its selling efforts. The customers would be unhappy, and the governments would crack down. And that is what happened to the House of Cornfeld.

The Fall of the House of Cornfeld

The first crack in Bernie's house appeared in the spring of 1969 when, as a result of the more contractive U.S. monetary policies designed to reduce the U.S. inflation rate, U.S. equity prices began to fall in what proved to be the worst decline in the New York Stock Exchange since the Great Depression. Selling mutual funds when the net asset value is declining sharply is not a rewarding experience; the promise of gains in the long run is modest balm for the short-run losses. Some holders of the funds began to voice their dissatisfaction with the hard sell, now that they were no longer protected from their hasty investment decisions by rising net asset values. The German government began to make anxious noises about IOS. But the sales pitch had not changed—the direction of stock price movements had.

At the same time, the high administrative costs incurred by the management company in expectation of future sales led to profits much lower than expected when these sales failed to materialize. So the price of the management company's shares fell sharply.

Even under the best of circumstances, maintaining IOS's growth rate over an extended period would have become progressively more difficult. Once it became clear that not all salesmen could become super-salesmen, and relatively few could become superdupers, motivating the sales force was bound to be more difficult, since the salesmen could no longer be "paid" with the promise of high future incomes.

Most firms—even those with skillful management—find it hard to adjust to a reduction in their growth rate. Adjustment from an annual growth rate of 40 percent to 10 percent is inevitably traumatic. Budgets have to be cut; pretty or handsome secretaries have to be laid off.

In an attempt to maintain the momentum, the IOS managers engaged in some colossal hanky-panky; they sought to disguise their lousy investment results by revaluing underdeveloped Canadian land from $17 to $119 million. The shareholders were accordingly "richer" by $100 million; the management company was richer because its fees increased as assets under its control increased. Nevertheless, its earnings were still far below expectations, with the result that the price of its shares fell even further. When these shenanigans became public knowledge, new customers became wary of the "water" in the net asset value.

As the shares of the management company plummeted, some of the IOS employees who had borrowed greatly from IOS banks to buy these shares were forced to sell them to repay the banks. Distress selling depressed the share prices further, and the salesmen lost whatever was left of their enthusiasm.

In retrospect, the failure of IOS was inevitable and predictable. The villain was not, as Cornfeld thought, envious competitors or hostile government regulators. Rather, the mechanism of his success provided the basis for his failure. Systems based on the chain letter principle cannot maintain their growth rate forever; they necessarily falter when the momentum weakens. The IOS system was designed to deal with success; it was poorly equipped to handle difficulties.

The collapse of IOS should not obscure Cornfeld's insight about the inadequacies of the options then available for investors in Europe. The lack of information about European equities and the absence of a broad base of investors reinforced each other, and European equity prices were more volatile than U.S. equity prices.

Cornfeld's purchases of U.S. shares had a marginal impact on the United States and a major impact on Europe. Even without his operation, European firms had been at a financial disadvantage in relation to U.S. firms. Directing European savings to U.S. investments increased the handicap.

There is another lesson. The U.S. equity market is so large that Europe cannot escape the U.S. impact. Europe is affected by its own forces—student riots in France, Russian pressures on Berlin, inflation—but the financial markets in most European countries are so small relative to those in the United States that these factors make little difference to the U.S. market. So Europe combines its relatively inadequate financial structures with a substantial dependence on the United States. And as chapter 17 suggests, the factors which made it possible for Cornfeld to establish an army of salesmen in fourteen years may help to explain why U.S. firms have had such a great advantage in buying up European industry.

P.S. Cornfeld is living well on the West Coast now although he has had some minor legal skirmishes about payment of his telephone bills.

17

Why Are Multinational Firms Mostly American?

In the late 1960s one of Europe's best-selling books was *Le Défi Américain—The American Challenge*. The author was Jean-Jacques Servan-Schreiber (JJ-SS), publisher of *L'Express,* the French imitation of *Time;* of *L'Expansion,* the French version of *Fortune;* and for a while, of *European Business,* the French counterpart of the *Harvard Business Review.* Servan-Schreiber was energetic, if not original. By 1981, *Le Défi Américain* was obsolete, but JJ-SS came forth with *Le Défi Mondial.*

The central thesis of *Le Défi Américain* was dramatic; after the United States and the Soviet Union, the third economic power in the world was U.S. business firms in Europe. As evidence, JJ-SS cited the increasingly important position of U.S. subsidiaries in European industry, especially in such technologically advanced fields as computers and electronics.

These U.S. firms, moreover, were at that time well ahead of their British, French, and German competitors in integrating their production and marketing across European borders. International Harvester's French plant produced tractor transmissions, and its German plant produced tractor motors; each exported its product to the other. And IBM-Europe produced its computers using components made in various plants across the continent; indeed, its production line in Europe was at least seven countries long.

Servan-Schreiber advocated numerous changes to help Europe meet the U.S. challenge. European business should become more like American business—more graduate business schools like Harvard, more professional management like that of Exxon, greater decentralization of corporate decision making as at ITT, and more expenditures on research and development like IBM. To meet the American invasion, Europeans should become more nearly American—as had JJ-SS.

One of the not-so-best-selling books in London in 1902 was *The American Invaders* by F. A. McKenzie, a modest Englishman worried by the American threat to British industry. Americans, he wrote, were "succeeding in Europe because of advantages in education, their willingness to accept new ideas, and their freedom from hampering tradition." In part this supremacy was reflected in U.S. exports, in part by the growth of subsidiaries of U.S. firms in Europe. McKenzie especially noted the dominance of Americans in the new industries: "applications of electricity to traction, the typewriter, the automobile, and the machine tools."

Servan-Schreiber never acknowledged McKenzie or *The American Invaders*. If he had, he would have had to explain why sixty-five years and two world wars after 1902, U.S. firms owned only 5 percent of corporate assets in Europe and accounted for 10 percent of European imports. And he would also have had to explain why the ratio of U.S. foreign investment to U.S. national income in the early 1970s was not substantially larger than in 1913.

McKenzie was somewhat premature in predicting American dominance of European industry. So was Servan-Schreiber. While a few U.S. firms had set up branches in Europe as early as 1850, direct U.S. foreign investment was modest until the

1920s, and largely confined to firms engaged in mining and producing crude petroleum. In the 1920s U.S. investment in manufacturing abroad jumped sharply. From the 1930s through most of the 1950s, foreign investments were modest because of the Great Depression and World War II; many U.S. firms sold their European subsidiaries. But beginning in the late 1950s, direct U.S. foreign investment soared; U.S. firms purchased foreign firms or set up new plants of their own.

By 1970 a substantial part of total manufacturing in Canada and several other countries was foreign-owned, especially by U.S. firms. In some Canadian industries more than three-fourths of the local plants were foreign-owned; however, in many industries, such as public utilities and retailing, foreign ownership was minimal. The industry mix of firms that invest abroad is varied. U.S. firms in the "new" industries continue to invest abroad extensively, much as they did in McKenzie's day; the major difference is that the names of the new industries are pharmaceuticals, computers, and electronics rather than the application of electricity to traction and automobiles. But U.S. firms are well established abroad in traditional industries, like hotel keeping and food processing, automobiles and tires, soaps and toothpaste. London has a Playboy Club, and the numbers of Hilton Hotels and Holiday Inns outside the United States are growing very rapidly.

Altogether, direct foreign investment for firms in all countries totalled about $350 billion in 1982, of which about 60 percent was undertaken by U.S. firms and 10 percent by British firms. Foreign investments by Germans and Japanese firms were small until the early 1970s, when they began to increase rapidly (one cost of losing wars is that the foreign subsidiaries of domestic firms tend to be expropriated). From 1973 to 1978 the value of U.S. direct investments abroad increased by two-thirds; during the same period, foreign investments in the United States doubled. Forty percent of U.S. foreign investment is in manufacturing, 30 percent in petroleum, and nearly 10 percent in mining.

Firms based in a small number of countries—the United States, Great Britain, the Netherlands, Switzerland, and Sweden—account for most of the direct foreign investment. Foreign investment is extensive in some industries (aluminum, petroleum) and minimal in others (textiles and steel). Dutch firms (Unilever, Shell, Philips) are large investors abroad, while Belgian firms are not. Swedish firms are big foreign investors, and Danish and Norwegian firms are not.

In the late 1970s foreign firms set up U.S. subsidiaries to compete in the U.S. firms' backyard. British Petroleum bought up Sinclair Oil and has a complicated arrangement that eventually will lead to increased ownership of Sohio; Imperial Chemical, the leading British chemical firm, acquired Atlas Chemical, which ranks about twentieth in the United States in sales; BASF (a German chemical company) acquired Wyandotte Chemical. Panasonic, one of the top three Japanese electronics firms, bought Motorola while Sony bought Warwick. A subsidiary of Nestlé, a Swiss firm, successfully bid for Libby, McNeill & Libby. Grand Union, one of the largest food retailers in the United States, has been acquired by a French-British firm. The Imperial Group in London bought up Howard Johnson's. Renault, the French auto firm, is becoming the owner of American Motors. Volkswagen has set up an assembly plant in Pennsylvania to turn out 200,000 "Rabbits" a year. Two of the major drug suppliers in the United States, Ciba-Geigy and Hoffmann-La Roche, are Swiss. Petrofina, the Belgian petroleum firm, is beginning to refine and distribute in the United States. The European penetration of the U.S. market has gone so far that the Good Humor Company is part of the Liverpool-based Thomas Lipton tea empire. Still, the list of foreign firms investing in the United States is shorter than the list of U.S. firms abroad; U.S. direct investment abroad is three times as large as direct foreign investment in the United States.

U.S. foreign investment surged in the late 1950s and the

1960s, not in response to any plan, but rather in response to market forces. Many firms were undoubtedly playing follow-the-leader in their industries, but this game could be expensive if market opportunities were inappropriate. Fortunately, the economic growth of Western Europe during this period was rapid, partly because of the bounce-back from World War II and partly because of the optimistic expectations generated by the development of the Common Market.

Then, in the late 1960s, the growing overvaluation of the U.S. dollar, caused by the more rapid inflation in the United States than in Europe, further induced U.S. firms to invest more abroad, to protect their export markets. Earlier, these firms had supplied foreign markets from U.S. plants. But as U.S. costs and prices increased, these U.S. plants lost their competitive edge—in the U.S. market as well as in the foreign market—and the firms felt obliged to produce abroad to protect market share. Some U.S. firms began to invest abroad to protect their position in the U.S. market; perhaps the best examples of this were the U.S. electronics firms which set up manufacturing and assembly plants in the Far East to protect their position in the U.S. market from the competitive thrust of Japanese firms.

The depreciation of the dollar relative to European currencies and the Japanese yen in the 1970s reduced the incentive for U.S. firms to invest abroad. German and Japanese firms began to invest more extensively in the United States; the decline in Volkswagen's market share and profits in the United States led to the decision to establish a U.S. assembly line. Volvo committed itself to a $100 million assembly plant in Tidewater, Virginia. Just as U.S. firms had increased their foreign investment as the dollar became overvalued, so German, Japanese, and other foreign firms increased their investment in the United States once the dollar appeared undervalued. Foreign investment in the United States began to grow three times as rapidly as U.S. investment abroad—the foreigners were coming.

271

The relation between foreign investments and the national interests of the host countries—and of the source countries—came under critical attack as nationalist pressures increased. By the late 1960s, when Servan-Schreiber's book came out, ownership of domestic factories and resources by foreign firms—especially by U.S. firms—had become a sensitive political issue in many countries. Was Canada worse off because such a large part of Canadian production occurred within U.S.-owned firms? Many Canadians thought so. Canada and other host countries feared that the activities of the giant multinational firms, especially those based in the United States, were a new form of imperialism, more insidious than the gunboats of the late nineteenth century. Nationalists in many countries—primarily in developing countries, but also in industrial countries like France and Canada—complained about a loss of sovereignty to the large international companies. Nationalist pressures were especially directed against firms engaged in extracting resources in developing countries. Peru expropriated International Petroleum, the local subsidiary of Exxon and also some of the local properties of W. R. Grace. Bolivia took over the local operations of Gulf Oil. In Chile, the Christian Democratic government of Eduardo Frei purchased 50 percent of Anaconda mines; subsequently, the Marxist government of Salvador Allende nationalized the rest of Anaconda's share as well as the mines of most other companies. Mexico has restricted foreign ownership to participation in joint ventures with Mexican partners; the share owned by foreign firms, once limited to 50 percent, is being further reduced.

The home countries are also concerned about foreign investment, especially about its possibly harmful effects on the balance of payments, on unemployment, and on tax revenues. Firms that wish to invest abroad may find it increasingly difficult to obtain approval from the governments of their own countries as well as from the would-be host countries.

Patterns of Market Penetration

By almost any measure, the foreign investments of U.S. firms are nearly twice as large as the foreign investments of all foreign-based firms combined. And if anything, this statistic underestimates the economic incentives for U.S. firms to invest abroad, since part of the "overseas investment" of British, French, and Dutch firms originated as domestic investment. For example, French companies held extensive assets in Algeria in the late 1950s; Algeria was then a geographical component of metropolitan France. When Algeria became independent, these domestic investments were counted as part of French foreign investment. British foreign investment is extensive in former colonies and the outposts of empire—Australia, South Africa, and Canada.

Why U.S. firms invest extensively abroad cannot be answered without first considering the unique qualities of each firm. A firm consists of individuals whose activities are coordinated by central management. The managers buy certain inputs to produce a variety of outputs. Most of the productive activities within the firm *could* be purchased, in modular fashion, from other firms. The managers might hire one company to develop new products, a second to produce them, a third to market them. The choice of whether to conduct an activity within the firm or to acquire the product of the same activity in the market is usually made on the basis of cost; competition forces the firm to choose the low-cost alternative. Some magazines—for example, *Playboy* and *Penthouse*—are primarily cut-and-paste jobs in that a very small editorial staff buys most of the stories and photos from free-lancers. *Time* and *Newsweek,* in contrast, maintain much larger staffs who write most of the stories.

Each type of firm has certain advantages—managerial and financial skills, marketing and engineering know-how, customer loyalties, and so forth. Firms are identifiable as repositories of marketing skills, financial skills, or organizational skills; these tags denote their advantages in relation to their competitors. Each firm continually seeks to exploit its advantages in the most efficient way. Since competitors are constantly trying to erode its advantages, the firm must continually strive to maintain its market position by developing new advantages and exploiting its established advantages in new markets, including those abroad. A firm may exploit its advantages directly, through sales to other firms, or indirectly, by selling goods which embody the advantages.

When a firm considers expansion into foreign markets, it must decide on the most efficient way of exploiting its advantages: it might export from domestic production, produce in the foreign market, or sell its know-how and other advantages. If the firm decides to produce abroad, it must consider whether to enter into a partnership with a host-country firm. The choice will depend on a variety of economic—and perhaps political—considerations.

Initially, the firm may supply the foreign market by exporting the output of its domestic plants. Then, after the foreign market has become sufficiently large, a plant may be established abroad. At first, the production in the foreign country may involve only the assembly of imported components, so as to save on transport costs and tariffs. The drug companies, for example, repackage drugs from large containers into smaller bottles; the auto companies assemble cars and trucks from imported components. As the host-country market expands, more of the inputs to the product may be locally produced, although the parent may continue to supply senior management, technical knowledge, and some financial assistance. As the scale of output in the host-country plant increases, production costs are likely to decline; the output of this subsidiary may supplement and perhaps ultimately supplant exports from the home-country plants.

At some point, costs in the subsidiary may fall below those in domestic plants, and the firm may begin to supply part or all of the domestic market from foreign subsidiaries. Ford imports motors for the Escort for the U.S. market from its English and Belgian subsidiaries. And some U.S. electronics firms produce part or all of the components for particular products in Taiwan, South Korea, Singapore, and Malaya; these components are then shipped to the United States for assembly into the final product.

The extensive integration of manufacturing activities in different countries is a relatively recent innovation. Initially the market for many products was local or regional; most of the local needs were satisfied from nearby production. Imports were minimal. Every town had its butcher, baker, and candlestick-maker, as well as its cobbler, tailor, and cigarmaker. The potential for cost reductions associated with large-scale production was small. And even where savings in production costs were possible, the extra costs of controlling a large-scale operation with activities in widely separated locations dominated the savings. The change in the last 150 years is that technological developments have both greatly increased the savings associated with large-scale production and reduced the costs of coordinating distant activities. Thus, bauxite mined in Jamaica is shipped to eastern Venezuela for refining to take advantage of extremely low-cost electricity. Some U.S. electronics companies fly partially assembled radio receivers to South Korea for further processing by skilled, relatively inexpensive labor. The combination of increasingly sophisticated products—higher unit values—and declining transportation and communications costs has reduced the pressure on firms to locate productive activity near either the market or the source of raw materials. As in banking, these changes in technology have increased the size of the market; regional markets are grouped into national markets, and national markets into the international market.

Enlargement of the market has encouraged firms to integrate their activities in different countries. In some countries a firm may both produce and market, in others it may only market, and in still others it may only produce. Thus, it is necessary to distinguish between the share of the world's market for a product held by U.S. firms, British firms, and Swiss firms, and the share of total production in each country undertaken by domestic firms and by foreign firms. The factors which explain where particular goods are produced are likely to differ from those which explain market shares, and both may differ from those which explain output shares. Servan-Schreiber focused on output shares, which is what U.S. industry in Europe is all about. Whereas U.S. firms produce largely in Europe to satisfy the European market, European firms traditionally satisfy the U.S. market by exporting European output. General Motors and Ford have major subsidiaries in Britain and Germany, while most of the European and Japanese auto companies supply the U.S. market from their domestic plants.

Why Firms Invest Abroad

Some reasons for overseas investments are noneconomic. General Leonard Wood established Sears, Roebuck stores in Mexico and elsewhere in Central America because he wanted to plant the U.S. flag in Latin America. A few firms may invest abroad because the corporation president likes semiannual trips to Madrid or Florence. Some firms invest abroad because of the bandwagon effect; their competitors are investing abroad, and they fear being left behind. The list of ad hoc explanations is long, and some individual investments may indeed be explained by one or several of these factors. But since the patterns of foreign investment do not appear to be random among countries, there is probably a systematic explanation for most—but not necessarily all—foreign investments.

U.S. firms competing in the European market are usually at a disadvantage in relation to their host-country competitors, since they incur costs their host-country competitors do not—albeit costs that have declined over the past fifty years. Thus, the activities of European subsidiaries must be managed from New York or Des Moines if they are to be integrated with those of the parent; the costs of plane travel across the Atlantic and international phone calls mount. And the salaries and expenses of U.S. managers in Europe may be several times higher than those of comparable European managers. Because of this cost disadvantage, firms with foreign subsidiaries must possess some offsetting advantages if their profit rates are to be comparable to those of their host-country competitors.

Similar statements might be made about European and Japanese firms which have set up or bought subsidiaries in the United States. These firms believe that it is more profitable to satisfy the U.S. market by producing in the United States than by exporting.

Three possible and nonexclusive advantages are attributed to the home-country firms. According to Servan-Schreiber, the U.S. advantage is a product of the combination of managerial know-how and a flexible business system. The United States often has superior businessmen; each manager may combine an undergraduate degree in engineering from MIT with a graduate degree in business from Harvard.

Superiority theories imply that Mother Nature plays favorites in the distribution of talent. If Americans were superior managers, the low-cost response for European firms would be clear: they should hire more American managers. Few do, although the success of the U.S. management consulting firms in Europe—the McKinseys, Booz Allens, and Boston Consulting Groups—is a substitute for hiring American managers. Other objections to the superiority hypothesis include its failure to provide insights about why foreign investment is so large in some industries and so small in others—and its failure to explain why the Dutch and Swiss invest extensively abroad, unless the Dutch and Swiss are also superior. Indeed, this "theory" is really a tautology. All it really says is that firms based in home countries are superior, and the evidence of their superiority is that they invest abroad.

A second explanation is that home-country firms have an advantage in the form of a patent or technical know-how or marketing skills, or other firm-specific advantages. In a few industries, these advantages may derive from large U.S. government programs in defense and space; however, this argument is irrelevant for the foreign activities of Playboy Clubs, Holiday Inns, Coca-Cola, or Pepsi. Of course, the advantages might reflect that relatively high U.S. wages compel U.S. firms to give greater attention to reducing their costs by developing labor-saving processes, while intense competition forces U.S. firms to develop new products for both old and newly created needs. So U.S. firms tend to develop "advantages" more rapidly than firms in other countries. Once these new products and processes have been developed to satisfy the domestic market, U.S. firms then seek to exploit these advantages to satisfy demands in foreign markets. So this explanation is directed to the market share question.

Presumably, the factors which explain why U.S. firms develop these advantages might also explain why firms in the Netherlands, Switzerland, and other countries also develop advantages which they then use to increase their sales abroad. So the question of what home-country firms have in common becomes a question of what characteristics do firms that develop advantages that have value abroad have in common.

The trouble with an explanation based on firm-specific advantages is its incompleteness about why firms in some countries develop more of these advantages than firms in other countries. Moreover, U.S. firms could sell their patents, know-how, and product advantages to foreign firms rather than incur the costs of managing subsidiaries located abroad. Indeed, many U.S. firms do exactly that by licensing their advantages. Coca-Cola sells franchises and its concentrate to foreign producers. If the sales prices for advantages were sufficiently high, few U.S. firms would ever incur the cost of establishing subsidiaries abroad.

So the reluctance to sell the firm-specific advantages to host-country firms must be explained. One suggestion is that firms fear that such sales might facilitate the growth of foreign firms which would later become their competitors. An alternative suggestion is that firms may find it difficult to sell the advantages, perhaps because they are ill-defined, especially if research and development lead to continuing changes in the advantages or if they involve marketing know-how. Thus each time the "know-how" changes, a new negotiation between producer and buyer would be necessary. The more general reason for their reluctance to sell their advantages is that the firms believe their income will be higher if they exploit them through wholly owned subsidiaries.

A third explanation is that firms invest abroad when further expansion within their traditional industries in the domestic market becomes difficult or expensive. One reason might be that demand for their products is growing more slowly, perhaps because the domestic market is saturated. In this situation, the firms might expand into other industries in the domestic market—that is, they might cross the borders between industries. Alternatively, they might cross national borders, expanding abroad with their traditional products. For many firms, crossing national borders may be easier than crossing industry borders, given their expertise in producing or marketing particular products. This view explains why firms seek foreign markets, but not why they produce abroad. It may explain market shares, but it does not explain output shares.

A fourth explanation of the pattern of direct foreign investment—the capital market view—is that U.S. firms and those based in other home countries have an advantage in the world capital market: they can borrow at lower interest rates and sell their shares at higher prices than firms in the host countries. These firms benefit from country-specific advantages.

Interest rates on dollar bonds have been lower than those on debts denominated in nearly every other currency for most of the last half-century, and especially when U.S. firms invested abroad extensively. Since the dollar is their domestic currency, U.S.

firms are able to borrow on more advantageous terms than their foreign competitors. Canadian and European firms have come to New York to borrow, not because they want to spend the funds in the United States but because U.S. interest rates are sufficiently below their domestic interest rates to justify incurring the exchange risk.

One consequence of the general preference of investors for dollar securities is that U.S. firms are willing to pay more for an advantage—for an income stream—than non-U.S. firms. And given an opportunity to increase its income by undertaking a new project, a U.S. firm will generally pay a higher price for the same anticipated income stream than a non-U.S. firm. The other side of the coin is that if a U.S. firm buys a French firm, even though the earnings of the French subsidiary remain unchanged, investors will pay more for the equities because of their preferences for dollar-denominated assets.

This suggests that the advantages of U.S. firms are inherent in investor preferences for assets denominated in dollars, just as the advantages of Swiss firms are inherent in investor preferences for assets denominated in Swiss francs. U.S. firms are *identified* with dollar equities, just as Swiss firms are identified with Swiss franc equities, and Dutch firms with guilder equities. A firm cannot change the currency denomination of its equities without changing its national identity. And firms almost never change their nationalities. As long as interest rates on dollar assets are low relative to those on assets in other currencies, U.S. firms will have a country-specific advantage, an advantage that foreign firms cannot buy since it is inherent in the system rather than in the behavior of individual firms.

The implication of the capital market view is that the home countries for foreign investment are those with relatively low interest rates. Casual observation suggests that the countries other than the United States which have been large exporters of direct foreign investment—Switzerland, the Netherlands, and Great Britain—have traditionally been low interest rate countries. The

280

Netherlands was the low interest rate country in the eighteenth century, when the Dutch empire was expanding abroad and Dutch trading firms were setting up overseas offices. In the nineteenth century, Great Britain was the low interest rate country, and British firms followed the growth of the empire. Even though both political empires have shrunk markedly since then, the large international businesses like Unilever and Shell in the Netherlands and in Great Britain have continued to flourish.

The capital market view also explains the pattern of ownership in different countries—whether individual countries will be home countries or host countries. As long as the dollar is the preferred currency, U.S. firms will establish foreign branches and buy up foreign firms. Foreign ownership of plants in the United States and foreign takeovers of U.S. firms may increase, but the capital market explanation suggests that the growth of U.S. investment abroad will be substantially larger; more importantly, the output shares of U.S. firms will increase.

The test of any theory is its ability to explain observed events. One of the most demanding phenomena to explain is the surge in investment in the United States by European and Japanese firms in the late 1970s and the early 1980s. How capable are these theories of explaining the takeovers of Howard Johnson's and A & P and Marshall Field & Co. by firms headquartered abroad? The Servan-Schreiber view would be that—all of a sudden—the Europeans and the Japanese developed superior abilities to combine technical and managerial skills. In contrast, if the theories that emphasize firm-specific advantages are correct, the implication is that European and Japanese firms must have surged ahead in developing such advantages—yet the relevance of these advantages to the foreign takeovers of U.S. firms is questionable. There are newspaper stories which suggest that foreign firms invested extensively in the United States because they wanted to participate in the largest consumer market in the world; however, many participate in the U.S. market by exporting their domestic production. Some firms are said to have invested in the United States as political insurance; they feared that military events in Europe or moves toward governmental ownership would handicap their survivability. Yet the advantage of these foreign firms relative to U.S. firms in the U.S. market remains unexplained.

TABLE 17.1
Flows of Direct Foreign Investment
(Billions of U.S. dollars)

	United States	France	Germany	Great Britain	Japan	Canada
Outflows						
1970	7.6	0.4	0.9	1.3	0.4	0.3
1975	14.2	1.6	2.0	2.4	1.8	0.9
1978	16.3	2.0	3.6	4.6	2.4	1.8
1980	20.6	2.9	4.5	6.7	2.4	2.3
Inflows						
1970	1.5	0.6	0.6	0.9	0.1	0.9
1975	2.6	1.6	0.7	1.2	0.2	0.7
1978	7.8	2.9	1.7	2.4	0.0	0.0
1980	8.2	3.2	1.4	3.2	0.3	0.5

SOURCE: U.S. Department of Commerce, *International Economic Indicators* (September 1982).

Thus few theories do a good job of explaining why the incentive of U.S. firms to invest abroad has declined in the last several years, while the incentive for German and Japanese firms to invest abroad has increased. The change in the low-cost location of investment is explained by the changes in exchange rates which are larger than the changes in relative costs of production. During the same period that the mark and the yen appreciated, interest rates on assets denominated in these currencies fell; and so firms headquartered in both countries had less of a disadvantage—and more of an advantage—than firms based in the United States.

Two factors explain why U.S. firms still seem to dominate the lists of multinationals, despite the Japanese and German surges in the 1970s and early 1980s. One is that because the dollar was more or less continuously overvalued from the 1920s to the 1970s, U.S. firms were obliged to invest and produce abroad if they were to be competitive in foreign markets. The second is that U.S. firms have had a modest advantage in the international capital market. This advantage disappeared in the late 1970s when interest rates on dollar assets rose significantly above interest rates on assets denominated in the German mark and the Japanese yen.

The Costs of Direct Foreign Investment

One of the paradoxes of the recent decade is that both home-country governments and host-country governments have questioned the economic advantages attached to the activities of multinational firms. That these firms have grown and expanded suggests efficiencies greater than those of the smaller domestic firms they have supplanted. The benefits of these efficiencies must be distributed among their employees as higher wages and salaries, or among their customers as lower prices, or among their shareholders as higher profits and dividends. All three groups may gain. Either the home country or the host country may gain as a result of their activities, or both may gain; it is implausible that both home and host countries could be worse off at the same time.

The home countries have several major criticisms of multinationals. One involves runaway jobs; unions often find that international firms circumvent their national monopoly over the supply of labor. Foreign investment affects the distribution of jobs among countries, just as changes in trade patterns do. Belatedly—fifty years belatedly—the unions are becoming interested in the international labor situation. Hence, the choice for the unions in the home country is whether to merge with unions in the host countries or to develop some other fraternal relationship with these unions.

A second criticism involves taxes: the foreign income of the domestic firm is taxed initially by the foreign government, and in most cases there is little left over for the domestic tax collector. For example, the United States has double-taxation agreements with many other countries. These agreements provide that the income is taxable first in the country in which it is earned, and that the combined tax rate of the foreign host and the U.S. government cannot exceed the higher of the two national rates. Assume the British tax rate is 40 percent and the U.S. rate is 50 percent. If a U.S. firm invests at home, each dollar of profit generates 50 cents for the U.S. tax collector. If the firm invests in Britain, each dollar of profit generates 40 cents for the British tax collector and only 10 cents for the U.S. collector. So the British have an incentive to attract foreign investment—their tax payments.

A third concern involves the adverse balance-of-payments consequences. Foreign investments mean that exports decline and imports increase more rapidly than might otherwise occur. While the payment of dividends may counter the loss of exports, the offset may be partial rather than complete.

These criticisms imply that the home-country firm faces a choice between producing at home or producing abroad, when the effective choice for some firms may be producing abroad or not producing at all. The shift in the production of many electronics products to Southeast Asia occurred because production costs there were much lower than in the United States; if U.S. firms had not joined German, Dutch, and Japanese firms in this move, they would have lost both their export markets and the domestic market. The loss of U.S. jobs, the shortfall in U.S. tax revenues, and the adverse impact on the U.S. balance of payments would have been even sharper. Even if U.S. firms might have retained the domestic market, at least for a while, without shifting to offshore production, their long-run competitive position would have been weaker.

There are other criticisms. During the dollar crises, the multinationals moved funds to avoid losses from the changes in exchange rates; some may have also sought to profit. Some critics even suggest that the crises resulted from the behavior of the firms, and not from the mismanagement of the system.

An even more sensitive issue involves the alleged political involvement of the multinationals in the host countries. Multinationals may contribute to political parties, much as host-country firms do. ITT tried to forestall the election of Allende in Chile. Again, the firms say they act to protect their interests. The criticism is that the interests of the firm may be identical neither with U.S. national interests nor with the interests of the host countries.

Home-country governments—or at least the U.S. government—may be embarrassed and inconvenienced by disclosure of the political activities of the multinationals. But the managers of the firms are paid to protect the firm's interests. And they have on occasion found that the methods of decision making and persuasion that are typical, or at least not uncommon, in the host country would not be generally accepted at a New England town meeting.

Host-country attitudes toward multinational firms are ambivalent. Many countries compete to attract foreign firms, for they bring employment, on-the-job training, and tax revenues. In many products, these firms provide access to world markets. Yet foreign investment has been much criticized within the host countries. Some of these criticisms are vague and reflect simpleminded xenophobia; foreign investment is equated with imperialism. Having nationals work for foreigners or having foreigners own domestic resources is said to demean the nation. Other criticisms are more specific: the foreign firm exploits the nation's patrimony of nonreproducible petroleum or copper or bauxite or tin, or reduces employment, or evades taxes, or stifles domestic entrepreneurship. The host-country government may feel that foreign-owned firms diminish its sovereignty and may resent these firms' involvement in the domestic political process.

Appraisal of these criticisms requires a benchmark, a view of what would have happened to growth, income, employment, and corporate development had foreign investment not taken place. Assume that the Canadian government had progressively restricted the operation of foreign firms in Canada. More of the Canadian market would now be supplied by the domestic production of Canadian firms. And Canadian imports from the same U.S. firms which now have Canadian subsidiaries would increase. Canadian incomes would be lower, or at least would have grown more slowly, since the supply of capital and knowledge would have been smaller or more expensive. But determining the relative size of each of these adjustments is virtually impossible on an a priori basis. The Canadian firms that replaced the U.S. firms would import some of the resources that the Canadian subsidiaries of U.S. firms now get from their parents, and they might pay higher prices. As a group, Canadians would be worse off. But whether they would be worse off by 1 percent or 5 percent is difficult to estimate. Perhaps they might gain more control over their destiny—or their culture might remain purer—but these factors too are difficult to measure.

One of the major concerns of small countries is that they might become technological backwaters; these countries fear that because their own science and technology and industries do not offer attractive careers, highly educated and trained nationals will migrate to the larger countries. Multinational companies often centralize their research and development activities in a relatively few locations, which is why government officials sometimes view the large international firm as impeding the development of a viable local scientific community. The underlying presumption is that in the absence of the multinational company, domestic firms would undertake research and development comparable to that done abroad by the foreign firm. Perhaps. But it is equally possible that the domestic firms might import their research and development because the import costs would be less than domestic production costs.

Host-country governments worry that multinational firms diminish their sovereignty. Occasionally the head office of a firm may, in response to pressures from its own government, direct the subsidiary to cease exporting to certain markets or to shift funds to the home office. Host countries fear that the power and influence of the state may not be used directly against a foreign firm, perhaps because it enjoys the backing of its more powerful government. The host-country government would like to be able to rely on foreign as well as on domestic firms to increase exports or boost employment, or to take other measures that may not be in the firm's interests. Foreign firms may be less amenable to such measures than domestic firms would be. Perhaps. But foreign firms know they can be asked—or forced—to leave the country. For this reason, they may be less able than domestic firms to withstand the pressures of the government.

To the extent that firms offer access to the world market, they are likely to be the "pawns" of competing national governments. For example, when Canada adopted a set of measures to induce U.S. auto companies to produce more cars in Canada, U.S. employment and U.S. tax revenues declined. When Malaya adopted a set of measures to attract foreign electronics firms, Singapore and Taiwan began to worry, much more than did the United States and Japan.

Foreign firms are sometimes accused of making excessively high profits, especially in the extraction of nonreproducible resources. Host-country governments know that mines or wells will eventually be exhausted, so they want to maximize national gains from these resources. Typically, the host-country governments have auctioned concessions to exploit the resources; they may receive a lump-sum payment or a contingent payment based on the profits. If a concession proves attractive and profitable, then a host country may seek to revise the contract in its own favor. But the game is asymmetrical; if the firm fails to discover oil or the concession proves unprofitable, the company never gets a refund. In some cases, of course, the arguments for reopening the contract may be strong; perhaps the state issued the concession under duress. Or a minister may have been bribed and thus have betrayed the interests of his government. Since most resource-owning countries manage to attract foreign firms to exploit their resources, the threat of contract renegotiation cannot be too severe. And increasingly, the firms may recognize the likelihood of expropriation or contract renegotiation as they determine how much—or how little—to bid.

In manufacturing, the profits earned by a foreign company reflect its efficiency. High profits mean that the firm can satisfy the market demands more efficiently than its domestic competitors. High profits also mean higher taxes to the host-country government. And higher efficiency allows the firm to use fewer domestic resources, which are thus available for other uses. Most governments, of course, would like to get the taxes and the efficiency, but at a lower cost in terms of profits to foreign firms.

The arguments are inconclusive. At various times (like nearly every year), the Canadians have set up study groups to determine whether Canadian interests have been served by the presence of multinationals. There is a supply of anecdotes about the misbehavior of the multinationals; the critics have a point or two, if not a case. The virulence of the criticism is more evidence of the increasing nationalist sentiment so evident in monetary policies.

Various governments have set up foreign investment review boards to screen desirable foreign investments from less desirable proposals. The United Nations has developed a code of conduct for multinational firms, a sort of Emily Post guide to behavior. Why the code should apply only to multinational firms is unclear; fairness suggests that all firms be affected.

Whither the Conflict?

The conflict between governments and multinationals is likely to become more intense. Problems arise because the firms are dynamic organizations and respond to developments in technology and markets, while political organizations—states—remain largely static. Firms grow and consolidate and expand their activities around the world in response to changing profit opportunities, while the states are locked into a more or less fixed set of boundaries. Reductions in the costs of transportation and communication increase the mobility of business firms, but this increased mobility may be viewed as a threat by the governments of host countries.

In many industries the growth and expansion of multinationals has increased competition and reduced the monopoly power of the dominant domestic firms. The U.S. automobile industry is much more competitive because of the eagerness of foreign firms to export to the U.S. market, and the German automobile industry is more competitive because of the presence of General Motors and Ford. Sony and Panasonic have greatly increased competition in the electronics industry, so there is now an international electronics industry. In drugs, chemicals, and numerous other industries, trade and investment have substantially increased the number of participants. And evidence of unusually attractive profits would be expected to induce other firms to enter the market.

Inevitably, pressures to regulate the multinational corporations—and to regulate the capacity of states to regulate these corporations—will develop. Because the issues are complex and the interests of various states and corporations highly diverse, ambitious efforts at a regulatory code are not likely to succeed. Three changes are possible. The first is an agreement among governments to limit their reach into the foreign activities of firms which they identify as "their corporate citizens"—or into the extraterritorial span of national control. This change would be directed primarily at the United States. The second, a set of rules governing the entrance of foreign firms into manufacturing, would be much like the rules governing the access of foreign goods to the domestic markets. These rules might specify when access should be unimpaired and when the firm might be required to join with a local partner. The third is a set of rules about compensation for foreign firms when their property is expropriated or when they are otherwise deprived of the full value of their advantages.

Yet the likelihood of meaningful rules is small, at least in the near future. And the reason is that governments in both the home and host countries appear to find more political support in what is effectively an ad hoc approach to regulation. In other words, the economic issues interest them less than the domestic votes.

18

Japan: The First Superstate?

In 1970 Herman Kahn, physicist and nuclear theorist, predicted that Japan would become the first superstate—Japan's GNP would double between 1970 and 1975; and again between 1975 and 1980— a fourfold expansion in a decade. Between 1970 and 2000, annual average growth rates would reach 9 percent a year, so that by the year 2000 GNP would be nearly sixteen times the 1970 levels. The news was heartening to the Japanese and frightening to most other countries because of the competitive impact of Japanese goods in world markets.

No country has presented more of a challenge to international trade and monetary arrangements. Yet a prediction about the Japanese challenge would have seemed absurd in 1950 or 1960. Japan had been bombed extensively in the last several years of World War II, its factories ravaged. Its colonies in Manchuria, Korea, and Taiwan had been lost. Japan had very few raw materials and needed to import most of its energy and much of its food. It almost seemed as if Japan would remain forever on the international dole—if there had been any donors.

Within a generation, Japanese exports were the most rapidly growing component of international trade. Japanese producers dominated world markets for consumer goods, cameras, and supertankers. By the early 1970s the Japanese seemed a threat, more insidious than during World War II, for the Japanese were playing by the rules of the system and winning.

Early in the 1960s the Japanese government had adopted a ten-year "Doubling National Income" plan. With a population growth rate of 1 percent a year, per capita incomes would double in a decade if the growth rate of economic production were 7 percent a year. Actual economic performance beat the targets of the plan, in contrast to most other countries, where economic performance has almost always lagged behind the target. By 1967 Japanese per capita incomes were twice as high as in 1960.

Kahn's prediction was based on the extrapolation of the growth rates of the 1960s through the next thirty years. In the 1960s, Japan had grown at the rate of 12 percent a year; in contrast, the United States had grown at the rate of 3 percent, and Germany and France at rates of 6 to 7 percent a year. Simple arithmetic suggests that if a country with a lower level of income grows more rapidly than a country with a higher level, the rapid-growth country will eventually overtake and surpass the higher income-level country, no matter how large its initial disadvantage.

In the early 1980s, a new industry appeared—books which sought to reveal the secrets of the Japanese economic miracle. The story in *Japan as Number One,* by Ezra F. Vogel, is one of tradition, literacy, social cohesion, and a Puritan or Confucian work ethic. *The Art of Japanese Management,* by Richard T. Pascale and Anthony G. Althos, and *Theory Z,* by William Ouchi, emphasized the skill of industrial managers in developing a consensus among workers before introducing any change. *The East Asia Edge* highlighted the "Gang of Four"—Korea, Hong Kong, Taiwan, and Singapore—who were achieving gains in economic well-being as rapidly as Japan. *Shogun,* by James Clavell, had its own story, at least by implication; business firms in various industries competed extensively for market share, just as several centuries earlier feudal war lords had competed for power and fame and attention. Some explanations gave priority to "Japan, Inc.," asserting that the economic success was a result of cooperative planning between business and government leaders. Probably each of these explanations had some validity—and so the problem was to determine their relative importance.

Increases in national income result from increases both in the number of man-hours (and woman-hours) worked, and in labor output or productivity per man-hour. Increases in the volume of capital equipment and technological improvement lead to increases in labor productivity; the workers are smarter and have more powerful machines to work with.

In most industrial societies, labor supplies grew rapidly during the 1960s as members of the post-World War II baby boom graduated into the labor force. Yet, in all of these economies, the work week was becoming shorter, vacations were becoming longer, there were more holidays with pay, and the retirement age was lowered. All these changes were normal economic responses to growing material affluence, so the number of hours of work per year probably declined. Increasing absenteeism and more voluntary unemployment also led to a reduction in the effective labor supply. So differences in growth rates largely reflected differences in productivity growth. Somehow the Japanese did something better—while they may have worked harder, they could not have worked progressively harder year after year for a decade and a half, or else they would have been able to run the mile in under three minutes.

The arithmetic of growth should be distinguished from the economics of growth. What was needed was a story that explained why Japanese firms invested so much, and whether the high productivity growth rate was closely tied to the high rates of saving and investment. The high savings rate—three times as high as in the United States—was explained in institutional terms. Because Japan lacked adequate social security, individuals saved to provide for their old age.

Then the willingness of firms to invest had to be explained.

One story centered on the Japan, Inc. concept—that the Japanese business and government leaders planned the penetration and takeover of world markets. Government greatly facilitated business expansion, so the story went, or maybe it was the other way around. Moreover, the Japanese took advantage of the low tariffs abroad, but did not allow easy entry of foreign goods into their domestic markets.

For fans of the market system and free trade, these ideas were heretical. The first implied that a planned economic system could deliver a higher growth rate than a market system. The second implied that a country could gain if it maintained tariffs and other import barriers, whereas the free trade argument is that such barriers retard growth. According to the fans of free enterprise and the market system, planning and import barriers should have led to a lower growth rate.

Soon after Kahn's book appeared, the Japanese economy began to falter. There was a sharp recession in 1971. In the context of the world inflation of 1972 and 1973, the Japanese price level increased by 30 percent a year. In 1974, Japan was hit by the world recession. It began to appear that the cyclical behavior of the Japanese economy mimicked the swings of the world business cycle, but in a highly exaggerated fashion. When world business was booming, the Japanese economy purred. But when the world economy burped, the indigestion in Japan was severe.

In the 1970s, Japanese growth was still higher than in other industrial economies. But the excess of the Japanese growth rate over the U.S. growth rate in the 1970s was significantly lower than in the previous several decades.

The slowdown in the Japanese growth rate was almost certainly inevitable. Those who had projected a continuation of rapid growth had failed to recognize that no element in the system can grow more rapidly than the system for an extended period. Rapid growth in Japanese income requires a corresponding rapid growth in Japanese imports, because Japan lacks raw materials and foodstuffs. Imports, however, must be financed by an approximately equal rapid growth of exports. If Japanese exports grow at 8 percent a year while world exports grow at 4 percent a year, then Japanese exports would eventually be larger than world exports.

The second factor that is usually overlooked is the contrast between Japanese economic growth after World War II and before. From the late nineteenth century until the beginning of what is sometimes euphemistically called "The Great Pacific Confusion" in Tokyo, economic growth in Japan averaged between 4 and 4.5 percent a year. The increase in the growth rate shortly before the turn of the century resulted from a commitment to industrialize, undertaken to prevent or withstand the rapacious Western powers who coveted spheres of influence and turf in Japan as they had in China. This economic growth rate, which consisted of productivity gains of about 3 percent a year and increases in the labor force of about 1 percent a year, was not significantly higher than the growth rates of most other countries during the early stages of their industrialization.

The data suggest per capita incomes in Japan were unchanged during World War II. Immediately after the war, however, cut off from supplies, extensively damaged by massive bombing, short of foods, and bereft of foreign markets, Japanese per capita income fell sharply.

In the late 1940s and early 1950s, economic growth in Japan began to increase rapidly, more so than at any time in the previous sixty years. Much of this growth was "making up arrears" and recovering from the calamitous economic consequences of the war. By getting the railway switches to work, the railway system was put back to work; small investments appeared to have tremendous potential in increasing output. However, not until the mid-1950s did per capita income in Japan reach prewar levels. Incomes in the United States had more than doubled over the same fifteen years.

Assume, in the absence of a war, that Japanese income had continued to grow at the historic rate of 4 percent a year. Then

295

per capita income would have doubled from 1940 to 1958 and doubled again from 1958 to 1976. However, in the mid-1950s, per capita incomes were only one-half of what they would have been had there been no war. The rapid growth in the 1960s meant that Japan actually achieved the income levels it would have attained had there been no war with the projection of the pre-1940 growth rate into the 1940s, the 1950s, and the 1960s.

TABLE 18.1
Japan's Growth Rates: Real GNP
(Average annual rates of growth, percentage)

Terminal Year	Base Year							
	1900	1910	1920	1930	1940	1950	1960	1970
1910	3.3							
1920	3.9	4.5						
1930	4.3	4.8	5.1					
1940	3.5	3.6	3.2	1.2				
1950	3.3	3.3	2.9	1.8	2.3			
1960	3.8	3.8	3.7	3.2	4.2	6.1		
1970	4.8	5.0	5.1	5.1	6.4	8.6	11.1	
1980	4.8	5.0	5.1	5.1	6.1	7.4	8.0	5.0

SOURCE: Bank of Japan, *Hundred Year Statistics of the Japanese Economy* (1981).
NOTE: The figure in each cell shows the average annual growth from the base year at the head of each column to the terminal year noted at the far left.

Thus far, the story is one of arithmetic. Any number of stories might be devised to explain why the growth rate was so much higher after the war than before. One is that once the labor force, the savings rate, and competitive spirit were organized to achieve an 8 percent growth rate, momentum alone would lead to a continuation of the rate. The increase in the growth rate in the early postwar years could be viewed as a counterpart to the increase in the growth rate in the late nineteenth century, when the campaign to industrialize was first undertaken.

The competing scenario is that the Japanese economy had tremendous excess capacity immediately following World War II, and that rapid growth could be maintained as long as there were no bottlenecks. In the early postwar period there was in fact substantial idle capacity in industry because of the shortages of switches, spare parts, raw materials, and markets. But once this idle capacity was utilized, continuing the growth momentum would become progressively harder. Similarly, the skills of the labor force may have been less than fully utilized if many individuals were working at jobs below their potential as gauged by their education. Once their skills were fully utilized, it would be more difficult to maintain the growth rate.

Japan, Inc.

All economies face the same questions—what should be produced, in what volumes, and by what techniques? In some economies, decisions about what to produce and how to produce it are made in a highly decentralized way by the managers in tens of thousands of firms in response to their views about consumer demand. In other countries a few government officials, perhaps at a planning agency or the finance ministry, make these same decisions; if they err, some goods will be in short supply and others will pile up in the stores. In both cases there is always the concern that if too many firms invest in the plant and equipment designed to produce similar goods, productive capacity will be excessive, prices will be cut, anticipated profits will evaporate, and some firms will incur substantial losses.

Adam Smith once said that businessmen rarely meet without deciding how to "carve up" markets—how to ensure that competition is not so excessive that it leads to lower prices. In the United States, legislation limits business practices intended to stifle competition, including price-fixing agreements and mergers which reduce the number of competitors in an industry.

Few other countries have such legislation. The concern is that as a consequence of the more stringent U.S. antitrust policies, foreign firms have an advantage—they can be confident that investments will be profitable, and that supply will not be excessive, because they can meet and discuss the measures to limit excessive competition. In contrast, managers of U.S. firms are subject to greater uncertainty about whether contemplated investments will prove profitable.

Somehow the view became pervasive that the Japanese success in penetrating world markets with textiles and steel and autos and electronic equipment was unfair. Partly the criticism centered on the imbalances in trade. Japanese imports were largely raw materials, which were noncompetitive with Japanese production. In contrast, Japanese exports to the industrial countries were almost always competitive with goods produced in those countries. Japanese imports of manufactured products were very low, leading to charges that the import barriers were both formal and hidden in Japan. There was also continuing concern that the Japanese were subsidizing exports or otherwise dumping them—selling them abroad at prices below Japanese prices and transport costs. Or perhaps the Japanese had an unfair advantage in the way their business system was organized.

The Japan, Inc. metaphor developed while Japanese economic growth was flourishing. Businessmen and officials of two powerful government agencies were supposed to meet to formalize market-sharing arrangements. One agency, the Ministry of Finance (MOF) was the ultimate controller of the supply of credit and the owner and manager of the Bank of Japan. So MOF was in a powerful position to secure business cooperation because of its ability to allocate credit to the commercial banks which in turn supplied credit to industrial borrowers. The second agency, the Ministry of International Trade and Investment (MITI), controlled import licenses and hence was in a strong position to influence firms to limit investments. If they didn't listen, MITI would be unresponsive on import licenses. Thus, the story went, businessmen responded readily to government initiatives, suggestions, and requests. According to this model, government officials were relatively strong and in a powerful position to affect business decisions.

An alternative model of competition within Japan is a twentieth-century version of struggles among feudal war lords for power, authority, prestige, and standing. According to this view, the descendants of these war lords, the *zaibatsu* or *keiretsu*—the Sumitomos, the Mitsubishis, the Mitsuis—are a family of firms in a variety of industries, including a trading firm, a bank, a steel firm, a shipping line, a petrochemical firm, a subset of textile firms, and so on. Each group engages in extensive mutual support, favoring other members of the group in buying inputs, selling outputs, and supplying credits. There are interlocking share ownerships—the Mitsui Bank lends funds to firms that are primarily attached to other *zaibatsu*.

Moreover, within each industry, every firm is extremely conscious about its market position—whether it is the number one firm or the number five firm. Each firm accepts its market position, but each is very reluctant for its position to decline because of the loss in prestige. Finally, unlike other competitive industrial countries, few large firms go out of business, and mergers are very infrequent.

The second model differs sharply from the first. The first suggests that rapid growth is a result of effective central planning or coordination; the second implies that rapid growth is a result of much more extensive competition than in other industrial countries. The number of firms in the major industries is much larger than in Western economies. For example, there are six or seven major automobile firms in Japan, whereas there are only two or three in the United States. In photoequipment there are Yashica, Asahi, Mamiya, and Fuji; in the United States, Kodak and Polaroid. The Japanese motorcycle industry includes Honda, Suzuki, Kawasaki, and Yamaha. In hifi equipment, Kenwood, Matsushita, Sony, Toshiba, Hitachi, Sanyo, Sharp, and AIWA compete for market share. Industry by industry, there appear to be many more firms than in the United States or Western Europe, even though the Japanese economy is substantially smaller than the U.S. economy and the Western European economy. Rapid economic growth has not led to a sharp reduction in the number of firms in Japan as it has in other industrial countries.

To maintain its market share, each firm must obtain the capital necessary to finance increases in its plant and equipment. If losses are incurred, financial support is from related firms in the *zaibatsu*. And the workers accept smaller than average wage increases, for they know their futures are intimately linked with that of their employers. If the firms were to go bankrupt, the future of the employees would be bleak because the lifetime employment system means that job mobility is low.

The implication is that the roles of capitalists and bankers and workers in Japan are reversed from those in other market economies. In the United States and Britain, the workers have the first claim on the revenues of the firm; firms go out of business when wage rates and labor costs are too high relative to revenues to repay the bankers and other lenders. In Japan, by contrast, workers divide up that part of the revenues which remains after the bankers are paid. So there is a substantial difference among firms in wages paid workers of similar skills. And this is possible because wages within each firm are determined by seniority rather than by job classification. Moreover, part of the wage payment consists of a semiannual bonus, and the size of the bonus can be varied as revenues vary.

The stability of market shares might seem consistent with the planning model or with the competitive model. If the planning model were dominant, it might be inferred that government would have attempted to have rationalized the business system by reducing the number of firms. Such changes have occurred—but in a very modest way. To the extent that the planning model is relevant, the Japanese growth rate has been reduced and the impact of Japanese competition in world markets has been dampened.

The External Impact of Japan

The rapid increase in the size of the Japanese economy has had an increasingly disruptive impact on the economies of the nation's trading partners. In the 1950's and 1960's, during the pegged-rate exchange system period, Japan had a stable balance of payments cycle: three years of increasingly larger payments deficits were followed by a year of payments surplus. The story is that as the business cycle developed its momentum, the rate of growth of imports increased while the rate of growth of exports declined, so that the annual payments deficits became larger and larger. The payments deficits were financed by annual increases in the amounts borrowed abroad. As the ability to borrow in the United States and Europe to finance the payments deficits decreased, the Bank of Japan was forced to contract credit, and the growth in Japanese demand and income became sluggish. Import demand dropped sharply and export supply soared, for firms were much more eager to sell abroad once domestic growth slackened. The payments balance responded quickly and a large surplus developed so that the loans used to finance the deficits in previous years could be readily repaid. And, because export sales were usually only 20 or 30 percent of domestic sales, a small reduction in domestic demand led to a several times larger percentage increase in exports. The story was simple; once Japanese firms had the productive capacity in place, goods could be produced; if they could not be sold at home, they would be sold abroad at the prices necessary to clear the market. Better to sell at discount—or even distress—prices abroad than to engage in price competition in the domestic market, or not to produce at all.

From time to time, whenever Japanese domestic growth faltered, the rest of the world was subjected to a sharp increase in Japanese sales. The growth of Japanese exports was countercyclical to the growth of Japanese income. The ability to sell in foreign markets enabled Japan to cushion the movements of its own business cycle. In a way, Japan was exporting inflation when it was booming because of the surge in its demand for imports, and it was exporting deflation whenever its own growth slowed significantly.

In the 1950s and 1960s, the international monetary system could readily adjust to the payments deficits that resulted whenever the Japanese wanted to have payments surpluses. As long as Japan was reasonably small, the rest of the world could accommodate the surge in Japanese exports. Many of these exports were directed to the United States, which was a large and reasonably open market. Marketing in the United States was substantially easier than trying to sell the same goods in smaller economies. Individual firms and groups of firms in the United States complained about unfair competition; they continually asserted that some Japanese firms were dumping. The Japanese had two responses—that they were not dumping, and besides, even if they were, cutting prices was the only way they could increase their sales in the U.S. market. So the U.S. response was to lean on Japan to follow "orderly marketing procedures."

In the 1950s and 1960s, after the contractive monetary policy had shifted the payments balance into a comfortable surplus position, the Bank of Japan relaxed its monetary policies and the economy resumed its rapid growth rate. However, in the early 1970s, there was a sharp change; when the Bank of Japan loosened monetary reins, the increase in effective demand was weaker. Because domestic demand in Japan was not growing nearly as rapidly as productive capacity, Japan continued to earn large payments surpluses as exports boomed. In effect the Japanese were selling Toyotas and Sonys and buying U.S. Treasury bills, not because this was intended, but because they could not manage their economy to reduce exports relative to imports. In both 1969 and 1970, the current account surpluses were 4 to 5 percent of national income in Japan; in 1971 and 1972, the ratio approached 10 percent. Since for every surplus there is a deficit, the inability of the Japanese to manage domestic demand relative to its productive capacity meant it was exporting very large payments deficits to its trading partners, principally to the United States.

The resulting U.S. payments deficits were a major factor in the breakdown of the Bretton Woods system. Even in the absence of the more rapid inflation in the United States than abroad, the Japanese surpluses would have threatened the stability of the system. Theory suggests that revaluation of the yen in response to the excessively large Japanese payments surplus would have reduced the Japanese surplus. If a small revaluation would not have been effective, than a larger revaluation might have succeeded. In 1971, however, Japan was reluctant to revalue; any decline in exports relative to imports would have intensified unemployment in Japan.

In 1973, as the world economy boomed and prices of raw materials imports increased, the trade surplus declined. Japan's oil import bill alone went up by $15 billion a year. Japan had a modest payments deficit in 1974. When the world recession hit in 1975, domestic demand in Japan grew sluggishly, and once again Japanese producers began to ship more abroad. Comparisons across countries indicated a much greater cyclical variation in the payments balance in Japan than elsewhere. The story was simple—when the growth in Japanese income was rapid, Japan's exports would grow slowly, and when Japanese income grew slowly Japanese exports would grow rapidly. Variations in the growth of domestic income were the major factors in explaining the changes in Japanese trade balance.

With the move to floating exchange rates, the textbooks predicted that Japan would always be in payments balance, if the Bank of Japan would not buy and sell dollars. Yet in 1977 and 1978 Japanese payments surpluses were extremely large, because the Bank of Japan was a massive buyer of dollars. Paradoxically, these payments surpluses were much, much larger than had ever been experienced under the pegged-rate system;

when the rules of the Bretton Woods system were abandoned, the system was left without rules. Without intervention, the yen would have appreciated sharply, and the Japanese exporters would have been obliged to cut export prices sharply, or else forgo sales. The problem was the same as under the pegged-rate system—if domestic income was growing sluggishly, then excess productive capacity would have to be geared to export sales.

In a mercantilist world, the Japanese payments surpluses might represent the success of economic policy. But the proposition is not convincing: the excessively large surpluses represent the failure of policy. The managers of Japan, Inc. had failed to design a system which was able to cope with cyclical imbalances without placing great strain on its international trading relationships. The likelihood that Japan will bear out the Kahn prediction is low.

 19

Optimal Bankrupts: Deadbeats on
an International Treadmill

Deadbeat—Someone who deliberately avoids paying his debts.

The third edition of this chapter began:

If history is a guide, then in 1984 the structure of public international credits will collapse. A number of developing countries will threaten to default on a substantial part of their debts to government agencies in the developed countries and to international institutions. New York bankers will propose an international financial conference in Paris. The World Bank will call for borrowers and lenders to sort out their problems amicably. At the end of the conference, the terms on the $400 billion owed by the governments of developing countries will be renegotiated. A new international agency, Development Refinance International, will be established to help the borrowers consolidate their debts.

For some of the poorest of the developing countries, some of the debt will be forgiven—converted into a grant or a gift. For others, the annual debt service burden of the borrowers will be eased; the maturities on these debts will be extended and the interest rates reduced. Yet the debt obligations held by the lenders will continue to be listed in the annual reports of the national treasuries and international agencies and the commercial banks at the same face value as before the negotiations. Face will be saved all around. The economic statesmanship of the ministers of finance in the lending countries will be applauded. The international institutions will appear to have emerged unscathed.

Once the debt negotiations are complete, the borrowers will increase their credit-financed imports. Six or seven years later, the external public debts of the developing countries will again be renegotiated. And so it goes.

By the time of the September 1982 meetings of the International Monetary Fund and the World Bank, the debt of the developing countries (LDC) was the major topic. Mexico had had a major financial crisis and had threatened to delay payments on its external debt for three months. Argentina was falling behind on its ability to make interest and amortization payments, a result of its abortive and costly attack on the Falkland Islands—or, as they say in Buenos Aires, the Malvinas. By the end of 1982, the external debts of the developing countries totalled $800 billion—the volume of debt had increased much more rapidly than had been projected in the third edition.

Within domestic economies, bankers shy away from deadbeats. Lending money when the probability of repayment is low is an inefficient form of charity. Nevertheless, loans sometimes go sour. Businesses fail. Some borrowers are incompetent, some untruthful; a few are incompetent *and* untruthful. Credit bureaus run an elaborate intelligence operation on the habits of borrowers—who repay promptly, who repay slowly, who rarely repay. Lenders pay for this information as a way to reduce their loan losses; they recover the costs by scaling interest rates to the riskiness of the borrowers. To further protect themselves against loss, the lenders frequently require that the borrowers pledge real property—houses, land, cars, or rings—as surety for the loans. If the borrowers do not repay according to schedule, the lenders may take title to the property—the borrower's car is repossessed, rings go to the pawnshop, and the sheriff arranges a foreclosure sale on the house. The borrower's income may be garnisheed—that is, the courts may direct the borrower's employer to make a direct payment to the lender.

Lending among nations is an altogether different proposition. Most such loans are either public loans or publicly guaranteed loans; perhaps two-thirds of the external debts of the developing countries have been issued by governments, or government agencies, or with the guarantee of the government borrowers.

Perhaps one-third of the lender's loans are government or government-guaranteed loans; the rest are loans from commercial banks and exporting firms. (The careers of the lenders are not likely to be directly affected by whether or not the loan is repaid. The glory is in making the loan, not in securing its repayment.) Some of the loans may be politically inspired: the lenders want something from the borrower, like an air base or support in a UN vote. There are no credit checks, for the rules and practices of international diplomacy rule out an analysis which might suggest that Haiti is not so good a credit risk as Finland. Finland, after all, was the only country that repaid its World War I debts. When Finland borrows from an international institution at an interest rate of 6.5 percent, so does Haiti. The income of kings cannot be readily garnisheed. Kings no longer mortgage their castles—and even if they did, the U.S. Marines are no longer used for debt collection, as they were before World War I.

The most important distinction between domestic and international loans is that governments may abrogate contracts with foreigners; this is the essence of sovereignty. A government cannot be sued, except with its permission. Failure to repay, a legal problem within a country, becomes a political problem internationally. Domestically, the law specifies the options open to the lender; if the borrower defaults, there are bankruptcy proceedings that operate in accordance with established rules. But no such rules are available internationally; the procedures are largely ad hoc.

Moreover, borrower and lender governments are also usually involved in a web of other relationships—trade issues, airline landing rights, military alliances—and the lenders are reluctant to demand repayment on overdue loans because to do so would endanger the whole skein of the two countries' relationships without increasing the likelihood of repayment. Thus, the U.S. government may be reluctant to be hard-nosed about a country's failure to repay, perhaps because some U.S. firms are negotiating for oil concessions or because the U.S. Air Force has valuable air bases there. Borrowers and lenders within the domestic economy are rarely involved in such a complex set of relationships with each other.

Fifty years ago, international credits were primarily commercial; since then, they have become increasingly governmental, with political overtones. Yet the terms of commercial credits are retained. Commercial loans are supposed to be repaid. The lenders, and to a lesser extent, the borrowers, kid themselves that much of the post–World War II government-to-government credit is commercial.

International Lending—The Background

Lenders have long been fascinated by foreign securities, partly because the yields have been higher than those on domestic securities. On the free lunch principle, higher yields are matched by greater risks. During the nineteenth century, British investors were severely burned on their loans to U.S. borrowers—first when the canal companies failed in the 1840s, then when state and local governments defaulted in the 1870s. French investors incurred substantial losses after World War I on their extensive loans to the Russian czars and the Austro-Hungarian kings; neither group was around to repay.

By 1920 the risks of international lending were increasingly obvious; in an era of nationalism the political risks were compounding the commercial risks. The European investors' demand for foreign securities declined, partly because of defaults on prewar loans to Eastern European countries and partly because Great Britain retained exchange controls on the purchase of foreign securities by its residents. The center of the international capital market shifted to New York, continuing a development that began during the early years of World War I, before the United States entered the war. Americans paid little recognition to European experience as they became the new international lenders. During the 1920s the U.S. public acquired billions of dollars of foreign securities. Some were issued by reputable borrowers. Many were issued by German cities and minor rather than major governments; most of these securities became worthless during the Great Depression. With the principal exception of purchases of Canadian securities by U.S. lenders, the international bond market remained dormant for thirty years.

One principal change since World War II is that public institutions—both national and international—have taken the initiative in lending to the developing countries. During the Great Depression, most national governments established export loan or loan guarantee agencies to stimulate exports and promote domestic employment. Today, loans and loan guarantees are often tied to the purchase of domestic products by foreigners. In effect, cheap credit is used to stimulate export sales. If buyers are short of cash or if they have domestic money but lack foreign exchange because of exchange controls, the availability of export credits may be the crucial factor in the choice between buying from U.S. suppliers, or European suppliers, or Japanese suppliers. Indeed, the advantage of easy credit terms may often compensate for the disadvantage of a higher sales price. Suppliers— the export firms within each country, and their employees—are subsidized by these credits, since the larger the line of credit, the larger their sales and the higher their profits. Consequently, firms lean on their governments to ease credit terms on export sales. The process is competitive. Firms in countries with relatively high prices request their governments to provide attractive credit terms to offset the price disadvantage. Their competitors in low-cost countries then lean on their own governments to match these easier credit terms.

One consequence of these export credit arrangements is that foreign customers frequently can obtain loans at a lower rate than domestic customers. Thus, in the summer of 1975, the U.S. Export-Import Bank in Washington financed the sales of Boeing 747 jets to various airlines in Western Europe and Asia at an interest rate of about 6 percent, or about 0.5 percent above the interest rates on medium-term U.S. Treasury securities. The interest rates paid by U.S. commercial airlines, when they borrowed to finance the purchase of the same types of aircraft, were at least 1 or 1.5 percentage points higher.

The postwar period has also seen the establishment of multilateral agencies designed to facilitate the financing of economic development. The International Bank for Reconstruction and Development (IBRD), or World Bank, set up in the mid-1940s to finance postwar reconstruction in Europe, was the first such agency. After the defaults of the 1930s and the exhaustion of the war, European countries were poor credit risks and could only borrow if some other country cosigned the note.

The World Bank is an international financial intermediary: it borrows money by issuing its own securities to private parties and to national governments, and it then lends these funds to its members. Initially the major reason why the World Bank's securities proved so attractive to private lenders was that the United States was the effective residual cosigner; as the credit standing in international markets of Germany, Japan, and other countries improved, so did the number of available effective cosigners for the bank's bonds. If the lenders failed to repay the World Bank and the Bank proved unable to repay its debts as they matured, then the creditors had ultimate recourse to the United States and the other cosigners.

In the immediate years after World War II, the World Bank made relatively few reconstruction loans, largely because the

Marshall Plan placed the financial needs of the European countries on a grant basis. In the 1950s the Bank turned increasingly
to development financing as part of a worldwide effort to stimulate economic growth in nonindustrial, low-income countries.
The development needs of these countries were legitimate; besides, it was only natural—for a bureaucracy—to find another
client when the first client graduated.

Regional multinational lending institutions, such as the Inter-
American Development Bank, the Asian Development Bank, and
the African Development Bank, have been modeled after the
World Bank. These institutions are also international financial
intermediaries: they sell their own bonds in the world's capital
markets and lend the funds to their members. Their success reflects the fact that the credit standing of each institution is higher than that of the individual borrowers; most borrowers from
these institutions would find it virtually impossible to sell their
securities directly to private borrowers in the world market. Increasingly, the major industrial countries have participated in
each of these regional institutions as lenders.

During the early 1950s, much of the financial assistance from
the United States to the developing countries was on a grant
basis, a carryover from the Marshall Plan. But in the later
1950s, there was increasing pressure within the United States to
place assistance on a businesslike basis. And the synonym for
"businesslike" was loans. The idea was that the borrowers would
then use the funds for productive projects—projects which would
earn rates of return higher than the interest rates on the loans
issued to finance the project. If aid is extended on a grant basis,
so ran the argument, then the recipients have no strong incentive
to use the funds efficiently; they might use the money to finance
imports of Coca-Cola. A loan, on the other hand, would force
the recipients to pay much more attention to efficiency and
costs, since they would be obliged to repay the funds—with
interest.

A number of the developing countries have successfully made

the transition from borrowing from international institutions to borrowing from private lenders, initially from the major international banks on short-term loans, and subsequently, by the sale of long-term bonds. Perhaps in time, other countries will be able to borrow from private sources. Much will depend on whether private lenders retain confidence in the idea of extending credits to the developing countries, or whether the defaults of a few will sour the lenders, much as in the 1930s.

The Current Imbroglio

In 1970, the external public debt of ninety-six developing countries was $55 billion; in 1975, the total had increased to nearly $190 billion. In addition, the external private debt had increased from $10 billion to over $50 billion during this same interval. Because of the higher cost of oil imports and, perhaps more important, the decline in both the volume of exports and export prices in the world recession, the external debt of the developing countries soared to $250 billion at the end of 1977 and $800 billion by the end of 1982.

The rapid increase in the size of the external debts reflects a convergence of several factors. Governments in the lending countries, especially in the United States, wanted to stay in the foreign aid business. But since their citizens were reluctant to engage in "giveaway" programs, aid was shifted to a loan basis. Whereas in the late 1950s, as much as 50 percent of aid was in the form of grants, by the end of the 1960s the grant component was down to 10 percent. Moreover, in their scramble for balance-of-payments surpluses, the developed countries frequently subsidized credit on exports. But these export credits were on hard terms—short maturities and relatively high interest rates. Besides, interest rates throughout the world rose sharply in the 1960s and 1970s, so that the repayment burden was greater for all loans.

The developing countries borrowed in the hope that economic growth would resolve many of their domestic and external problems. The 1960s was a decade of grandiose expectations about the development process; borrowers incurred substantial external debts because they believed that they would soon be on a self-sustaining growth path. In a few cases, national leaders with imperial ambitions—Sukarno of Indonesia, Nkrumah of Ghana, and Nasser of Egypt—mortgaged the future export earnings of their countries.

The sharp rise in the oil price increased the oil import bill of the developing countries as a group from $10 billion in 1973 to $120 billion in 1980. Yet, because of the large payments surpluses of the OPEC countries, the developing countries were able to increase their external loans sufficiently rapidly so they could—as a group—readily pay for their imports of oil. Indeed, the combination of the OPEC surpluses and the worldwide inflation led to a decline in the real interest rates they were paying on their debts.

World inflation has eased the debt-repayment problem for developing countries as a group, since inflation always tends to bail out the debtors. Thus while the annual debt-service payments increased from $6 billion in 1970 to $13.3 billion in 1974, the increase in constant 1972 dollars was from $7.1 billion to $7.9 billion. But what was true for the group was not necessarily true for each of its members, and some were still candidates for write-downs and write-offs.

The much more rapid increase in the debts to commercial banks reflected several factors—the banks had the funds to lend because of the combination of the large increase in petrodollar-deposits and the sluggish loan demand from borrowers in the industrial countries during the world recession. The interest rates on the loans were attractive. The developing countries were eager to borrow to offset the drop in export earnings.

As external debt of the developing countries grew rapidly, the inability or unwillingness of borrowers in the developing countries to repay on schedule led to fears about the collapse of the banking system. The scenarios usually began with a standstill in the debt service payments of a few borrowers. Argentina won't repay because of ill-will resulting from its Falkland adventure. Mexico can't repay because the oil price went down when it was supposed to go up. The liquidity of the banks having substantial loans out to these borrowers would decline. These banks would be reluctant to extend credits to other developing-country borrowers. And, because of the inability to obtain credits, these countries then would find it difficult to repay on schedule.

The economics of debt service is straightforward. Once committed to the external debt, borrowers frequently sell new loans to get the funds to make interest and principal payments on outstanding loans. Assume that a country needs an excess of imports over exports of $100 million per year for ten years if it is to achieve its targeted growth of domestic income; the import surplus will provide resources to build dams, factories, and schools. The import surplus can be financed in a variety of ways, including grants, soft loans at long maturities and low interest rates, and hard loans at short maturities and high interest rates. In this example, an annual grant of $100 million per year will enable the country to finance its import surplus. If the country borrows $100 million in year one to finance the desired import surplus, then it will be obliged to make interest- and loan-reduction payments in each subsequent year until the loan is repaid. These payments are a charge against its export earnings. So if it wishes an import surplus of $100 million in year two, then it must borrow somewhat more than $100 million in year two; the year-two loan must be greater than $100 million by the amount of the interest- and loan-reduction payments on the year-one loan. Similarly, in year three the loan must be greater than $100 million by the amount of the interest- and loan-reduction payments on the loans arranged in years one and two. And so it goes.

The simple proposition is that the harder the loan terms, the larger the size of the new loan required each year so that the country can have the same import surplus. The higher the interest rates and the shorter the repayment periods, the more rapidly total indebtedness rises. The more rapidly indebtedness grows, the more vulnerable the country becomes to a credit crunch.

The combination of a larger volume of external debt and harder terms meant that a crunch in debt service was inevitable; the major uncertainties involved which country would be the first to be unable or unwilling to repay on schedule. Argentina provided the answer in 1955—and so its external debts were renegotiated or rescheduled. Rescheduling involved the stretching of maturities. Over the next twelve years, eight countries found themselves in the same predicament of being unable or unwilling to make the interest- and loan-reduction payments on schedule. This meant, of course, that they were unwilling to cut imports or to take measures to increase exports to obtain the foreign exchange to make the debt service payments on schedule. Rather than incur the domestic political costs of these Draconian measures, they threw the ball to the lenders. The lenders had several options: they could cancel all or part of the loans, or they could reschedule the loans. One consequence of the decision to reduce the annual debt-service payments of the borrowers was, paradoxically, that the borrowers became more attractive recipients for new loans.

In retrospect some of these debt-relief activities were shortsighted; Argentina's debts were rescheduled four times in a ten-year period (see table 19.1). Once the debt burden was rearranged for one borrower, other borrowers wanted their own debts rescheduled too, since they would then be able to obtain a larger volume of new loans. India's debts were negotiated eight times in eight successive years, beginning in 1971. The creditors were reluctant to be too liberal in the reduction of the debt-service burden: they wanted the borrowers on a short string. But if the string was too short, then the borrowers could force the next rescheduling by not repaying on time.

TABLE 19.1
International Debt Reschedulings

Country	Year	Total Amount Rescheduled (in millions)
Argentina	1956	$ 500
	1962	270
	1963	72
	1965	274
Brazil	1961	300
	1964	270
Cambodia	1972	4
Central African Republic (CAR)	1981	55
Chile	1965	90
	1972	258
	1974	460
	1975	230
Egypt	1971	145
Ghana	1966	170
	1968	100
	1970	18
	1974	190
India	1968	100
	1971	100
	1972	153
	1973	187
	1974	194
	1975	248
	1976	200
	1977	120
	1978	200
Indonesia	1966	310
	1967	110
	1968	180
	1970	2,090
Jamaica	1979	149
	1981	103
Liberia	1980	30
	1981	25
Madagascar	1981	142
	1982	115
Malawi	1982	29

TABLE 19.1 *(continued)*

Country	Year	Total Amount Rescheduled (in millions)
Nicaragua	1980	562
Pakistan	1972	236
	1973	107
	1974	650
	1981	280
Peru	1968	120
	1969	100
	1978	500
Poland	1973	32
	1978	450
	1981	2,900
Romania	1982	4,800
Senegal	1981	61
Sierra Leone	1977	52
	1980	25
Sudan	1979	373
	1981	538
	1982	174
Togo	1979	48
	1980	69
	1981	169
Turkey	1959	440
	1965	220
	1972	114
	1978	1,400
	1979	1,200
	1980	2,600
Uganda	1981	27
Yugoslavia	1971	59
Zaire	1976	280
	1977	400
	1979	147
	1980	402

SOURCE: Updated from "Debt Relief Extended to Developing Countries," 1956–1982.

The Optimal Bankrupt

A country's debt-service payments cannot increase forever in relation to export earnings; if they did, eventually all export earnings would be required to service the debt. At some point, the volume of the borrower's external debt must reach a ceiling relative to its export earnings. When this stage is reached, the value of the annual flow of new loans is about the same size as the debt-service payments. In effect, the receipts on the new loans are being used to finance interest- and loan-reduction payments on the outstanding loans; these new loans do not bring additional commodity imports or real resources to the country. At this stage, the borrowers have a greater incentive to default.

The principal reason for the borrower to repay outstanding loans is to continue to be eligible for new loans. When the funds available under new loans are smaller than the debt-service payments on the existing loans, the incentive to default is high. By defaulting, the borrower reduces the debt-service payments; a much larger share of export earnings is now available to buy imports. And the borrower may be able to sell more new loans to eager exporters in the industrial countries.

Some of the borrowing countries are practicing the art of optimal bankruptcy. The optimal bankrupt lives well by borrowing. First the country borrows as much as it can from low-cost lenders; when that source is exhausted, the country borrows as much as possible from high-cost lenders. The borrower uses funds from new loans to pay the interest and amortization charges on outstanding loans. The only reason the country desires to service the debt at all is to protect its credit rating—its ability to borrow more. So it will continue to make payments on outstanding loans only if the flow of new loans is rising. If the country's export earnings decline sharply or if the new loan seems too small, the borrower will threaten to default. At that point, the lenders will usually offer a debt renegotiation to save themselves the embarrassment of being caught with worthless loans; the borrower may demand new funds before agreeing to the renegotiation.

Of course, the optimal bankrupt knows that creditors are reluctant to throw good money after bad. But the borrower also knows the injury it might do them by defaulting. The larger the possible damage, the larger the amount of new credits the borrower can probably secure. But the larger the volume of new credits the lenders extend today, the more severe will be the borrower's debt-service problems in the future.

Some lenders might seek to avoid the embarrassment of a default by placing all future aid on a grant basis. But in that case, many of the developing countries would borrow as much as they could on subsidized export credits and loans extended for political objectives; the debt would still rise and the process would be repeated. The only constraint on the amount they *do* borrow is the amount they *can* borrow.

The irony is that attempts to make U.S. financial assistance more businesslike have made it less businesslike. And the efforts to gain an advantage for U.S. exports and the balance of payments have been largely self-defeating, since other countries have adopted similar measures. If both lender and borrower act under the presumption that a loan is on hard terms, less can be demanded of the borrower. Stricter conditions may be attached to the use of grants.

But it is naïve to believe that changing the terms of aid could now make any great difference. The fact is that politicians in the aid-receiving countries do not have the same interests as the development planners in the donor countries and the international agencies; nor do they have the same constituencies. And so, even if the borrowers should promise—and keep their commitments—to use the external assistance wisely and frugally, domestic and other non-tied resources would still have to be used to accomplish their political interests. Why, then, do the lenders continue to be manipulated by the borrowers? The answer is that, on margin, continuing the game seems attractive: the cost of new loans always appears lower than the losses that would occur if the borrowers defaulted, for the point of no return has already been passed.

The developing countries are not the only borrowers that sell new debts to refinance existing debts; so do the U.S. government and many U.S. corporations. Even though the developing countries are caught on a treadmill, it does not follow that they have borrowed too much abroad. Whether a country has borrowed too much depends on the relationship between the interest rates it must pay on external loans and the productivity of the investments financed with these loans. Some developing countries probably have not met this test. Of the six countries that account for a large part of the external indebtedness of the group—Argentina, Brazil, Korea, Mexico, Peru, and the Philippines—Brazil, Korea, and Mexico have all achieved very impressive records in terms of the growth of their economies and of their exports. Mexico, however, encountered a severe foreign exchange crisis as a result of the combination of the decrease in the price of oil and its own inflationary financial policies.

As the external debts of the developing countries mount, the obvious question is whether the debts will be repaid at all. A few countries have succeeded in repaying their international debts— France after the war with Germany in 1870 and Finland after World War I. And the reconstruction loans of various European countries after World War II have been repaid. But these repayments were all from the relatively wealthy countries. Many of the developing countries today have achieved impressive growth records and will be in progressively stronger positions to repay. Some, however, are now so poor compared to the developed countries that refinancing—and eventually some form of cancellation or forgiveness—seems inevitable. Loans to these countries are likely to be converted into de facto grants.

Part of the risk of lending to these countries originates with mismanagement; being poor and underdeveloped means they are undersupplied with effective managers and sometimes oversupplied with political demagogues. A larger risk comes from a world recession and declines in the developing countries' prices and volumes of exports. The combination of higher real interest rates and lower export earnings sharply reduces the likelihood of repayment, and greatly increases the likelihood of more debt relief and reschedulings.

Zlotys, Rubles, and Leks

Hjalmar Schacht was Hitler's chief financial adviser, a wizard of money. The term "Schachtian policies" has become a synonym for economic policies used by a large country to exploit its smaller neighbors. Under Schacht, the Eastern European (née Balkan) countries paid above-market prices for their imports from Germany and received below-market prices for their exports to Germany.

Schacht is dead, but Schachtian policies live on. For a while, the Soviet Union exploited its smaller neighbors in Eastern Europe. Now the tables are turned, and the Russians are being exploited. Paradoxically, the change is not that the Russians are now good guys, remorseful about their past. Rather, despite the strictures of Marx and Lenin, exploitation is inevitable in planned economies—as long as prices in the world economy are used as a benchmark.

Market Prices and the Planned Economy

Marxist doctrine predicts that Socialist societies will one day function without money. That day does not appear imminent. Stocks and bonds went out with the czars, and most productive assets—and many nonproductive assets—are owned by the state. But government-owned banks in the Soviet Union and in Eastern Europe produce money, workers receive much of their incomes in money payments, and most of their consumption expenditures are financed by money payments. Indeed, within the Soviet Union, Poland, and the neighboring countries, the banks are among the most efficient of the productive enterprises. They can produce money much more rapidly than the farms and factories can produce the food and consumer goods that the workers would like to buy with their money.

In the West, with a few exceptions—postal services, railroad passenger services, and other government-provided goods and services—prices are set to cover costs. At the core of a market economy is the belief that a good should be produced if the consumers will pay a price sufficiently high to cover its production costs. And in competitive industries, profit-maximizing firms expand output until selling prices fall to the level of costs of production. The managers of the firms make the decisions about which goods to produce and in what amounts in response to their estimates of consumer demand.

Within planned economies, in contrast, government bureaucrats determine which goods will be produced. Then they make an independent decision about the prices at which these goods will be sold. If they set the prices too low, then queues and shortages develop and a large number of customers remain unsatisfied. If they set the prices too high, then the goods pile up on the shelves waiting to be sold. In planned economies, selling prices cover production costs on a much smaller range of goods than in

323

market economies; there are many more "loss-leaders"—goods whose prices are below their costs of production. The planners recognize the needs and the preferences of the public, although they believe that they know what the public wants better than the public does—which is why they were chosen to be the planners.

Thus many goods and services are sold at nominal prices—at prices much below their production costs. Housing, medical services, university education, and air transport are cheap in the Soviet Union. But not all goods can be sold at prices below their costs. Indeed, for the economy as a whole, the excess of costs over revenues in some industries must be matched by the excess of revenues over costs in other industries. Thus, as a general rule, for every loss there must be a corresponding profit. Except that, as in the West, if the losses dominate, the planners go to the central bank to get newly produced money to pay for the losses.

The differences between market economies and planned economies in their approaches to setting prices become important when they trade with each other. Within the West, international trade reflects the decentralized decisions of numerous firms in different countries. Firms export if their costs are low enough for them to be able to undersell the domestic producers in foreign markets. And they import if foreign prices are sufficiently below the prices of domestic producers. The planned economies import and export for the same reasons the market economies do—it is cheaper to import some goods and to pay for them with exports than to produce these goods domestically. So the planned economies import industrial products, raw materials including gold and petroleum and hams, machinery, computers, turbines and other high-technology items, wheat, coffee, and tea, as well as goods which may be temporarily in short supply. Their exports consist largely of raw materials, a few industrial products, and IOUs—promises to pay in the future because they are not able to pay in the present. Like good capitalists, they are eager to borrow to finance; they need more imports than they can pay for from their current export earnings and their gold sales.

In the planned economies, prices are less useful as guidelines for deciding which goods to import and which to export. If prices were used as guidelines, then the goods exported would be those which were priced far below their production costs, while the imported goods would be those which were sold at prices much above costs. Arbitragers would make a fortune exploiting the differences between prices in the market economies and prices in planned economies. So planners must decide which goods to import and which to export. Decisions are centralized to fit the plan—and the breakdowns in the plan.

The centrally planned economies (CPEs) conduct their foreign trade through state trading organizations (STOs). When the CPEs trade with market economies, they deal at world prices, more or less; their exports must sell at or below prices of comparable Western goods, regardless of the cost of producing them. Similarly, the planned economies pay world prices for imports, unless they are successful in obtaining special deals, as they did with the purchase of U.S. wheat in the summer of 1972.

The monetary counterpart to the monopolization of imports and exports in state trading organizations is that there is no freedom for consumers in these countries to hold monetary assets in the West, and no freedom for firms and individuals in the West to hold money and financial assets in the East—even if they had a reason for doing so. Both the monopoly on trade and the monopoly on money are necessary complements to ensure that private decisions of the consumers cannot undercut the public decisions of the planners.

Much of the trade between countries in Eastern Europe involves a series of bilateral exchanges—Russia sells 1,000 3½-ton trucks to Czechoslovakia in exchange for 1,650 6-inch lathes. World prices can be attached to these barter exchanges to determine whether Czechoslovakia gets a better deal than if it had sold the lathes in the West at world market prices and used the proceeds to buy comparable trucks from Italy or Germany.

The Eastern Europeans believe the prices they pay the Soviet Union for their imports are generally higher than the prices the Russians would get for the same goods if they sold them in the world market. And they also believe that the prices they receive on their exports to the Russians are generally below those they might receive in the world market. Paying more for imports and receiving less for exports is what Schachtian policies are all about. And the Rumanians and Bulgarians participated in these policies in the 1960s and 1970s for the same reason they did in the 1930s.

While state trading organizations are a logical counterpart to central planning, the individual STOs are not branches of the Salvation Army—each is a maximizing agent, constantly calculating whether it is more profitable to sell in the Western markets than to STOs in other Eastern European countries, and whether it is cheaper to buy in the West than from other STOs. Trade between STOs in the various planned economies is on a barter basis. Each STO can calculate the world market price of the goods it wishes to export and the goods that it might import from other STOs. So, Western market prices become the reference. As political barriers have diminished, STOs have done more trading with the West and less with each other. The ability of the Russians to exploit their smaller neighbors has declined.

Indeed, when the world price of oil increased, the Russians did not raise the price on oil exported to their East European neighbors correspondingly. So the East Europeans benefited by being able to obtain oil at lower prices than most other oil-importing countries. Almost certainly this benefit to the East Europeans resulted from the slow pace of change in the plan.

The Ruble Is a Heavy Currency

The Russian currency—the ruble—and the currencies of other Eastern European countries are not included in the world hit parade of currencies, since individuals are not free to sell rubles and zlotys against dollars, Swiss francs, or marks. Transactions in Western currencies by residents of Eastern countries are strictly controlled. Investors do not buy or sell rubles because they expect that the ruble may be revalued or devalued in terms of the dollar or of gold. Comparisons of interest rates on bank deposits in the Soviet Union and the United States are not meaningful, since the interest rates on financial assets in Communist countries are set by the plan rather than by the market. Because the state banks are monopolies, they have no incentive to raise interest rates to attract funds from other financial institutions, spending on current consumption, or even mattresses.

When the Russians and other Eastern Europeans export, they are paid in dollars, marks, or some other major currency; they are apt to deposit these funds in the Moscow Narodny Bank in London, in the Banque Commerciale pour l' Europe du Nord in Paris, in Wozchod Commercial Bank AG in Zurich, or in another Western branch of one of the Russian banks. Similarly, when they import, they write checks against their deposit balances in one of these banks. Trade with the market economies is financed in one of the Western currencies, largely because Western firms would have neither the incentive to hold the ruble nor the means to sell it.

Perhaps a better indication of the Russian position in finance was the large grain purchases in the 1970s. Whenever harvests have been poor, wheat imports have been necessary. The wheat came from the United States in its role as the residual supplier in the world grain market. Part of the imports were financed by credit, part by sales of gold. In bad crop years Soviet gold sales

327

are unusually large. Gold sales are last-resort financing, for when it comes to gold, the Russians are at the top of the list of mercantilists.

The Russians fantasize that the ruble is at the top of the hit parade—the financial market counterpart to their claims to having invented the sewing machine, the typewriter, and baseball. The ruble needs a price in terms of the dollar, the mark, sterling, and other Western currencies. Foreign embassies in the Communist countries need the local currencies, and so do foreign tourists. Moreover, a peg is necessary for the ruble; it cannot float in the exchange market because the necessary conditions for a floating exchange rate—that buyers and sellers meet freely to exchange national monies—are not present. Since no Western country has been willing to peg its currency to the ruble, the Russians must peg the ruble to a Western currency.

In 1937 the ruble was pegged to the U.S. dollar at 4 rubles to $1. During the cold war, the Russians did not appreciate the implication that the U.S. dollar was four times as valuable as the ruble. So in 1950 the ruble was pegged to gold at a rate of 140 rubles per ounce of gold. Actually, the peg could have been 1 ruble per ounce or 1,000 rubles per ounce; in the Soviet Union the gold price has no significance in determining how much gold is produced, how much to pay the workers in the gold mines or how many people choose to become gold miners, what gold is used for, and when gold is sold abroad. But once the ruble was pegged to gold, a ruble-dollar exchange rate could be readily calculated. Given the then U.S. gold parity of $35, the exchange rate was, once again, 4 rubles to the dollar.

In 1961 the Soviet Union underwent a currency reform; all outstanding ruble notes were declared worthless and had to be exchanged for new notes at the rate of 1 new ruble for 10 old rubles. (This "reform" was really a tax on holders of bank notes, especially those who held large amounts of notes.) At the same time, the Russians set a gold parity for the new ruble at 32 rubles per ounce. Then the exchange rate between the new, heavy ruble and the U.S. dollar could be readily calculated as the ratio of the price of one ounce of gold in terms of each currency. And so the new rate was $1.11 U.S. equals 1 ruble.

Now the ruble was worth more than the dollar—or at least so it seemed. Since the ruble price of gold had no economic significance, the Russians in effect had first decided on the dollar-ruble exchange rate they wanted, then set the ruble price of gold accordingly. If they had set a gold parity for the new ruble at 7 rubles per ounce, the exchange rate would have been $5 U.S. to 1 ruble; with a gold parity of 1 new ruble to the ounce, the exchange rate would have been $35 U.S. to 1 ruble.

The currency reform at the ratio of 10 old rubles for 1 new ruble suggests that all ruble prices should have fallen by a factor of ten; each new ruble would then be ten times as valuable as each old ruble. Thus, the ruble price of gold should have fallen from 140 rubles per ounce to 14 rubles; the dollar-ruble exchange rate would then have been $2.50 U.S. per ruble. But in terms of purchasing power, the ruble would have been grossly overvalued. So the Russians used the commotion of the currency reform as a smoke screen to devalue the ruble in terms of the dollar from 1 ruble equals $.25 U.S. to 1 ruble equals $.11 U.S., a 125 percent increase in the ruble price of the dollar.

This dollar-ruble exchange rate was largely symbolic: no private holder of rubles could buy dollars at this price. Since Soviet trade with the West consists largely of swapping bundles of exports for bundles of imports, the exchange rate was irrelevant for balancing Soviet payments and receipts with other countries.

When the dollar price of gold was increased in 1971 and 1973, the ruble got heavier relative to the dollar, since the ruble price of gold was unchanged. Moscow gloated. But the Russians had an exchange rate problem: they had to decide whether to peg the ruble to the dollar, thereby allowing their currency to float in terms of the mark, the Swiss franc, and sterling, or to peg to the German mark and allow the ruble to float in terms of the dollar and sterling. One thing was clear. They could not rely on market forces to bail them out; the planners had to make a decision. So they stuck with gold and continued to revalue the ruble in terms of the dollar, first by 8 percent at the end of 1971, then by nearly 10 percent in early 1973. The Russians were striving to make the ruble respectable. But at the same time they were revaluing the ruble, the price of the dollar was increasing significantly in terms of the ruble in the black market.

The Lek and the Leu Are Not Heavy Currencies

The lek, the leu, and the ruble are greatly overvalued; their purchasing power is much less, at the official exchange rates, than that of Western currencies. From the point of view of the planners, overvaluation has the advantage of taxing the foreign diplomats and tourists who must acquire these currencies. Because the exchange rates in the Soviet Union and other Eastern European countries are so out of line with market reality, their gov-

TABLE 20.1
Exchange Rates of Eastern European Currencies,
1979[a] *(Currency units per U.S. dollar)*

Country	Currency	Basic Rate	Capitalist Tourist Rates	Black Market Rates[b]
Albania	lek	4.14	7.00	30.00
Bulgaria	lev	0.97	1.32	2.57
Czechoslovakia	koruna	5.97	9.54	27.00
East Germany	mark	1.842	1.65	8.75
Hungary	forint	9.73	20.3	34.10
Poland	zloty	3.32	31.16	111.75
Romania	leu	4.49	12.00	29.45
Soviet Union	ruble	0.746	——	4.50

SOURCE: *Pick's Currency Yearbook* (New York: Pick Publishing Corporation, 1981).
[a] As of December, 1978.
[b] The black market rate is approximate.

ernments have set up special exchange markets for tourist transactions where the rates are half or less than half the official
rates. Moreover, a black market has developed in U.S. dollars.
Thus, the official rate for the Bulgarian lev is 0.97 per $1, the
tourist rate is 1.32 leva per $1, and the black market rate is 2.57
leva per $1. The official rate for the Albanian lek is 4.14 leks per
$1, the tourist rate is 12.5 leks per $1. The premium in the black
markets—the percentage spread between the black market rates
and the official rates—varies from 200 to 400 percent, and suggests how unreal the official rates are. That the exchange rates
for tourists from capitalist countries may be 150 to 250 percent
higher than those for tourists from Socialist countries is one indication that each Eastern European country recognizes how
grossly overvalued are the currencies of its neighbors.

The Ruble–Dollar Seesaw

From time to time, individual Eastern European countries have
made cautious moves toward increased trade with the Western
countries, moves which might be associated with an increased
role for market-determined prices in their economies. Yugoslavia
has gone much further in this direction than the others. Thus,
Yugoslavia belongs to the International Monetary Fund and has
sought to make its currency convertible. The Yugoslav dinar is
readily traded, and Yugoslavs can hold foreign currencies and
readily travel abroad. The foreign exchange value for the dinar
is set at a level which—together with a variety of import controls—balances Yugoslavia's payments and receipts with the rest
of the world. Several extremely large devaluations of the dinar
were necessary in the early stages of Yugoslavia's opening to the
West to offset the previous substantial overvaluation. Czechoslovakia was moving in the same direction when the Russians returned to Prague in the summer of 1968. Hungary, Poland, and

Romania have joined the International Monetary Fund. Other countries in Eastern Europe may also move toward greater decentralization of decision making, although a substantial easing of restrictions and moves to greater payments freedom will require extensive devaluations of their currencies.

On occasion, the Russians and other Eastern Europeans, stimulated or threatened by the success of the European Economic Community, have announced plans for a common market of their own. For planned economies, a common market might mean free trade within the associated economies; stores and factories in each country could import from foreign sources as well as domestic sources. But this approach would require that each factory know the foreign as well as the domestic demand for its product. A common market for planned economies would require integration of the planning systems of the member countries.

The exchange rate relationship between the Soviet Union and its Eastern bloc neighbors would have little significance once the planning systems were integrated. The currencies of other Eastern European countries—the Polish zloty, the Hungarian forint, the Romanian leu, the Albanian lek—have parities, usually expressed in terms of gold or occasionally in terms of the Russian ruble. However, expressing parities in terms of gold (like the ruble's parity in terms of gold) is meaningless, since no individual, firm, or agency deals in gold at this price. But the exchange rate for the zloty in terms of the ruble might be computed from the parity of each of these currencies in terms of gold. Given the parity of the Polish zloty in terms of the dollar—about 3.4 zlotys to $1—and the ruble-dollar rate of $1.24, the price of the ruble in terms of the zloty should be 4.2 zlotys to the ruble. But the Poles peg the zloty at 13.8 zlotys to the ruble.

Zlotys are cheap in terms of rubles, and that is good for the Russians. Nearly all of the Eastern European currencies are cheap in terms of the ruble, which is even better for the Russians. The foreign exchange costs of the Russian diplomatic establishment in Eastern Europe—the thirty-eight divisions of the Russian Army that sit between the Vistula and the Oder—are thus reduced.

Poland collects a large supply of rubles from its sale of zlotys to the Russians. And these rubles are used to settle imbalances in the barter trade—to pay for Russian oil and steel. The exchange rate structure is favorable to the Soviet Union and costly to the smaller Eastern European countries. Capitalism may have gone out with the czars, but imperialism did not.

Barter, Credits, and Détente

Moscow has a Pepsi-Cola franchise, as well as branches of one or two New York banks. Pepsi arranged a barter deal: it would import Russian vodka for sale in the United States while the Russians would import Pepsi. The U.S. demand for vodka has been growing rapidly; whether the Russian demand for Pepsi will grow as rapidly remains to be seen.

Pepsi for vodka is only the frosting on a much larger cake: the extensive efforts to facilitate industrial growth in the Eastern bloc. Fiat built a massive automobile plant in the Soviet Union, and the Russians have already begun to export the Russian Fiat—not to be confused with the Polish Fiat or the Spanish Fiat or the Fiat Fiat. Mack Trucks was involved in a similar program to build a turnkey factory. For numerous industrial products in Eastern Europe, Western firms have built the plants from scratch and trained the local managers.

In a few cases, the Eastern Europeans have paid by exports to the West; in many cases, however, credits available from the West have been the financing mechanism. The Hungarians, the Poles, and other Eastern Europeans have been nibbling at the fringes of the Eurocurrency market; at the end of 1981 their outstanding borrowings totaled $60 billion.

Initially, the largest source of financing was the Western governments, which were eager to promote exports—and the employment associated with such exports. While the same credits might have been used to finance investments in the industrial countries themselves, the demand was inadequate; there were enough automobile and steel plants in the West already. Subsequently, commercial banks, especially those headquartered in Germany, France, and Italy supplied the credits.

The breakdown in the Polish economy associated with the Solidarity crisis led to an external debt crisis; labor unrest led to significant declines in production on the farms and in the mines and factories, so that Polish exports did not increase as rapidly as anticipated. Yet it seems likely that Poland would have had an external debt crisis even without its labor problems, for it would not have been able to earn the foreign exchange to pay interest on this debt on schedule.

The Soviet Union and the other Communist economies are almost certain to repay promptly as long as they wish to maintain their credit ratings. To the extent possible, these countries, just like the developing countries, will use funds from new loans

TABLE 20.2
Eastern Europe's Debt to the West

	Hard Currency Debt (Billions of dollars)		Debt-Service Ratio (Ratio of debt-service payments to hard currency earnings)	
	1975	1981	1975	1981
Bulgaria	2.1	2.2	.44	.23
Czechoslovakia	1.2	3.4	.11	.26
East Germany	4.8	12.8	.24	.44
Hungary	2.3	7.2	.20	.45
Poland	7.7	22.6	.32	1.02
Romania	3.1	10.1	.21	.35
U.S.S.R.	7.8	10.2	.19	.25

SOURCE: Wharton Econometric Associates, "Eastern Europe's Burden of Debt," *New York Times,* May 26, 1982.

to repay outstanding loans. At some stage, however, the lenders may decide that the outstanding debts of these countries are too large to justify extension of any more refinancing loans. Or, if the Communist countries decide they no longer wish to increase their debts to the West, they will have no incentive to repay. Even if they did wish to reduce the total volume of their debts to the Western countries, their exports would have to increase relative to their imports. And the Western countries would have to be willing to take these imports. The surge in Polish debt reflected a policy decision that the way to keep workers content was to provide more consumer goods, both imported goods and goods produced in Poland with Western equipment. So the Poles gambled that if they borrowed extensively to finance imports from the West, they would be able to increase domestic production by enough to keep the workers happy and to meet the debt-service payments on schedule. They lost the gamble—at considerable cost to themselves, to the Soviet Union and other countries in Eastern Europe, and to the bankers that hold $60 billion of Eastern European loans.

Fitting the Pieces Once Again

Someday, perhaps, the international money problem will disappear. Perhaps the nation state will be phased out as the basic political unit. Or, less likely, independent countries may merge their currencies into a common international currency.

Neither event seems imminent. Over the last fifty years the number of countries has increased sharply as colonial empires have broken up. Nearly all the newly independent countries have opted for their own currency, and some of them have gradually moved to monetary policies directed at their domestic objectives. Many other countries, long independent, have also oriented their monetary policies to domestic objectives. Now there are 130-plus members of the IMF, five times the initial number.

The nation state appears unlikely to be phased out in the foreseeable future as the basic unit for organizing political activity— for supplying law and order and deciding on income distribution and economic priorities. Nor is there any indication of a broad-based movement toward the merger of monies. While there is a plan for monetary integration in Western Europe, such moves are still in a preliminary stage. And this plan stands alone. No other group of nations seems close to planning seriously for a common currency.

A merger of national monies makes economic sense only if the economic structures of the participating countries are similar—if their business cycles have similar phasing, if their labor forces grow at a similar rate and are similar in terms of skills, and if their preferences for price stability and full employment are also similar. Even then, vested interests within the several countries, both economic and political, would strongly oppose the merger, since the use of a national money is closely linked with the exercise of sovereignty. Control over the growth of the money supply is one of the most effective measures available to government leaders as they seek increased support from their constituencies.

National monetary policies result from political forces within individual countries; the level of interest rates, the rate of growth of the money supply, and the rate of increase in the price level are still issues in national elections. For this reason, prices rise more rapidly in some countries than in others. So payments imbalances are inevitable. Usually the countries with the most rapid increases in prices incur payments deficits. Eventually adjustments are needed to restore the payments balance. Either exchange rates must change, or else some other variable that will balance international payments and receipts must be altered.

Inevitably, the anticipation of changes in exchange rates leads to conflicts, for profit-oriented business firms, anticipating these changes, seek to achieve profits or at least avoid losses from such changes. But if some firms earn profits, then losses must be incurred by someone else, either the central banks, commercial banks, or individual investors. And these shifts of speculative funds sometimes take the initiative away from the authorities; they may be forced to alter their exchange rates, economic controls, or monetary policies earlier than they had planned. Moreover, authorities in the deficit countries and in the surplus countries are frequently at odds about who should take the initiative in reducing the imbalance. And they also disagree about the best policies to use, especially whether market forces are superior to bureaucratic decisions.

337

The increasingly domestic focus of national monetary policies led to the breakdown and collapse of the IMF rules. These rules were a guide to national behavior: they indicated when countries could change their exchange rates and when they could not, and when they could use controls on international payments and when they could not. The purpose of the rules was to ensure that in attempting to solve its own economic problems, a country would not dump the problems in the laps of its neighbors.

That the IMF rules became obsolete should not be a surprise, for the history of most international agreements is that they last for only a decade or two. Then, when the economic circumstances for which the rules were intended change, the rules become passé. While it might be possible to design sets of rules sufficiently broad to cope with changes in these circumstances, such rules would almost certainly be so general that they would have no bite or impact. What the rules can do is increase the confidence that each country can have about the future policies of its trading partners. Few countries, however, are likely to accept severe constraints on their future freedom of actions—or to abide by the constraints if doing so is very expensive.

Two events occurred in the 1970s that were not contemplated when the IMF rules were drafted thirty years earlier. One was the world inflation and the greater reluctance of Germany to accept price increases than the United States. The second was the decline in the relative economic position of the United States, evidenced both by the more rapid growth in Germany and Japan and the decline in the competitiveness of U.S. exports.

New sets of rules might be negotiated to deal with a variety of issues. Such rules could be directed to exchange market intervention practices of national central banks, even in the context of a continuing inflation. Or the rules might be directed to the acquisitions of international money by various central banks.

In the absence of new rules, the system will increasingly rely on ad hoc approaches. Then each country will adopt the measures that suit its immediate needs and interests, with minimal regard for the external consequences. The new rules would have to provide for greater flexibility among national currency areas; they would have to find a balance between enabling countries to follow policies appropriate to their domestic objectives and minimizing the possibility that some will pursue "beggar thy neighbor" policies and complicate the price, employment, or payments problems of other countries.

Designing the arrangement most likely to work requires foreknowledge of the types of economic problems that are likely to be dominant in the next five, ten, and twenty years. Unemployment? Inflation? Unemployment and inflation simultaneously? Will recessions and booms occur at the same time in the United States and Western Europe, or will they occur at different times? Will nationalism continue to become more powerful, or will the pendulum swing? And what about national attitudes toward market forces and bureaucratic regulation? Will the worldwide move toward more conservative policies continue? The types of rules most likely to be effective vary with the set of answers to these questions.

One frequently mentioned alternative to new rules is to rely on authority: to endow those who manage the international monetary institutions—the IMF and its successors—with the power to make the necessary decisions. But this approach seems untimely, for one counterpart to the increased attention to domestic objectives is most countries' increased reluctance to delegate substantial decision-making power to an international institution; they fear constraints on their domestic policies. Almost inevitably, the important decisions are likely to be made in national capitals. The managers of international institutions are increasingly responsible to committees of representatives from national capitals; the international civil servants will police the rules, but they will not make the rules, nor will they determine when the exchange rates must be changed, or by how much. The counterpart to the increasing concern with domestic objectives is that power has moved from international institutions to national capitals.

Crises—especially over changes in exchange rates—are inevitable in a multiple-currency world. While U.S. authorities, German authorities, and many economists favor floating exchange rates, many countries, especially the smaller ones, appear committed to a return to pegged rates. The more important foreign trade is in a country's economy, the stronger this commitment is. The authorities in many countries have concluded that floating rates have worked less well than they had hoped. The United States and Germany believe that a return to pegged rates will impose constraints and complicate the attainment of their employment and price-level objectives; the Germans are concerned that once again they will import inflation from their more expansive neighbors, while the Americans are concerned about once again taking on an external constraint on domestic policies.

The alternative to changes in exchange rates as a way to balance international payments and receipts are direct regulation of international payments through one or another form of exchange controls, or adjustment of prices and incomes to the payments imbalance. One attraction of this approach to the authorities is that the political costs are smaller. The objection to the controls approach is that it fragments the international economy, for each type of transaction tends to be subject to its own form of control, especially if relatively few transactions are controlled. The more comprehensive and uniform the controls over imports and exports of goods as well as securities, the more nearly this approach is equivalent to a change in the exchange rate. The distinction is that bureaucrats rather than market forces determine when the controls must be changed. But while academicians talk about the attractions of controls as long as they are comprehensive, the bureaucrats and politicians are likely to find compelling reasons for numerous exceptions to comprehensive controls. Eventually, the rules must deal with the issue: What are the acceptable forms of controls, when can they be used, and how do they relate to changes in exchange rates?

As the system moves from floating rates toward some form of

pegged rates, the adequacy of international money will again be of great concern, despite the surge in the dollar holdings of central banks in Europe, Japan, and the developing countries. Central bankers will again struggle with the problem of whether gold should have a monetary role. A closely related issue is whether the dollar holdings of foreign central banks will be convertible into gold or some other asset. Now, any central bank is free to acquire gold, but at the fluctuating price in the private market.

As long as foreign central banks hold more than $300 billion in liquid dollar assets, the U.S. Treasury will be reluctant to accept convertibility of the dollar into other international monies out of fear that if conversion is possible, there will be a run to convert.

Either gold will increasingly lose its monetary role or central banks will tend to formalize arrangements to deal in gold at prices nearer the market price. Gold demonetization could occur passively; central banks in deficit countries would sell their gold in the commodity markets at the market price, rather than to each other at the monetary price. Such sales are likely to be minimal until the conviction spreads that gold will be demonetized. Some central banks might even be buyers in the commodity market.

The gradual demonetization of gold is likely to require agreement on a comprehensive arrangement to produce a new international money; otherwise the system will eventually be subject to a severe shortage of international money. The paradox is that the decline in credibility resulting from U.S. gold demonetization may make it more difficult to obtain agreement on alternatives. In any negotiations, the Europeans would be preoccupied with the concern that if the United States could effectively demonetize gold, it might also "demonetize" the new international money by refusing to buy the money in exchange for dollars.

The alternative to gold demonetization—a worldwide increase in the price of gold—seems less impractical and unlikely than it did several years ago, even though most economists and editorial writers deplore the use of such a barbarous relic as money. While the continued use of gold as money may be barbarous, the continued demand for gold reflects the fact that some countries lack faith in the commitments of others. And so they put more value in a commodity money than in a paper money. Their decision may be wise or unwise—but it *is* their decision. Most of the objections that stalled the necessary increase in the monetary price in the 1960s are already irrelevant because of the sharp increase in the market price of gold. Relatively little attention was given to the implications of a higher gold price (or of gold demonetization) for the monetary system. And while taking gold out of the mines of South Africa to bury it again in the vaults of central banks is stupid, at least those who acquire gold pay most of the costs.

If once again there were a monetary price for gold, more gold would be available to satisfy the monetary demand. The increase in the monetary value of existing gold holdings would enable central banks to move toward the preferred combination of gold, dollars, and SDRs in their international money holdings. An increase in the gold price would not resolve all international monetary problems forever; no price can be fixed forever and, on the international scene, no agreement lasts forever. And few last more than a decade or two.

A U.S. initiative to increase the world gold price has some strong arguments in its favor. Many Europeans prefer this solution, and they would bear nearly all the economic costs. There may even be some favorable impacts on the relationship between the dollar and other currencies, for the ratio of U.S. gold holdings to foreign holdings of dollars would increase.

The European preferences are conditioned by the monetary events of the last decade and especially by their dependence on the United States—and their interpretation of this dependence. The countries in Western Europe want greater control over their own monetary policies. But their attitudes are ambivalent; these countries want to achieve payments surpluses while ensuring that the United States does not have a deficit. Such attitudes are inconsistent. They want to achieve price stability while maintaining pegged exchange rates, two objectives which are consistent only if the United States also achieves price stability. Perhaps the United States will. But the U.S. price-level performance will almost certainly be determined by U.S., not European, needs. And the U.S. price-level performance is not likely to be affected by whether gold remains in the monetary system.

Just as no price can be fixed forever, no currency is likely to be at the top of the hit parade forever. The shift from dollars into gold and to other currencies in 1970 and 1971, a result of U.S. inflation and speculation against the dollar, may suggest that the dollar's tenure as the top currency may be over. Yet the shift from dollars may have been short term, largely an anticipation of the change in the exchange rate. Some diversification in reserve holdings is likely, primarily to supplement rather than replace the dollar.

Political pressure will certainly develop to diminish the international role of the dollar. Foreign countries do not like the asymmetry of having to revalue or devalue their currency relative to the dollar. In effect, they hope that a revision of the arrangements might protect them from U.S. inflation; they hope either for an external constraint on U.S. policy, perhaps in the form of a limited amount of gold to finance payments deficits, or for a U.S. initiative in reducing its deficits. The move toward a paper gold arrangement is an effort to use political power—the force of numbers—to provide an external constraint on the United States and to reduce the impact of U.S. policies on other countries. The political route is taken because economic forces are still likely to keep the dollar in the top spot.

This conflict is not unusual; it is what the international money game is all about. National interests conflict, on both major issues and minor issues, and the bureaucrats and politicians know their own roles require that they achieve gains for their constituents. So each will agree to modify institutional arrangements only if their constituents gain. The conflict is inevitable as long as there are national monies; changes in the rules and structure cannot eliminate it. The various solutions—eliminating gold, raising the gold price, relying on paper substitutes for gold, or letting exchange rates float—do not resolve the conflict; instead, they shift the arena in which the conflict will occur.

INDEX

Index

Index

Index

Index

Index

Index

Index

Index

Wages, 8, 300; ceilings on, 106, 108
Walston, 116
Wars, 177; financing, 76, 170; and floating rates, 76; and foreign investment patterns, 260, 269; and inflation, 17, 22–23, 34–36, 44–47, 100–101, 174; nuclear, 78; *see also* Civil War, American; Vietnam War; World War I; World War II
Warwick, 270
Watergate economics, 105–9
Westdeutsche Girozentral, 53–54
West Germany, *see* Germany
Wilson, Harold, 62
Wood, Leonard, 276
World Bank, 118, 126; functions of, 305, 310–11
World War I: and the gold standard, 145–46, 171–72; inflationary impact of, 17, 23; sterling displaced by dollar during, 151–52; U.S. economic

power stimulated by, 36; *see also* Wars
World War II, 23, 291, 295; reconstruction loans after, 310–11, 320; *see also* Wars
Worchod Commercial Bank AG, 327
Wyandotte Chemical, 270

Yamaha, 299
Yashica, 299
Yen, *see* Japanese yen
Yom Kippur War, 121
Yugoslavia, 184, 331; debts of, 317

Zaibatsu, 299
Zaire, 317
Zambia, 194